NORFOLK AFRICA & ME

by
Mike Cringle

best wishes
Mike Cringle

First published in Great Britain in 2007
by
Mike Cringle

Copyright © 2007 Mike Cringle

Names, characters and related indicia are copyright and trademark
Copyright © 2007 Mike Cringle

A CIP Catalogue of this book is available from the British Library

ISBN 978-0-9557759-0-1

Printed and bound in
Great Britain by Biddles Ltd,
King's Lynn, Norfolk

Cover design and page layout by
Chandler Design
www.chandlerdesign.co.uk

CONTENTS

FOREWORD

This book follows on from 'The Gamekeeper's Boy', and takes up the story with his grandson Mike, who is a schoolboy during the second world war and who spends his period of National Service in the R.A.F.

We then follow him to Africa in chapters filled with adventure and keen observation of farm life in Kenya. Back home in Norfolk again, Mike and his wife settle down to become antique dealers, pursue the trade through its many changes over the years, and raise their own family on the North Norfolk coast.

DEDICATION

To my wife Anne, without whose constant encouragement this book might never have been printed .

NORFOLK, AFRICA & ME

1
The Dugout

My friend George and I quite enjoyed the beginning of the war. It was exciting, even if there were some inconveniences, like not always being able to go to the beach. We spent a lot of time gazing up into those blue summer skies, closely watching any aircraft that happened to be passing, telling each other that we were witnessing a ferocious dogfight. In fact in those days, though there was plenty of talk about the war in the air, it was all happening over the fields of Kent which was far, far away from our home town of Holt, in Norfolk. That was a foreign country to us and we only had a vague idea where it was, but we felt that if boys in Kent could watch Spitfires and Messerschmits zooming round in the sky, then we should be able to as well. We could see it all in our minds eye, if not in reality, and used to perform a sort of ballet in the school playground, running round with arms outstretched and making suitable noises for the roaring of engines and much stuttering machine gun fire.

We also invented new and exciting games, like pretending to be spies, or being saboteurs and blowing up trains. There was an especially convenient place for this, where the Melton Constable to Holt train, usually carrying a few local people and a couple of bicycles in the guard's van, had to pass through a narrow cutting quite near our school. There was a wood there where we often played, and when you heard the train coming, puffing slowly up the long incline out of the Glaven valley, you could dash out from cover and take up position on the edge of the cutting. Then, as the train chuffed and rattled on its way down below us, imaginary bombs could be thrown with impunity, wiping out whole divisions of equally imaginary Nazi troops at a stroke. There were also wild strawberries growing there in profusion amongst the tussocky grass, which made this a particularly attractive pastime.

We added these war games to the ones we usually played there and on the adjoining Spout Hills, a piece of common land just outside

Holt. It was an area of gorse bushes and short turf, grazed down by sheep and horses, and bounded on the side away from the town by the railway. There were several small steep hills, very good for tobogganing when there was any snow; a pond, and a stream running from it which we used to dam, and then let go with a great rush of water which we hoped would flood the vicarage garden further downstream. In the summer we paddled in the cold clear water of the pond and you could almost swim in its deepest end, if you were small enough and the day hot enough. A freezing cold spring gushed from a spout in the hillside to feed the pond, and that spring water was more refreshing than any fizzy drink.

There was also a building we called the Water Works, from which the town water supply was pumped up to a tall brick tower in the middle of Holt. Inside this little old Victorian pumping station there was an ancient machine which kept up a slow, steady thump, thump, thump, most of the time, and which exhaled warm air through a grating; very useful for drying wet socks or even trousers. During the war those in authority decided to build a few courses of bricks round our pond, to make it into a reservoir for the fire brigade to use in the case of air attack. This was quite exciting, and even though the rain of fire bombs never came, the deepened pond was better for swimming.

School activities had also become more exciting. We had a headmistress at the junior school, possibly a bit over excited about the war, who convinced us that we could be attacked by German paratroops at any moment; or failing that, balloons might be dropped on us filled with explosives or gas. We used to look for these balloons, which sounded interesting, but never found any however carefully we looked. For a time our walks to school through the town, habitually through all possible alleys and byways rather than along the main street, were occupied in careful searches for such items. Perhaps some people wondered what we were doing, poking about behind dustbins and in dark corners, but these were not matters that you discussed with grown-ups.

We were issued with gas masks and had to go into a dark, mysterious caravan sort of thing, presumably full of gas, to try them out. We were pushed in, half excited and half frightened, stumbled around trying to see through steamed up eyepieces, and were then let out. Everyone who went in duly came out again, so the gas masks were proved to work.

At school we had a special drill when air raid warnings sounded. There was a siren on top of a tall post at the police-station, and when this began its warbling, which was quite often in those early days, we were told to get under our desks. The first time this happened the excitable headmistress rushed into our classroom shouting, 'Get under your desks! Get under your desks!' Of course no one moved, we just sat there with open mouths and bulging eyes. No schoolteacher had ever said anything like that before to a class full of eight year olds, at least not in our experience. She had to get hold of one or two children and almost wrestle them down to the floor and then under their desks, before we could believe what was actually required.

Our classroom windows had already been covered with crisscross sticky tape over every pane, to stop us being showered with flying glass; but someone must have decided that this, and sitting underneath our desks, was not the ultimate in air raid precautions, so we started a new drill. From then onwards when the siren sounded we were all required to stand up in an orderly fashion, pick up our work books and march out of the classroom into the corridor. There we arranged long forms to sit on, and proceeded with our work well away from those tall fragile windows. As ideas go, it was better than nothing, but little work was ever done, and usually by the time all the classes had been reorganized, separated, persuaded to sit in the right place and open their books, the siren had sounded again for the All Clear. At that the whole performance had to be gone through again in reverse, until each child was back in its own classroom, sitting at its own desk, and with its own books. As time passed and no-one bothered to bomb us, enthusiasm for all this waned, and someone in authority must have decided that for the sake of continuing our education we would have to take our chance with the Luftwaffer. After that we just stayed where we were and got on with our lessons.

In the end few bombs ever descended anywhere near us at Holt. Just two or three fell fairly close, almost certainly dropped by some totally lost German pilot who felt he had better unload his bombs somewhere, anywhere, before heading back to the Fatherland. One night one of these exploded about a mile away, and Dad had us all out of bed and 'taking cover' of a sort downstairs, where we sat under the table in our dark dining room for an hour or two. After the muffled thump that had woken us up, nothing more happened. We just sat about in the miserable chill of early morning, surrounded by total darkness and the dank sooty smell from the cold fireplace; and then we went back to bed again.

The following day everyone had an enjoyable time telling each other how long they had been awake, and how it had been impossible to get to sleep afterwards. George and I went on our bicycles to look at the place where the bomb had fallen and were told by an air-raid warden on guard not to go any nearer. That was disappointing, because we would dearly have loved to acquire one or two pieces of shrapnel, which could have been gloated over and possibly swapped for all sorts of things like matchbox covers, or cigarette cards, or other collectibles.

Our little town had its own official air-raid shelters by this time, but no-one, apart from the odd courting couple, ever used them. They stood in strategic positions on street corners; oblong brick structures with a slab of concrete for a roof, dark and dank inside, and the subject of many caustic comments from people who knew about such things, concerning cheap construction and war profiteering. We boys merely used to poke the mortar out from between the bricks on our way to school. My father who had been in the Great War and knew all about such things, had built us a very smart private air raid shelter, but that was a mile or so away on some land he owned at Letheringset. This land was really just a small-holding of a few acres, but it was always called The Farm.

There Dad used to keep chickens, and grow all sorts of vegetables, and tomatoes in greenhouses. There was also a barn filled with sacks of grain and meal, and tools and wheelbarrows, and odd bits of machinery. A big springer spaniel called Paddy also lived there, because Mum said she wouldn't have him in the house up at Holt. But this arrangement didn't work very well, because although Paddy was perfectly happy on the farm when Dad was there or when they went shooting, when he was left there by himself in the barn he got bored, jumped out of the window and trotted up the hill to Holt. Then Dad had to be found to take him back again. What made it even worse was that Dad was quite likely to use Mum's little Austin Seven for this exercise, and the car was her pride and joy. Paddy was a very big, and usually muddy, dog, to get into a small car; so the dog and Mum were not friends. But as Dad and Paddy spent a lot of their time on The Farm, it didn't matter much.

In those early days of the war everybody expected to be bombed sooner or later, and it must have been this that led to the idea that we, as a family, would go and live on The Farm for the duration. 'For the Duration' was a favourite phrase that everybody used all the time, to describe things brought about by the war that made life temporarily inconvenient. Rationing was for the Duration. Train services on the railway were reduced for the Duration. So we would go and live on The Farm for the Duration, and this notion gave Dad his excuse for designing and building a dugout.

He had been an engineer in his war, knew all about digging trenches and dugouts in the most scientific manner, and obviously enjoyed putting the theory into practice in the peaceful Norfolk countryside rather than the mud of Flanders. He used a ground plan that probably came straight out of some military manual, and The Dugout itself was a square underground chamber, roofed with stout beams and turf, and from which two trenches emerged at opposite corners, bent in the middle like the arms of the swastika. Thus there were two entrances or exits, in case one should become blocked, and the bend in each trench made it impossible for a bomb fragment hurtling along it, to enter the actual shelter. Paddy, lending a hand the way dogs do, had tunnelled into the side of one of the trenches and excavated an extra small cave which was referred to as Paddy's Air Raid Shelter. There is no record that he ever used it.

In the end of course, no one was ever saved from the horrors of Hitler's blitzkieg by this beautiful bit of field engineering. It is true that we were all taken down to the farm for a night or two when it was finished and ready for use, and we spent a good few uncomfortable and sleepless hours in the barn on beds that Dad had knocked together from some odd planks with wire netting stretched between them. We were ready to scuttle down into The Dugout the moment the bombs began falling on Holt, but they never did, and we never availed ourselves of its shelter. After a few nights of this Mum decided that we would be better off at home, war or no war, and back we went.

We were able to do this shuttling back and forth, because although petrol was in short supply, Dad was still able to get some. He had a lorry, used in the family business, which I used to ride in some times, usually bumping and jolting along farm tracks delivering loads of meal, or collecting sacks of grain from one of the many local farmers that Dad knew. It was quite an old lorry, built mainly of wood, and had hand brake and gear levers made of brass, and highly polished from constant use.

Paddy rode in the open back with the sacks, leaping from side to side, barking, and taking a lively interest in everything along the road. Everybody used to say that it was a miracle that he didn't fall out, and one day when I was having a ride too, he did. Dad, when he noticed eventually that it was unnaturally quiet in the back of his lorry, realized that the dog was no longer there and had to turn round and drive back miles, looking for him. But Paddy came to no harm. The familiar curly, brown and white creature reappeared at last, trotting quietly along the road, dusty but apparently unperturbed; but he had learned to be more careful, and never fell out again.

Sometimes I went with Dad to the water mill that was just a short distance from the farm. This was a rather frightening sort of place to me, vast, and full of great turning wheels and rumbling machinery noises, and the dry, dusty smell of the meal that spouted out of shoots to fill sacks when ropes were pulled. There was also a very narrow plank bridge, with the mill stream rushing past below it, which I was too nervous of to walk over in the usual way, and could only cross crawling on hands and knees. Teetering over on my two feet, while reaching up for the rickety handrail was just a bit more than I could manage. Dad, of course, strode across without touching the rail at all, with a sack of meal on his back, the plank springing beneath his feet and Paddy trotting behind.

Dad was also a member of the Home Guard. He had volunteered as soon as it was formed, being too old for the army this time, and was usually busy with its mysterious comings and goings when he was not running his businesses or shooting. What he did in the Home Guard was completely unknown to anyone in the family at the time, but still vaguely disapproved of by my mother. She particularly objected when sometimes he would bring home a heavy machine gun and park on the kitchen table; but I found it fascinating, as a boy would. Mum seemed to be less than enthusiastic about many things that Dad was involved in, and probably saw the Home Guard as a sort of extension of his shooting and wildfowling activities; which as Mum was all too aware, often meant his staying out till all hours, and coming home soaking wet.

The war caused Mum a lot of minor irritations. There was the occasion when George and I decided to be escaping airmen who had been shot down over enemy territory. Secrecy was obviously essential, so we didn't tell anyone, but one day during our summer school holidays we put some biscuits and a couple of apples in our pockets and set out. We had an old AA pocket book, containing a very small scale road map, and set out across country to Switzerland, or possibly a channel port. We were lucky with the weather, a fine late summer day, and walked nearly as far as Sheringham, which was quite a good stretch of about six miles; and then were not sure what to do next. We had long ago eaten our biscuits, the two apples, and some very unripe blackberries, were footsore and thirsty, and beginning to feel that perhaps we should go home. Evading the Gestapo seemed less important now. But then the difficulty was finding our way home again, because though we knew we were somewhere near Sheringham and also near the sea, apart from that we were not at all sure exactly where we were, or which road we were on. Of course all the signposts had been removed because of the war, on the theory that removing place names and sign posts would confuse an invading force so that they wouldn't know where they were, or where to go. It confused us quite a lot too, and studying our miniature map did not seem to help much; so in the end we just walked towards the west, which we worked out must be the right general direction.

We trudged along for a long time in what we reckoned to be the direction of home, but nothing looked familiar, and we still had no idea where we were. Nobody and nothing, but us, was moving on our road, the sun was getting lower in the sky, and then it began to seem to us that the afternoon was rapidly becoming the evening. We marched on, tried whistling a jolly tune, and then decided that walking in silence was better. Our mouths were really dry by now, and wondered if we might die of thirst quite soon; we had heard that sucking a stone was supposed to help, but it didn't. There did not even seem to be a house in sight, anywhere, and the road just went on and on into the hazy distance.

Then, as we trudged towards the westering sun, there was a distant, faint rumbling and whining noise on the road behind us. Something was coming along to overtake us and we briefly contemplated pretending that it was a German tank, and hiding in the hedge; but no, that game was over, and anyhow it was obviously a bus. It ground its way slowly up to us and stopped, the conductor looked down at us and we looked back; you have to buy a ticket on a bus and we didn't have any money. 'Are you boys goin' ter get on then?' inquired the conductor. We jumped on, the bus moved off, and we began trying to explain how we came to be there, not liking to admit that we were RAF pilots who had burned our uniforms and were heading for Switzerland. We also had to admit we were without the fare. He gave us a world-weary look, 'I reckon you boys hev bin up ter somethin', and you'll get wrong when you get home. You can stay on, I'll drop you off at the corner and you can walk home from there, that's only a mile.'

We were duly dropped off and trudged the last long, weary mile home. Mum may have been relieved to see us, but did not show it. 'Where do you two think you have been?' She said, 'With me worrying all day. Your father has been looking for you, George, you'd better run home.' She turned on me, 'You can go straight to bed. I'll tell your father, and he'll have something to say to you when he comes in.' I scuttled off to my bedroom and George disappeared to his own home, which was just two hundred yards away, and from which he was not allowed to emerge again to play for a couple of days. I drank a lot of water out of the tap and then sat on the edge of my bed feeling ill used after all my adventures; but I was soon let out of my room to have supper. Dad never said much about it, he hardly ever did.

My friend George was the son of a ironmonger, and lived in a very neat, new little bungalow near the bottom of a byroad that was simply called The Lane. It was next door to the cinema, which was also a brand new building. George's bungalow was a source of wonder to us, being so new, and neat, with a new and neat garden, and with a brand new indoor bathroom and lavatory. Our WC was of the old fashioned outdoor variety which was still the norm and we had no bathroom at all. Bath night, as far as most people were concerned, meant bringing out the tin bath and filling it from kettles full of boiling water; in front of the fire if it was cold. George, on the other hand had this amazing modern bathroom, bright with white tiles and glistening chrome pipes and taps, and usually full of swirling clouds of steam which you could hardly see through. I, on account of my privileged position as friend, was allowed to go and bath there too, taking my rolled up towel as though on my way to the beach.

George's father must have been a bit of an entrepreneur, because living next to the cinema he had this bright idea of building a long shed, and charging people a fee to look after their bicycles. Just about everybody who came to the pictures from beyond walking range came on their bikes, and many seemed happy to pay a few pence to have somewhere safe to leave them. It must have been quite a useful little source of income, as the long shed often overflowed, and bicycles were parked in clusters all over the garden.

George's dad was in truth a slight mystery to me. He did not seem to have been in the Great War, as my dad had. Nor was he in the Home Guard. I think he may have been an air raid warden, but air raid wardens did not have much to do in Holt, there being no actual air raids. Thus he did not really seem to fit into the war scene at all, and everything else in my life seemed to be related to the war in some way. Even the clothes I wore were a sort of juvenile version of the famous siren-suit in which Winston Churchill was frequently seen.

My sister Avril and her teenage school friends were also suitably engaged in useful jobs like collecting waste paper for the war effort, while she looked forward to joining the Land Army, being very keen on horses and the like. She was several years older than me, a big, well developed girl, and she had discovered the soldiers who were to be seen in the streets of our little town now, and whom Dad regarded with little enthusiasm in spite of his own military past. He probably knew only too well how soldiers' minds work. At all events he always wanted to know exactly where his daughter was, if she was still out at nine o'clock of a summers evening.

I noticed all this without much interest; teenager girls were usually doing silly and uninteresting things like giggling to each other on the telephone about tennis and dances and grown-up stuff. But it gave me respite from having the cleanliness of my neck and hands checked all the time, my big sister always being more interested in monitoring my activities than in toeing the family line herself. Occasionally a soldier or airman would be brought home to tea, but they were always far too well behaved to be much fun; they sometimes pretended to be flatteringly interested in me, but I could see through that.

As the war went on these boy friends came and went, as regiments came to our area and moved on, and airmen were moved about from one RAF station to another. The whole of Norfolk became dotted with airfields. Not the romantic fighter bases that we boys had spent so much time thinking about; but rather sinister places which showed little sign of activity during the day, but from which great fleets of bombers droned over our heads at night. One of Avril's assorted boy friends was a crew member on one of the bombers; a gunner, I informed my friends, as that sounded exciting. He seemed to be around for a long time, then he suddenly wasn't there any more; it was much later on that someone told me that he was dead.

One day, round about the middle of the war, we had a surprise visit from a jolly sort of young man in an American uniform. To everybody's amazement he turned out to be a close relative, a cousin in fact. He came from Canada, and was the son of Dad's sister Ruth, who had married a policeman from across the Atlantic many years before. He was called Buddy, he told us, though no-one thought that was a proper name, and he was a photographer. He wasn't the first American we had seen because by that time there were a fair number of Yanks about; they flew some of the bombers and gave you packs of funny looking chewing gum, but it was odd to find that we more or less owned one of them. He visited us several times, and was very pleasant and friendly, but no-one knew quite what to make of him. The smart uniform with a lot of shiny buttons and stuff made him seem too different to our own dull looking soldiers and airmen, and made us all seem shabby. The lack of a proper bathroom suddenly became embarrassing.

Dad, who had been to America as a young man, said never mind about that, because when he was where Buddy came from they all lived in wooden shacks. The trouble was that Dad was there before the first world war, and it was obvious that things must have moved on quite a lot since then. Then at Christmas Buddy sent us a card which incorporated a large, shiny portrait of himself. Nobody liked that, because we thought it seemed sort of conceited. In our little world people did not send Christmas cards with pictures of themselves on the front, so poor Buddy was never quite approved of after that, though he remained the same nice, friendly sort of person he naturally was. After a time he was moved on, as everybody seemed to be moved on in those days, and we did not see him again. We never knew exactly what part his photography played in the war or what he was doing, except that he died with many others on the Normandy beaches.

The war had been going on for a long time then, almost forever, as far as young boys were concerned. In a way it had passed us by, living as we did in the depth of the Norfolk countryside, far from any real danger; and to George and me it was by then just a background to our lives. The excitement of the early days was long over; almost forgotten, for instance, was that strange period when we had been descended upon by hordes of evacuees from London. Then, for a few weeks we had lived in a peculiar, divided world; half the familiar one inhabited entirely by local boys and girls we had always known, and half that of a crowd of complete strangers who talked with a funny sort of accent about things we didn't understand, and even played quite different games. Some of these games we soon learned to play ourselves, such as Tin Can Copper, in which one of them stood guard over a tin can, which every one else had to try to hit with a stick; a very popular noisy one, that.

Their arrival had seemed to take everyone by surprise, the adults as much as us. There was nowhere for them to go to school even, so for a time they had our school for half the day while we had it for the rest. Hence a half day holiday from school every day. It was too good to last of course and eventually the authorities got things organized, and that batch of evacuees moved on like a tribe folding its tents and departing in the night, and we had our school back, all day long.

My sister eventually joined the Land Army, as she had intended, but it didn't seem to involve working with horses very much. She did most of her war work on a chicken farm, but at least it got her away from home, which was probably a bit of a relief for both her and Dad, whose attitude to her military boy friends had never changed. Dad himself, after Home Guard alarms and activities had all faded away, found himself a niche working for the Ministry of Agriculture, as a sort of liaison officer between officialdom and the farming community. With most young men in the armed forces, there was a lot of organising to do getting farm work done by who ever else happened to be available, which often came to mean prisoners of war. This suited Dad down to the ground, as he already knew most farmers in the area, and soon became friends with the military men who ran the prisoner of war camps. One of these, an army captain, became a shooting companion, and they spent their time, when not arranging working parties to lift potatoes, in going round the coast on wildfowling outings. Mum's foreboding about the military, Dad, and shooting, had come true again.

By the end of the war all had changed, just as surely for us as for so many others. The family business that had been flourishing in the thirties, gradually declined through the war years. Dad never went back to it, but remained working with the Ministry of Agriculture for many years; the shop at Holt was sold, and he and Mum moved out of the town and went to live in a Victorian farm house at Glandford, a few miles away. I lost touch with my old friend George, but otherwise I loved this move to a new place. Instead of a little house in the middle of a town, with no garden, we were now living in this big old house with a cellar and all sorts of sheds to explore, a wild garden round it and over the wall the exciting countryside.

This house was in the Glaven valley, famous among country lovers for its quiet charm. As a teenager I was not particularly aware of its fame in this respect, but I loved it. There was the river not far from our house, and woods and small hills all round, so that I only had to step outside the door to be in a boy's paradise. During school holidays I was busy from dawn to dusk, and bitterly resented having to be away from home for any reason whatsoever; I simply did not have time to go anywhere else.

The river obviously demanded a boat of some sort, so I built a canoe. Suitable materials for boat building were in short supply at the end of several years of war, and anyhow I had no money to buy anything with, so it was constructed of some old scrap timber and roofing felt. The roofing felt seemed to me to be a brilliant idea, since it was obviously waterproof; unfortunately it was also very old and brittle and so tended to crack and split when you tried to tack it on the wooden frame. I eventually produced something that seemed to be fairly water tight, at least while it was in our yard; but when I carried it down to the river and carefully launched it my canoe and I both went straight to the bottom. The Glaven was only about a couple of feet deep just there, so I returned home again not much wetter than usual. But I gave up boat building, as it was obviously more difficult than it looked.

The water life in the river was fascinating too, so I built a small pond in the garden of our new home, and stocked it with water plants and assorted river life. Tadpoles, caddis larvae, water scorpions, small fish; anything that could be caught in a sort of large butterfly net. Some aspects of river life were too big to be brought home, and those I watched by the hour. Water hens, herons, king fishers could all be seen along our little river, where most of the time they were completely undisturbed by anything more alarming than a cow or a sheep, or sometimes me.

When life by the riverside palled, there was the woods. These were, strictly speaking, private and patrolled by a game keeper who lived near us, but either he did not patrol very carefully or perhaps he did not bother too much if he caught a glimpse of me flitting between the trees now and then. I was not a great hazard to the wildlife, apart from one unfortunate jackdaw that I stole from its nest and took home. I had this vision of a bird that would ride round on my shoulder and say amusing things, as jackdaws do in books; but it didn't live very long, probably because I had no real idea of how to feed and rear a young jackdaw. But I did have a tame hedge sparrow, which I fed more successfully, and which stayed with us for a long time.

Amongst the woods were several small hills which became Alps when we had some snow in the winter, and one year when we had a lot of snow I made myself a pair of skis. As usual I didn't have the correct materials to make anything properly, so used whatever came to hand. In this case two very ordinary planks of wood that happened to be lying about. They were too wide, and too heavy, and I shuffled about on them rather than flying through the air, but they were skis of a sort.

One of these little hills was about a mile from our house, more or less at the limit of my range, and it had the ruins of an old building on the top of it. It always seemed a very quiet and secret sort of place, and I never saw another human being near it. From the top, near the old ruin, you could look down on our house, and the village and river; and across the valley the fields rising to more woods and heathland on the far side of the valley. On the other side of this hill there was just more woodland. I was up there one day when it suddenly struck me how quiet it was. Just then there was no sound of any living creature; nothing from the valley below, no bird singing in a bush close at hand, no rasping cry from a cock pheasant in the woods. I suddenly felt uneasy, and started to walk away from the ruin, back down the hill towards home. Then from the corner of my eye I seemed to glimpse a tall figure dressed in black move and disappear behind one of the broken-down walls of the old house. I kept on walking, fast, and didn't look round or stop until I reached home.

Much later I heard that there was in fact a ghost story connected with the gamekeeper's house, which though invisible from the ruin was in the woods not far away. Perhaps there was some connection, or perhaps the whole thing had more to do with a teenager's imagination. At our own house down below the hill, we did quite definitely have a ghostly presence, just once. In the early hours of a bright, midsummer morning, I was lying awake in my bedroom when I heard footsteps walking along the corridor outside. The footsteps went past, apparently to my father's office which was just beyond my room; but then nothing, just utter quiet. I had thought it must be Dad getting up early for some reason, but then after a time with no further noise I felt I had better go and look. There was no one there, of course. I went the other way and peered into my father and mother's bedroom, and they were both still sound asleep.

Ghosts, or not, I had a wonderful time as a young lad at Glandford. We spent several years there, while I used to ride my bicycle up to school at Holt every day. Then Dad was sent to another district by the Ministry, and soon after that I left school and went away to my first job. I had no idea what I wanted to do to earn my living, but clearly had to do something, and mainly to please my mother, took an examination and became a civil servant in Finsbury Square in the City of London. I did not know it, but it would be many years, and I would have lived in many different places, before I made my home in Norfolk again.

2
Icarus

When I was eighteen, which was in the fifties, not many years after the war, there was National Service to be done. Every young man of my age had to do two years in the armed forces, theoretically helping to defend his country should war suddenly break out again. For most it was two years of boredom, while you did rather pointless things in an uncomfortable uniform, waiting to get on with your real life again; but I had been rather looking forward to it. I had been working in that Civil Service office in London for a few months, and had already decided that I'd had enough of the life, so it was quite a welcome thought that it must end as soon as I was called upon to take up arms. Moreover, there had always been the idea, tucked away at the back of my mind somewhere, that I would like to be a pilot. Of course most other young boys growing up during the war, who didn't want to be engine drivers, probably had similar vague ambitions. But then I heard that National Service might give me the chance to have a go at flying, and so one day I walked into an RAF recruiting office and asked them about it. Rather to my surprise, I was told that this was indeed possible. It seemed that a few suitable candidates were accepted as air crew for their national service and, I was given to understand, this became even more possible if one would like to throw in one's lot with the RAF for four years instead of two. Four years sounded a long time, but to one who had recently been facing the possibility of a lifetime spent in a civil service office, where the main subject of conversation each morning was what had been on the radio the night before, it wasn't too unattractive a prospect.

I decided to take the metaphorical shilling, and soon found myself invited to take a series of tests at an RAF station just north of London. I had a few days holiday due to me, so off I went and found myself in a crowd of a dozen other young hopefuls who fancied themselves in the blue uniform with wings on their chests. We were soon herded together by a young man already in that uniform, and taken from room to room and building to building to do all sorts of written tests, and then more on a bewildering series of machines. The machines were good fun, not too unlike games you might have found in an amusement arcade, on which the young would-be pilot had his coordination of hand, foot, and eye put to the test. Spatial perception came in for a lot of attention too, and we had to show that we could work out whether different shapes would, or would not, fit together. Finally we had to do intelligence tests and fairly simple maths. I seemed to be able to do most of the tests without too much trouble, and so was then passed on to a doctor, and was poked and prodded and told to cough, and listened to through a stethoscope. After all that there was a board of selecting officers who asked some questions, shuffled some papers, and then told me that I would be accepted for training as a pilot.

Later I found out that most of the others who had come through the same ordeal with me were offered the choice of pilot or navigator, not pilot only; so clearly the maths tests though fairly simple, had not been quite simple enough for me. They had quickly worked out that if I were put in charge of navigating a bomber to Moscow, it might well arrive at somewhere quite unsuitable.

While we were being put through this selection process, which took several days, we also had a mild taste of service life, and were given useful jobs to do, like cleaning out the station pigsty. An introduction to RAF food was included too, with hearty fried breakfasts of egg and bacon. The bacon was recognizable, and may well have originated from the pig accommodation we had been cleaning, but none of us had seen eggs in this form before; it was bright yellow, carved out from a large roasting pan, and we received a solid two inch cube each. The first time we met it there was an animated discussion at our rickety trestle table about exactly what it was, and if some form of egg, from what bird it had originated; but egg it was all right, and eatable if you carved it quite thinly. Those of us sitting round that table who went on to become real airmen soon came to accept it as the norm, and egg shaped eggs were forgotten.

It was briefly back again to our old lives again after that, and eventually for me a rather embarrassing interview with the head of my department in Finsbury Square, who had assumed that I was off to do my obligatory two years' national service like everyone else, and would be back again one day. He could not even begin to understand a young tearaway who, at the very beginning of a safe and cosy career in the civil service, could drop it all for the sake of four years in the RAF and a very uncertain future aloft. I was far from certain why I was doing it anyway, and so we had a few minutes of mutually incomprehensible conversation and then parted for ever.

My parents were not too pleased about it all either. Dad took it in his stride, and as ever got on with his own life, but Mum didn't like the idea at all. Having worked in an aircraft factory during the first world war she regarded aeroplanes as nasty flimsy things that often fell out of the sky. Also she had been delighted that her boy had joined the civil service; she had worked hard on that, and there it was, wasted. But she baked me a cake to take with me, and they took me to the railway station to see me off, and away I went. First to RAF Cardington to be kitted out, then to Driffield in Yorkshire, for no apparent reason, and then to Jurby, in the Isle of Man.

This was the place where future aircrew started their training, and began to learn what they had let themselves in for. Jurby, our new home, was a wild and lonely spot in the north west corner of the island. There was an RAF station, consisting of a few rows of wooden huts, some sand dunes, a very windy beach, and the sea. On the other side of the sea was Ireland or America, depending on exactly which way you were facing, and from that general direction came the wind. During the several weeks we spent there, doing what was described as basic training, that wind never stopped blowing. It blew day and night out of west as though someone had switched on an enormous fan, and forgotten to switch it off again. In our huts at night, with all windows firmly shut, you might forget it for a while; but you would emerge in the morning, walk a few yards in shelter to the corner of the hut, and then be blown off your feet.

One of the things they taught us there was how to give orders on a parade ground, it being assumed that pilots and navigators would end up as officers and therefore need to know about such matters, and this permanent howling wind provided the perfect environment. The method of teaching was simple. You were merely required to drill a squad of your friends and hut mates, who may not have been the most co-operative of subjects, upwind in the face of this steady Atlantic gale. We were all young innocents who had scarcely had any need to raise our voices hitherto, but we soon learned to shriek and bawl like a drunken drill sergeant; if you didn't, no one could hear a word.

Our time was spent in this and other basic matters, such as polishing brass and learning how to make up our beds each morning in the approved manner; and because we were considered potential leaders, also in the finer points of service life like dining in the officers' mess. This happened once a week and was probably the most worrying thing we had to do, what with being expected to behave like proper little gentlemen, and say the right things, and pass the port the right way round the table. We also learned how to tie a bow tie properly. But the problem there was that to appear in the mess with a properly fixed bow tie, you first of all have to own a suitable shirt and tie, and when we drew our kit at Cardington no one had thought of issuing bow ties and wing collars. So we all scattered round the island trying to buy suitable neckwear.

Looking back, I suppose this might have been some sort of initiative test. I had teamed up with a young Cockney called Alan, who had been working in a gentlemens' outfitters before becoming an airman, and this proved wise. To start with he actually knew how to deal with wing collars and bow ties; and he had probably acquired some sort of instinct for finding shops where they might sell such things. At all events we managed to get the right sort of gear at Peel, which was a good walk from Jurby, but seemed to be the nearest place with such items on sale. There were all sorts of things in Peel, unlike our benighted corner of the island; there was a cafe, boats you could hire to row round the bay, an allegedly haunted castle, even girls. Heaven on earth compared to Jurby, but we seldom had the chance of getting there; they kept us too busy, learning to be flyers and perhaps, gentlemen.

At the end of our time on the Isle of Man, and after a set of final exams, the sheep were separated from the goats, and then those on whose education the Air Ministry felt inclined to risk more money, were sent on to a flying training station at Cottesmore in Rutland. This was the real thing now, with lots of actual aeroplanes standing about on the tarmac in front of a row of hangars, and buzzing about in the sky above. Up till now we had not been near a flying machine of any sort, even the journey to and from the Isle of Man had been on the old steam ferry, and it was almost a surprise to find that suddenly we were really going to be allowed sit in the cockpits of these exciting things and actually fly them.

There were planes of all sorts, most prominent the very smart looking radial engined Harvards from the USA, which shot into the air like rockets with an earsplitting roar, and immediately gave rise to feelings of great inadequacy, carefully concealed. We were not going to have to fly those things, were we? Luckily, we weren't, at least not for the first six months, anyhow. The aircraft we were introduced to, as the one in which we would learn the basic essentials, was the rather old fashioned looking Percival Proctor, by comparison a dull, slow machine, in which student pilot and instructor sat side by side in a sort of little greenhouse on top of the fuselage. Still, however dull and slow it might look, it was our aeroplane, and we were going to fly it.

Then there was more excitement as we were issued with our flying gear. Leather helmet and fur lined boots, silk inner and leather outer gloves, flying overalls with large pockets on the leg for maps, goggles and oxygen mask, even a special wrist watch. We could hardly believe what was happening as bored looking ground crew at the stores handed out all this stuff to us. Free sets of flying gear exactly like that you saw in films. It was ours! We were pilots. Well, we soon would be. We could wear it, we could go home in it; well, no perhaps not, it would look a bit out of place on the train or the bus. Still, we could send photographs home; I had a camera, and Alan had a suitably dashing looking scarf, so we rigged ourselves out, found a quiet spot by a hanger, and photographed each other gazing with narrowed eyes into the sky. But then the real flying training started.

It was hard work, and perhaps more serious than we had imagined. There was no taking off with a casual wave to the ground crew, and zooming into the wide blue yonder. We had to learn all about aeroplanes, to start with, and there was an awful lot to learn, starting from how petrol engines work, and going on slowly but steadily from there. It was very thorough, too, and we soon knew exactly how and why the propeller went round; explained carefully to us by a grey haired flight sergeant who started our first lecture with the enquiry, 'Have any of you lot heard of the Otto cycle?'

We had not. I was still dredging around in my mind trying to remember what, if anything, I knew about auto cycles, when he began to explain the basics of the invention of the internal combustion engine, apparently by a German genius called Otto von Something. Our instructor had a lot of regard for Otto, who had first thought of the cycle of induction, compression, ignition, and exhaust; which is basically what a petrol engine does. Having passed on the good news about Otto, we were soon on to swept volumes, cubic capacities, super-chargers, how to detect a faulty valve, and how to remove it and grind in a new one. To this man the only thing that mattered in the RAF was the aero-engine.

But then we learned from similar grizzled members of the staff that the same might be said of wireless telegraphy, and navigation, and signalling, especially the Morse code as transmitted by a flickering Aldis lamp. 'An Aldis lamp?' we wanted to know, wasn't that what the Navy used, passing messages between destroyers and convoys in stormy seas? But we were soon made to understand that if we thought we were going to be pilots one day, the ability to read an Aldis message while flying, navigating, dealing with the odd faulty valve, and possibly passing the port decanter to an Air Vice-Marshall, was all just part of the trade.

When we did get into the air the training was just as thorough. The first thing we learned, while still at the stage of trying to work out whether one felt sick or not, was what to do if the engine stopped. I don't think any of us had considered that possibility. We knew we were sitting on a parachute, but the Air Force didn't seem to attach much importance to that; we had been given very perfunctory instructions about how to use it, 'You pull that thing there, right? Jump out and try not to be hit by the tail.' So what do you do if the engine stops? To clear up this point my flying instructor simply switched it off as we cruised along on our first flight and said, 'Look for a place to land.' I thought, what does he mean?, and looked round vaguely and hopelessly. It was suddenly horribly quiet, but we weren't actually falling, just gliding; then, with the wind rushing past, not so quiet, as ones ears become used to the lack of engine roar. He said casually, 'See that field over to the right, the green one near the railway?' I had no idea what he was looking at, but said yes. 'We'll just have a look at it.'

Our plane seemed to sort of slip down to the right, and then levelled out again. He said, 'Well, that looks all right, we'll leave it at that today, another time we'll go right down to do a practice forced landing.' I thought, what's he going to do now. Even I knew that our aeroplane didn't have a self starter; you started it with thick electrical cables from a special little truck on the ground called a trolly-ac. I watched mesmerized as he switched on, opened the throttle and adjusted a lever that I had just learned controlled the pitch of the propeller. Then he pushed his control column forward and we seemed to dive straight at the ground, the noise of the slipstream increased, and the propeller started to revolve fast as the air rushed past it. Suddenly the engine roared into life again, and we climbed away, and I was thinking that there was more to flying than I had realized.

Days and weeks passed, half the time flying and the other half sitting in classrooms and learning the theory behind it all. Soon we could converse, after a fashion, in morse code, and knew, more or less, what was happening inside that engine in front. Flying became routine. First we did lots of circuits and bumps; which was taking off, leaving the airspace above the airfield, rejoining it again, and landing. Then there were more ambitious exercises. Basic aerobatics like looping the loop proved to be simpler than they look from the ground, but less dramatic operations like simple navigation, much more difficult that we had imagined. The trouble, we found, is that up there the world underneath does not look as you expect it to. We could lay-off a course in the classroom at the drop of a hat, but up there, with a crumpled map sliding off your knee, and flying your aircraft with one hand, while trying to make sense of what was spread out hazily nine thousand feet below, it was all somehow different.

We soon learned that the world down below does not look like an ordinance survey map, and towns in particular are virtually impossible to identify, as they all seem to consist of the same endless rows of tiny houses. My instructor, who like most of them had been in the war and knew what navigating under stress was all about, explained early on that if in doubt one should follow the railways. They were the only features that normally stand out clearly in the landscape, and look the same as on the map. That bit of advice I found really useful when I was up there by myself, and wondering if I would ever find my way home again. One of our lot did get completely lost on one navigating exercise, and eventually landed, to everyone's surprise at the USAF base at Lakenheath, about a hundred miles away. He was returned the next day, sheepish, but a minor hero.

We were flying by ourselves, solo, surprisingly quickly. About ten hours flying time was considered quite adequate, and then at any time your instructor might tell you to land, calmly get out of his side of the cockpit, and say, 'All right, you go and do it then, one circuit and down, and try not to break the aeroplane'. After one had done that, usually with a good deal of bouncing about, solo flying soon became the rule; you went to the briefing room, were told what to do, and went off and did it. Then you came back and wrote it all up in your log book. The routine became second nature. You put your gear on, walked out to your designated aircraft, checked that all its control surfaces were moving about as they were supposed to, got in the cockpit, went through the preflight checks of all equipment, clipped on your microphone and started talking to the control tower. You waited to be told to taxi to take-off point, then signalled to the ground crew with the trolly-ac who connected the hose carrying the electric cables for your starting motor; switches to contact, the starting motor wines, then the engine stutters and bursts into life. You wait politely for the ground crew to remove the hose without being decapitated by the propeller, and then exercise the engine controls, let it settle down happily, then release the wheel brakes and move off.

Now came the really unexpected thing about these aircraft. You had vaguely imagined that on the ground it would be like driving a car, but no, there is no steering wheel and of course none of the flying controls have any effect. The propeller pulls it along, but the only way of steering it is by use of the brakes, which can be used independently, left and right; so you start by yawing about all over the place, but soon get the hang of it. You taxi to the end of your runway, line up, and sit there and wait; the control tower tells you that you are clear to take off. You watch a little hut with a window facing you, about fifty yards away, and an Aldis lamp flashes green. You check that your brakes are no longer acting independently, but both on together, check the flaps in take off position, adjust the propeller pitch, open the throttle, release the brakes and move forward.

The Proctor had a low take off speed, no higher than a fairly smartly moving car, and in no time the tail rises and you are coming unstuck from the ground; sluggish bumping about on mother earth is instantly forgotten and everything is very smooth. But remember that the air is moving, what we call the wind on the surface of the earth, so you have to start making sure that you are not being blown sideways like a bit of paper. To fly in the direction you want to go you have to take into account the direction of the wind in exactly the same way that a boat has to allow for the movement of the tide or the current in a river, so you start checking your compass and looking at your map.

One of the things you might be told to practice might be stalling and spinning, this being a 'get you out of trouble' exercise, like knowing what to do if the engine stops. In this case it is all to do with the aircraft going out of control as the result of a stall, which is when its speed is allowed to fall below a certain level, and it stops flying and starts to lose height. In a moment it is out of control, and then begins to gyrate helplessly like a falling leaf. From the ground this might look like an aerobatics display, but it is actually an aeroplane falling out of the sky.

We practiced this all the time, in the hope that we would react automatically and do the right thing if and when it happened to us in earnest. The remedy was simple, if you didn't panic. You merely had to increase the speed of the slipstream over your wing, and when it was fast enough your plane would begin to fly again. This involved diving steeply, and doing various adjustments with rudder and engine controls; all quite simple and straightforward, but the sensation was strange in the extreme. To the pilot practicing these manoeuvres it is the world outside that spins round and does other odd things; it is so disorientating that an odd feeling of unreality takes over, and it is necessary to concentrate hard, and even remind oneself that this isn't for fun.

There were stories about inexperienced pilots having been seen to go on spinning until they hit the ground, without apparently making any attempt to do anything about it, and I could believe it. At all events there were fatal accidents from time to time, and on more than one occasion the crumpled remains of one of our trainer aircraft was brought home on a trailer. They used to say that these wrecks were left standing about for a day or two so that we would all see them and be encouraged to try harder.

On one occasion in my early days in the RAF I was detailed with a few others to act as crash guard on a wrecked aircraft. A guard was always put on a crash, to make sure it wasn't visited by souvenir hunters or other undesirables, and it remained guarded until it could be moved to somewhere out of the public domain. On this occasion a plane from some other RAF station had come down a few miles away in the late afternoon, so it had to be guarded all night, and we were told to go and do it. It was dusk when we arrived, and found the remains of a Tiger Moth, from which we understood a body had been removed. The fuselage was a bit damaged but still reasonably intact, and with idle curiosity I went and looked in the open cockpit, wondered briefly what the small white objects were, scattered about on the floor, and then realized that they were someone's teeth. Everybody had to have a look, of course, and then wished they hadn't; and we spent a miserable night, huddled in our greatcoats, freezing cold, and pretending to take it in turn to sleep.

We all discovered another way of having a really bad night when we did escape exercises, acting as air crew downed in enemy territory; we had played at this as children, but now it was a lot more uncomfortable and went on longer. The idea was you were taken out in a closed van, driven several miles, and then heaved out into the countryside somewhere in the dark; you then had to find your way back home without being caught by 'enemy' patrols who were looking for you. It was more fun than guarding a crashed aeroplane full of teeth, but not much. You soon get cold, hungry, and generally very fed up, stumbling about in the dark, trying to find out where you were, but at the same time carefully avoiding any human contact that might turn out to be the enemy.

On one particularly cold occasion three or four of us had been doing this all night but were still miles from home when the unkind light of a freezing morning caught us, and we decided to hide up in an old wagon in some farmer's cart shed. In theory this was to wait until the return of darkness and then resume our escape, though we probably all secretly hoped to be discovered. We could then be 'captured' and return honourably to civilization, warmth, food, and something to drink. We were in fact duly discovered by the farmer, but he then to our horror, entered into the spirit of the thing and told us we could stay where we were and he wouldn't tell anyone; he even, kind soul that he was, arranged for his wife to bring us out a small piece of cake and an elegant cup of tea. A few loaves of bread and a saucepan of soup would have been more use, but we thanked her nicely, and then as soon as she had gone back to the house, scuttled away; a day spent huddled in that frigid cart shed was more than anyone could contemplate. We got caught anyhow, nearly everyone always was.

All this training went on day and night, for we did night flying too, for about a year. It was not a bed of roses, but even when you enjoyed it least you were still aware that it was very good training. Many of our instructors had been through the war, and we had a high degree of respect for them; you felt that they knew what they were about. They taught us very well, if sometimes with a dash of eccentricity, like the one who frequently came out with odd bits of advice, as for instance concerning driving along the country lanes around RAF Cottesmore. 'When approaching a crossroads, always accelerate to maximum speed; the faster you cross over, the less chance there is of someone on the other road hitting you'. But no one joked about flying, that was always serious, and you were always aware that if you did not reach the very high standard required, you could at any time be taken off flying, and given something very boring to do in an office.

This process of sifting us out went on all the time; well over half of our original complement had fallen by the wayside by now and you were always aware that those who did not reach the required standard could be dropped any day. One of our lot, who disappeared suddenly, was rumoured to have been seen flying low over his girl friend's house and waggling his wings at her. You might have got away with that sort of thing in 1940, but not in the fifties. It was made very clear to us that we were not carefree young war heroes, we were serious students learning to do a very technical job properly; we were also potential officers, and that was even more serious. Silk scarves and hats worn at rakish angles were definitely out; some of our instructors might have a whiff of wartime glamour about them still, but that was not for us. By the end of the first year, and it was reckoned to take two years to teach us our job, many familiar faces had disappeared from the course for one reason or another. The truth was that since there was no longer a war to be fought, the RAF was being very picky about the pilots it finally took on.

Alan and I had both survived thus far, and even become quite comfortable at Cottesmore. We used to go to village dances at weekends, and consume the odd pint of beer at local pubs. I had even found myself a girl friend, and got invited out to tea on Sunday, which was considered very crafty. They were a nice family, Jill worked at a local stables, this being very horsy country, and they lived in a comfortably shabby old house. We sort of quite liked each other, and even wrote rather aimless letters, in a desultory sort of way, after I had vanished from the scene. In fact my departure from the flying scene was, as with everyone who didn't quite make the grade, very sudden.

Perhaps I wasn't any longer trying hard enough; though I liked the flying, I had also begun to realize that I probably wasn't really cut out for the life in uniform, and someone may have noticed that. At all events, one day I found myself going through a set of tests with a new instructor, who didn't seem to be too thrilled by my performance. I was interviewed, told this officially and sent out to do some more flying tests. I managed to do everything badly again, and ended the performance with a landing that must have looked like a toy aeroplane bobbing up and down on the end of a piece of elastic.

This was followed by a rather frigid interview with my Wing Commander who in effect told me that I was wasting the time of my flying instructor, and I could go away and do something else. Within an hour or two I had handed in my flying gear, packed my kit, and was on my way to Cardington again. Long farewells were not required or expected; everyone who had been sacked from flying had vanished like a puff of smoke, and I had done the same trick. I sat in the train to Bedford in a state of shock, carefully unpicking the white aircrew flashes from the collar of my uniform; there was no need to advertise my ignominious fall. Flying was finished, and I was already trying to work out quite a serious problem. I had signed on for four years to be a pilot, and now I was not going to be a pilot, but I still had the rest of my four years to do with the boys in blue. The recruiting posters used to say that there were dozens of great careers to follow in the RAF, but there were also plenty of nasty dull little jobs too that you might get pushed into. I had the rest of a rather short railway journey to work out all my future plans.

3
Grounded

Cardington, at least to the ordinary recruit, seemed to be the mystical heart of the Royal Air Force. Perhaps the higher echelons of the service didn't see it like that at all; to them the epicentre may have been the RAF college at Cranwell, or the Air Ministry. But to the thousands of rather reluctant airmen who came and went as National Service dictated, that sprawling city of huts overshadowed by the great airship hangers was the true centre. That was where you took yourself to when the call-up papers and the rail travel warrant arrived; that was where you, in a long worried queue, were handed out your hairy, strange feeling, blue uniform and enormous square-bashing black boots; and that was the place you met your first drill corporal. You may have visualised that as a recruit you would soon be learning all sorts of new and interesting things, possibly being sent overseas to exciting places, even having to fight for your country; what you immediately discovered at Cardington was that for the present at any rate, your entire world was dominated by the point of view of your drill corporal.

He was not interested in your possibly brilliant future as an engineer or technician, he scarcely seemed aware that you, and he, were in a flying Service. His world, which he was determined that you would share with him, was dominated entirely by strange rituals to do with cleaning and polishing everything in sight, being neat and tidy in ones personal habits, making beds, and learning drill movements. He met you when you arrived on that first day, shepherded you through the routine of collecting all your assorted equipment, and then encouraged you to march, or at least walk smartly at that stage, to the hut that you and a dozen or so others would live in for your first six weeks. This was a long, wooden structure with iron bed frames along the walls, and two iron heating stoves in the middle; there were simple wooden cabinets between the beds for your kit, and the floor was covered by thick brown linoleum of a strange, almost mystical lustre. But the first thing you learned was that this unworldly lustre had no supernatural origin, just the tender loving care of all the recruits who had come and gone before you. The second thing you were required to learn was that this lustre would soon be reflected in all your kit, and especially in the great black boots with which you had been issued. As these were apparently constructed from some unusually dull and bumpy sort of black leather it was not easy to see how this desirable shiny finish would be attained, but the method turned out to be simple; you merely took a tin of boot polish and a duster, supplied at a reasonable price, and sat on the edge of your iron framed bed rubbing away at your boots until they did in fact shine. It took about a week, but as recruits were not allowed to leave the camp you had plenty of time to do it.

Bed-making was another important subject, and must have come as a strange revelation to many a young man with an indulgent mother. There would be no leaving unmade beds when you went to breakfast at seven thirty in the morning, or even a hasty pulling over of blankets, for that matter. Each recruit was issued with two sheets and four grey blankets, and each morning the bed would be stripped, and the sheets and three of the blankets folded into neat squares; they would then be made into a pile: blanket, sheet, blanket, sheet, blanket, like a large liquorice allsort, and the fourth blanket wrapped round them. This strange object then had to be left artistically placed at the head of the bed. After breakfast the contents of the cabinet beside the bed were also arranged according to an esoteric design; Knife, fork, spoon, plate, mug, shaving gear and all the rest of the kit, not merely clean and polished, but each item in exactly the preordained place. It is surprising how quickly all this can be done, when you get the hang of it.

The drill corporal, who introduced you to all this interesting ritual, lived in his own private room at the end of the hut, from which he could observe his little flock of recruits like a strict, somewhat obsessive, but not necessarily unkind, nanny. Except possibly first thing in the morning, when he might stride through the hut with a towel slung over his shoulder, offering useful advice about getting out of bed quickly, he never appeared in public other than dressed with the most extreme smartness. Uniform newly pressed, creases in the trousers you could cut yourself on, the same trousers tucked into gaiters above the sparkling boots; and weighted down cunningly by a circle of chain inside each leg so that they looked like rather long plus-fours. His job, having persuaded his charges to be clean and neat, was to teach them to obey orders smartly, and this was done on the drill square. Every one, whatever their future job in the airforce might be, had to learn to do drill first, and of course everyone muttered darkly about what a waste of time it was; but they had to get on and do it, and probably learned something or other in the course of it. In the midst of all this each recruit went through a selection process too, and after six weeks of concentrated learning of service ways, marching about, and taking a whole battery of tests, he was duly moved on to another RAF station to learn the trade to which he had been appointed.

I had missed most of this on my first visit to Cardington, having been already selected for pilot training; and on my way back there after getting the heave-ho from Cottesmore flying training school, a worry that occurred to me was that I might have to go through the whole process from scratch. However no one seemed to want me to do that, in fact no one seemed to particularly want me to do anything at all; I was outside the usual process of churning out recruits, and apparently in a sort of limbo, so I just went along to the personnel selection department and asked for another job.

I rather fancied the air-sea rescue service; zooming about in fast motor launches seemed as good as or even better than flying, but there turned out to be a snag. The young personnel selection officer I found myself talking to looked it up in his book of airforce careers, and said, 'Yes, good idea, but you'll have to sign on for eight years. It's for long service careers only.' We studied the book for other possibilities for some time, then he suddenly said, 'Why don't you go in for personnel selection? You go on a course, then you get made up to corporal straight away, which is not bad, you get a bit more money. You can just finish off your service doing that.' Why not, I thought. No sooner said than done, and thus after a year or so in the service of the crown I found myself back where I had started, but instead of taking aptitude tests this time, I was learning how to give them to others.

It turned out to be a long, very thorough, and surprisingly interesting course. It was back to school yet again, but this time instead of aero-engines and navigation it was psychology and the science of discovering the abilities and potential of airforce recruits. It was mainly done by giving many different sorts of tests, such as we had all done ourselves without too much idea of why we were doing them; and at the end of the process a set of figures was produced which allegedly told you all about the person going through the process. Much emphasis was given to the fact that this process, to be valid, must be exactly the same for each candidate, and most of the test papers were in the form of the sort of question and choice of answers, A, B, C, or D, which has become very familiar now, but was quite a new idea then. We also had to learn to talk to a room full of people, with at least an appearance of authority; and then, if the powers that be thought we could do it, we were pitched out and sent forth to help organise the endless stream of recruits being sucked in by national service.

As promised, passing out on this course earned automatic promotion to the rank of corporal. Possibly in recognition of our personal qualities, but more likely because someone realised that a corporal with a couple of stripes on his arm is the first thing that a recruit learns to respect; and that was going to be very useful in getting this work done in an atmosphere of reasonably good order. When you think that we were in exactly the same position as a very young and inexperienced school teacher, dealing with large crowds of young men of the same age, you appreciate the need for a bit of artificial authority. Anyhow at the end of the course, which was several weeks long, I duly found myself a corporal in the Personnel Selection branch instead of a trainee pilot, and on route to Melksham in Wiltshire.

This was another centre for recruits, and a sort of satellite to Cardington, and I found myself one of a group of about a dozen young men running the selection centre there. They were mostly of the undergraduate type doing their national service, and on the whole a noticeably unmilitary lot, probably selected by this very process as being well educated, but of little practical use in the service.

Our life was a curious one. We were corporals on an RAF station which otherwise seemed to be occupied entirely by very raw recruits, and drill corporals marching them about. Indeed, we had to march them about ourselves, since this was the only recognised way of getting recruits from one place to the next; but we were not very good at it really, while the drill corporals strode and swaggered about as though specially bred for the purpose. We often had to take two or three dozen new boys, who had just begun to learn how to march, from one end of the station to the other, to or from a personnel selection session; and that was usually more of a problem than putting them through the tests. It was especially tricky if one had to take them past the headquarters building, where Sod's law usually decreed that there was likely to be an officer emerging just as we all swung past the door. Getting a batch of very raw recruits to do a smart eyes-right, while saluting oneself; and getting the order out on the correct foot, is more difficult than you might imagine.

Apart from these slight problems, life soon settled down, as it usually does in the armed forces, to be a matter of fairly boring routine. At the personnel selection hut, which was in a remote corner of the camp near the medical section, a fact that turned out to be useful in the end, we did our school teacher act for varying numbers of recruits every day. They would be marched in to one of the classroom-like huts, one of us would assume a firm but not too severe stance in front of them, as required by our precise training, and go through the tests required. Then the papers would all be checked over, again by precisely laid down routine, so that each candidate had exactly the same chance, and the results passed on to the officers who did the final selection and allocations. Between these batches of worried, indifferent, or scared looking young men, depending on how they were reacting to service life, we had nothing much to do. Being usually left to our own devices, we spent a lot of the time playing Canasta; in fact after several months, when the supply of recruits seemed to be slowing down, we did little else. The key to making life more interesting seemed to be a bit of private transport, so that at least you could get away from the monotony of camp life when possible, and one or two of the others had a motorbike. So that became my next aim in life.

At home in Norfolk on leave, I studied the advertisements in the local paper, and saw an Arial three-fifty being offered for sale at £30. The address was in Norwich, thirty something miles away, I could easily get there by train, and I could just about run to that price, so acquired a pair of L-plates and set off.. The bike turned out to be a perfectly respectable example of an oldish, probably ex army dispatch rider's, machine. The owner demonstrated that it worked, and the engine seemed to be in good order; after all, I had been learning all about engines. He also explained about getting the registration changed, then I tied on the L-plates and prepared to set off home. I felt reasonably confident that as I could fly an aeroplane and ride a bicycle, I could probably manage a motorbike; but at this point the bike's vendor suddenly seemed to lose his nerve, and probably not wanting to see me hit something or somebody within sight of his gate, said the price included delivery. So we tied the machine on the back of his car, and he drove me back home, where we unloaded it and parked it in my father's garage for the night.

Mum and Dad were not very enthusiastic about the new acquisition, but reconciled to the fact that I was beyond advice or correction, merely told me to be careful, and turned their attention to other things. I arose early the next morning and went out to play with my new toy. In the cold light of dawn, and knowing that I had to deal with it all by myself, the motorbike looked more formidable than it had the night before, and bigger, and heavier to lift and move around; but it started after a few trial kicks, and the engine roared in a robust, if slightly frightening, way. I tried letting in the clutch and allowing it to move forward a few yards, which it did, and then stopped again obediently; I practised changing gear, which worked perfectly well, and then there was really nothing else to do but set out and see what happened, so I pushed it out of the gate, got into the saddle, put it in first gear and off we went down the street.

There was little traffic moving about in Wells that morning, and as I chugged experimentally along nothing untoward occurred. We got round the first corner, managed to change up into a higher gear, took a few more corners, and were soon buzzing cheerfully along through the Norfolk countryside. The first 'Halt at Major Road Ahead' sign was a bit tricky, but I managed to stop and start again, with only a few wobbles, and by the time we got home I felt I knew how to do it. I spent the rest of my weeks leave riding about North Norfolk, getting to know my new friend; painted it a nice deep red colour instead of its grubby black and khaki, and then holiday over, and its panniers stuffed with cake and sandwiches, set out on it back to Melksham.

It is quite a long way, sort of diagonally across England, from

Norfolk to Wiltshire; the journey felt like a world tour, and took all day, but we duly arrived and rode triumphantly into base late on a fine summer's evening. I showed my pride and joy to one of the other motorbike owners, and told of my epic ride across half a dozen counties; 'H'mm,' he said, regarding it thoughtfully, 'Yes, it looks like a thirty quid bike', and proceeded to enumerate all the things that would probably go wrong with it. But in fact very little ever did. It was old and rackety, but basically so simple that there was not much to go wrong. It went bumping along on its very basic springs all over the place, on many excursions with others from the camp round local pubs, and several more times all the way home to Norfolk. The worst that ever happened was the day the magneto, an old fashioned electrical component, fell off; probably shaken off by the normal vibration of the engine. I just had to walk back up the road, pick it up, and bolt it on again.

There was another occasion when the engine, single cylinder of course, was running so badly that I stopped by the roadside and dismantled the carburettor in the mistaken belief that the fuel supply was at fault. It wasn't, but in stripping it down I managed to break a small but vital part. A motorist stopped to see what the trouble was, and out of the kindness of his heart took me into the nearest town where I could get a replacement, and then drove me back to my bike again. I put it all together, but still the engine ran just as badly. In the end I got back to camp, late at night, after a long slow ride; then, because it was now dark, suddenly noticed a spark flashing where it shouldn't have been. The old high tension cable to the spark plug was worn, and it was shorting on to the cylinder head and causing all the trouble. But you couldn't blame an old bike for that, could you, and I had learned a valuable lesson in diagnosing engine problems.

Later on I once rode the old motorbike right back to Cottesmore, to see Jill again, but the visit wasn't a spectacular success. Her family seemed a bit taken aback to see me reappear out of the blue as it were, but gave me a meal and chatted away amiably enough. I gathered that Jill was out, but would be back soon; but there was a certain feeling in the air, a sort of uneasiness about something. I said I had better be on my way, a long way to go and all that sort of thing; but was told, 'No, stay a bit longer, Jill will be glad to see you.'

Eventually, late in the afternoon, Jill appeared; but no, she didn't seem to be that glad that I had turned up again. By degrees the story came out. She had taken up with a lad at the stables where she worked. Mum wasn't at all happy about it, neither was Dad. They seemed to have had some faint passing hope that I might take her mind off him, but Jill didn't see it like that at all. It was all a bit difficult, especially for me, and after a lot more general awkwardness I left. We wrote to each other once or twice after that, but I never saw Jill again; I believe she did get married, but I never heard if her family were reconciled to her stable lad in the end.

On the way back to RAF Melksham the bike got a puncture, and I arrived back late, long after I should have, forced to creep in past the guard room at the gate surreptitiously to avoid even more unpleasantness; not a successful outing at all. It was not long after this that my Melksham chapter ended unexpectedly and with a touch of drama.

There was another corporal in our section, called Phil, with whom I had a bit of a political feud. He was something of a left-wing intellectual and saw himself as Trotskyite, and we used to pass some of our more boring moments annoying each other. On this occasion we were horsing about over some subtle political point, when I stepped back, fell over a chair, and found I couldn't get up off the floor. At first nobody believed that anything was wrong, and thought that I was merely kidding Phil that he had knocked me out to win the argument; but it was obvious, at any rate to me, that one of my legs had stopped working. Eventually I managed to get to my feet, or at least to my good foot, and then could not get any further; and in the end had to be helped, hopping on that one foot, to the medical section next door.

There the non-functioning leg was looked at by one or two medical orderlies, who clearly didn't believe the story at all, and at last by a doctor who confirmed that yes, I had broken my leg by falling over a chair. Of course, no one said anything about what had been going on at the time. After a bit of a wait, because this had happened just before lunch time and the RAF medical emergency services were not available until they had finished eating, I was helped into the station ambulance and carted off to the military hospital at Swindon. The next day a worried Phil turned up with a very small box of chocolates to see what had happened, but I was able to reassure him that no one knew that a breach of good order and discipline had taken place. In the ward where they had put me I was just another case of a broken limb, of which there were several waiting to be looked at.

Eventually a surgeon studied one or two x-rays that had been taken of the leg, and then chattily explained that I had somehow managed to twist it in such a way that there was a long split in one of the bones between the knee and ankle. He was very pleased about this, he told me, because it gave him a good opportunity to try out some new stainless steel gadgets that he had just acquired for screwing together bits of bone, and he would have me in to the operating theatre in no time at all. He was so enthusiastic that one almost looked forward to the operation; and it turned out that in fact it was the good news, because after it was all nicely screwed up I would be able to get about on it again. I was already feeling that I had been immobilised a long time, at the mercy of nurses with bed pans and bed baths, and this seemed to be a very good idea.

Soon after I was duly wheeled in and hoisted on to the operating table, and was just looking round nervously when my surgical friend appeared with a hypodermic syringe in his hand and said, 'Don't worry, you wont feel a thing. This will knock you out in seven seconds, if you don't believe me, try counting up to ten'. I got as far as five, then woke up groggily, back in the ward again. The leg felt fine, and all the splints and stuff that had been wrapped round it was gone. I was in plaster from toe to thigh, but that seemed a good swap, and as promised I was allowed to get out of bed. I soon learned that the snag with being encased in plaster was that it generated the most horrific itching, but still I could get about independently again, while itching, and that was the main thing.

After a week or two at Swindon I was sent on to another hospital near London to do orthopaedic exercises, and was even allowed to go home, though that, given the difficulties of travelling by train with crutches and one leg in plaster, was not so much fun as it sounded. You had the choice, in those old carriages, of either stumbling over everybody else's legs to get near the window, or to sit near the door and have everybody else climb over your extended leg. It gave you a bit of insight about what it is like to be disabled, with everybody apparently unable to see the stiffly extended plastered leg until they fell over it, and then moving away embarrassed. So much for being a wounded hero, I thought. Eventually, after about six weeks, the plaster was cut off, and I was able to have a good scratch and a decent bath. It is difficult to convey the pleasure of that to anyone who has not had a limb encased in itchy plaster. Dealing with the itch was the main preoccupation with everyone in my ward, and great ingenuity was used in finding suitable tools to reach down inside the plaster cast; a dinner fork was the most easily available instrument, but too short to really help much. The trouble was that how ever far you could contrive to reach, the worst itch was always just beyond. In the end you believed that, whatever the medical staff might say, your leg inside the plaster was a mass of really nasty scars and scabs; and I was enormously relieved, and incredulous, when the plaster actually came off, to see nothing untoward there but a rather pallid and thin looking, but otherwise normal leg.

By the time I eventually got back to Melksham again, fit for duty, there was talk of the whole Personnel Selection section moving back to headquarters at Cardington. No one ever explained these things, but it was probably to do with the small number of recruits coming through, and the inordinate time the section was still spending in playing Canasta. At all events I was soon back in the shadow of the giant airship sheds yet again, for the third time, and still sorting out recruits.

The old Arial motorbike was still bouncing about gamely, but among the much larger group we were now part of, there was a man with a Morgan three wheeler which I looked at enviously. It had an air-cooled engine stuck out on the front, and looked like a small aeroplane without any wings. But if it had no wings, yet it did have a cockpit you could sit inside, and be fairly weatherproof; and I had learnt by then all about the main drawback of motorbikes, which is being completely at the mercy of the elements. On pretty well all my long cross country rides, home and back and elsewhere, at some stage it rained, and the bold motorcyclist got very wet indeed. The era of the smart and weatherproof leathers had not dawned, at any rate for us, and foul weather wear was a flat cap and raincoat, and possibly a pair of canvas leggings. You got very, very wet; and of course what ever was in the panniers strapped across the rear wheel suffered the same fate. I had several times arrived back from a weekend pass soaked, and with a cake from home and other goodies reduced to a sort of thick soup.

I looked thoughtfully at the three wheeler, and decided that I would find something like that. It was perfectly legal to drive such a vehicle on a motorbike licence, because having only three wheels it could be counted as a motor cycle and sidecar; and having spent several weeks in hospital, I had collected some back pay I'd had little opportunity to spend, so I was in funds. My course of action was obvious, and on my first day off I rode the old bike down to London to look round places where exotica like Morgans could be bought.

By luck, whether good or bad, it is difficult say, I found one straight away. At the very first dealer's showroom I looked around, there stood this strange looking object, a black Morgan Matchless Twin, of an undeniably sporty appearance; exactly what I wanted. Yes, it could be for sale, said the dealer, but it had only just come in and he hadn't had a chance to check it over. It may have been true, or perhaps it was just his way of saying that he did not want to be held responsible for it. It could be £150, he said. That was more than I had, so I suggested hire purchase. 'Right ho, gov. I'll give you a run round the block in it.' We ran round the block, it seemed to work, and that was that. Half an hour later I had handed over some cash, signed assorted forms, put some petrol in the tank, and there I was on the forecourt sitting in what was now my very own Morgan Matchless. All I had to do was discover if I could drive it, and find my way back to Cardington.

I let in the clutch and drove carefully on to the street; there was a lot of traffic, but it was moving quite slowly, heading out of London on the same road I had come in by, and I soon got the hang of moving along with it. Things went quite well until we came to a junction I couldn't remember seeing on the route in, and there I took what must have been the wrong road, then lost track of where I was altogether. At the next main cross roads there was a big, London type of pub, and I stopped and went in to ask exactly where I was, then couldn't get the Morgan started again. So back into the pub again to get some help; plenty of willing hands pushed me off on my way, and I went a few more miles; then realised I was once more lost. Again I got someone to show me the way in the direction of Bedford and give me another push. Something had gone wrong with the starter, or perhaps it was just my ignorance of the machinery. I didn't dare stop again after that, but just kept on going, and eventually got back on to the London to Bedford road. Ages later we arrived back in sight of the great black airship sheds, and with relief drew up at the main gate of RAF Cardington.

Then there was another ticklish problem. As a mere corporal I should go to the guard room, announce my presence to whoever was on duty, and ask to be let in; but if I left my new vehicle the engine would probably stop, and I would be in the embarrassing position of having to ask a military policeman, and they were all notoriously humourless, to turn out the guard to give me a push start. I felt I must be running out of luck, but as I drew up, to my amazement a figure came out of the guardroom hurriedly pulling on his cap, doubled over to the gate, flung it open and saluted. I waved cheerfully, and drove on. Who on earth did he think I was? Clearly someone important. I carefully kept well away from the guardroom for several days; there was no point in being recognised and embarrassing someone.

That Morgan was a strange vehicle. It looked like an outlandish racing car, with its twin cylinder engine stuck out at the front, tiny cockpit, low windscreen and wide spaced front wheels; but it had the performance of a pram driven by a lawn mower. It also had virtually no springing, and jolted and rattled along leaving a trail of nuts and bolts behind it. The drive was to the single rear wheel, via a long chain; and that rear wheel, being under the body, was almost impossible to get at if you happened to have a puncture. It also had brakes that it would be kind to describe as inadequate, and a driving position that was so low that you could often see the road ahead underneath other vehicles.

It was true that the cockpit did give some degree of protection from the weather, at least the legs remained dry, but in all other respects I was soon feeling quite nostalgic about the old Arial. It hadn't looked much, but it had worked better, and had chugged many miles with very little trouble. The Morgan on the other hand seldom went out without something going wrong. Its slow speed should have kept it out of trouble, as it seldom managed more than about forty-five miles an hour, but even so the braking system could not be relied on to stop it when required. Then when stopped for any reason on the road, as I had discovered early on, it was loath to get going again; it seemed to sense that movement meant trouble, and would have been happier in a museum as an example of early, interesting, but impractical motor design.

It, and I lived together for about a year, in the course of which time I appeared in court three times as a result of its uncertain ways. Once because of its inability to stop, once because I was trying to avoid stopping it in case it wouldn't start again, and once because someone else drove into it at night, probably because they couldn't see it, being very small and black with lights like bicycle lamps. In the end, as a result of one of these accidents, and being late getting back to camp, I had to leave it at a roadside pub and catch a bus. The owner of the hostelry where it had been left subsequently offered me £50 to take it off my hands, and I was happy to agree. It allowed me to pay off the money still owing on it and move on, like the wedding guest, a sadder but a wiser man.

In the mean time life in the Personnel Selection Section at Cardington went on, and my time in the RAF was drawing to the end of the four year engagement I had so rashly entered into. The officer in charge of the section at this time was doing his national service, and studying to become a barrister at the same time. He was older than the rest of us, in his mid twenties, his service having been deferred while he studied; and he received his legal qualification while he was with us. His wig, in its fancy box, had arrived shortly before one of my appearances in court, and he leaped at the chance of appearing in wig and gown as my advocate. This visit to the local magistrate's court was caused by the occasion when the Morgan's almost useless brakes had allowed us to drive, slowly but remorselessly, into the back of a butcher's van just outside Bedford. I knew I could count on a good defence, because I had been studying photography during my time in hospital, and had produced a portrait of my barrister, bewigged and in full plumage, which he really liked. But in the event, there wasn't much for him to do, as the magistrate just listened briefly to the story of a bent rear bumper from the butcher, said it was a case of careless driving, and fined me £5.

The final few months in the Airforce was spent in more of the usual uneventful routine, an which several of us all due for demobilisation did a modest amount of work, and filled in time otherwise with our own devices. At one time, for a few weeks, I took up politics seriously; mainly on account of a girl who was on the local Conservative Party committee. I went to party meetings and took her to the pictures quite a lot. Then there was a bye election, and it was all quite exciting for a time until our man won, thanked us rather grandly, and disappeared to London. End of political career, though my political activist and I still went to the pictures occasionally.

Back at camp our little group who were due to reach the end of our military service soon, often discussed what we would do next. Only one, a particular friend with whom I shared the interest in photography, had any very definite idea. Tony was determined to be a reporter on a London paper, and was studying the use of the camera to that end. We used to practice composing interesting newspaper type photographs, and using different cameras, even acquiring a plate camera of the ancient type that reporters use in nineteen thirties movies. He and I and the others also whiled away the time forming a music group, and dabbling in amateur theatricals; and one day, for no particular reason, we were all talking about the sea and sailing, and someone came up with the notion of us all going on a sailing trip together. I had been sailing on the Norfolk Broads, and reckoned I knew all about it, Tony had some experience, and the others just thought they would like to have a go.

In a week or so we had fixed everything up, and had booked a sailing boat at Wroxham in April. I would have left the RAF by then and, it was assumed, would be free to do whatever I liked, and the others would take a weeks leave. We were five to start with, but this became four in the way these things do; Tony and I, and Allan who was the musical one, and John, a tall vague young man, who thought he might quite like sailing if he didn't have to get up too early in the morning. We told him that the cook was always allowed to lie in bed except in emergencies, and he decided he would be the cook.

Shortly after these arrangements were made my four years of service life were up. I had an interview with a Careers Officer, who was supposed to help regular airmen with their approach to civilian life, and asked me what I was going to do. I said I rather fancied being a photographer, or a journalist perhaps, or maybe something else. I actually had no idea what I was going to do next, and neither did he; he was, I think, a bit tired of trying to give good advice to ungrateful airmen.

Next stop was the demobilisation centre, where I was offered the choice of the traditional demob suit that all time expired military men were given, or, as exciting alternative, a sports jacket and flannels, and took the latter. The flannels were all right, if not of fashionable cut, but the jacket was a strange russet shade that I have never seen since. I always intended to wear it, but somehow never did; it always seemed somehow connected with the life that was over, and now I wanted to leave that behind. In fact, I would have cheerfully taken anything they offered; the real object of the days work was to get on the train with my very last service pass, wave good bye to the RAF, and steam away into the future.

4

Interlude

The Norfolk Broads can be beautiful, or they can be unutterably dreary, depending on the weather, and your mood. On that particular day, a Saturday in April, at Wroxham, it was a lovely spring afternoon. The sun was shining, and a light breeze just ruffled the reflections of boats, waterfowl and cheerful holidaymakers, in the scarcely moving river. Tony, John, Allan and I were also being reflected in the water, if anyone was interested, as we trailed with our assorted luggage behind the boatman who was showing us our home for the coming week. 'There you are then', said our boatman, 'Tha's Dragonfly, in that cut there. She's a good comfortable boat, and' he added, looking at us thoughtfully, 'She's right easy to sail.' We stood on the edge of the wooden landing stage looking at Dragonfly. My first thought was that she looked very big, being about thirty foot long, broad with it, and with quite a large dinghy to tow behind; altogether a lot bigger than anything I had managed before. I was prepared to believe that she was comfortable, lying there at peace in her quiet little cut on a sunny afternoon, but I knew that conditions on the Broads were not always like that; still, it wasn't my place to worry the crew.

'She looks fine. Standard sort of Broads rig?' I enquired, trying to sound easy and knowledgeable. 'Oh, yes, you won't have no trouble with her, I'll just show you the motor, then you'll be off, no doubt.' He indicated the engine, which looked very small, located in one of the cockpit lockers. 'There it is, tha's a good little engine, you won't have no trouble with that. Just remember to grease her gland. Well, you'll want to get your stuff aboard and be away.' He seemed to want to get rid of us. 'Well, thanks very much,' I said, ' I'm sure we won't have any trouble......' But he was already out of Dragonfly's cockpit and running along the wooden staging to where a family party seemed to be trying to get a large, unwilling dog aboard a motor craft.

We heaved our assortment of very un-nautical looking luggage aboard, and began trying to stuff it out of the way. John started to change into a pair of white trousers, which he had apparently imagined were the correct rig for a sailing holiday, but was persuaded to take them off again. Like all Broads boats ours had very shallow draught, and seemed a lot smaller on the inside than she looked from outside, but we got everything stowed where you wouldn't fall over it if you were careful. Soon we were in the situation that someone would have to do something about actually sailing this large, lumpy looking craft. 'Well,' I said to Tony, the only one amongst the others who admitted to knowing anything about boats, 'We'd better get under way, I suppose.' He nodded thoughtfully, but did nothing. 'You'll be all right as long as you remember to grease her gland,' remarked Allan, lying on his bunk, while John looked carefully over the cooking pans that he had volunteered to manipulate. 'OK, all hands on deck then,' I said, 'Let's get this thing moving.'

It seemed a moderately worrying prospect to get Dragonfly underway and out into the river amongst all the craft that were occupying it. Numerous other parties were starting out on their weeks cruise, and the sunny afternoon had brought out plenty of casual sailors too, while ducks, swans and other waterfowl added to the general feeling of congestion. It was going to be quite a challenge to get sailing, and go off down the river away from Wroxham without hitting at least one or two other floating objects. I looked at the very stout mast, the various bits and pieces attached to it, and the boom about the size of a telegraph pole; this was not the moment to show indecisiveness. 'The wind's from upstream,' I said, looking towards Wroxham bridge, 'If we get the sails up, then give her a push out into the river, we should be all right. Lets get them up.' We sorted out the halyards from amongst the general tangle of ropes and cautiously hauled up the yard of the enormous mainsail, leaving plenty of slack in the mainsheet, and then raised the jib with its sheet free. Nothing untoward happened. Dragonfly still sat there quietly, hardly pulling at the mooring ropes while the very light breeze swung the boom out gently. Tony and I heaved the main halyard up tight, made it fast, then gave a hard push on the landing stage, and we moved ponderously out into the river. We hauled the sheets in, tweaked the tiller a bit, and we were sailing down stream; I just had time to think we had done that rather well before the great boom crashed over in a gybe, taking assorted ropes and a deck mop with it. It looked and felt very messy, but we were only moving very slowly and everything was retrieved out of the river as it floated gently by. The deck was soon tidied up again, and our cruise had begun.

Afternoon drifted into idyllic evening as the sun sank behind us and we sailed gently down the river towards Salhouse Broad, where we had decided to stop for the first night. It was so quiet and peaceful with the gentle breeze astern and no tacking necessary, that the crew soon became restive. Was this all we were going to do for the next week, they wanted to know? Sailing was boring. Allan returned to his bunk, and John clambered over the stern into the dinghy and said he thought he would sit there in peace and read a book until something interesting happened. The bustle that had been going on at Wroxham soon ceased as we left the village behind, and there were soon few other boats visible; just one or two others astern of us, and another sailing ahead that we were slowly catching up with. I watched it idly, thinking it seemed to be exactly like the yacht we were in and probably came from the same yard; it had probably left just ahead of us while we were working out how to get ours going. It made a pretty picture, as it glided along between the tall trees that line the river there, like us making use of the convenient tail wind that was just giving them steerage way. As I watched a girl climbed out of the cockpit, walked confidently along the side deck, picked up the heavy quanting pole that lay along the cabin top, and slipped the butt end into the water as casually as a hardened wherryman. She put her shoulder against her end of it, and 'walked' it aft, punting their boat along so that it began to pick up speed a bit and forged ahead again.

I noticed that their helmsman was also a girl, and then two more emerged from the cabin. John, from his position in the dinghy began to show signs of interest, and I remarked to the other two, who happened to be below, 'Let's race this other boat, shall we?' Allan glanced up the companion way at me. 'Don't be so boring. You can't race when there's no wind.' 'It's full of girls,' I said. He and Tony stuck their heads up and took in the situation, and in a flash they were on deck. Then Allan had a good idea. 'John can row the dinghy round to the front end and tow us along.' John, by now quite animated, began to start hauling oars out from the bottom of his dinghy, but obviously without any clear idea what to do with them. I could see this cruise ending abruptly, and John had said he couldn't swim. 'It wouldn't work,' I said hurriedly, 'Get back aboard, John; We'll have a go at punting too.' Tony took the tiller, and I climbed up on to the cabin top and untied our quanting pole, as our craft almost came to a stop too in the same place that the girls' boat had been becalmed.

A little pushing and heaving on the quant, and we were sailing again as the breeze reached us again between the trees; an impromptu race developed, and we eventually passed the girls with a jolly wave, noticing in passing that their boat was called Smuggler. A little later, and they passed us again with more jolly waves, and thus a certain relationship developed. After a bit more of this both boats reached Salhouse Broad more or less neck and neck, and entered the broad together; this was promising as we intended to moor there for the night anyway, and it looked as if the girls were stopping there too. Sure enough they did, and the boats came to a rest twenty yards apart. While Tony and I were lowering the sails and making everything neat and tidy, Allan suddenly announced that he felt he had better teach John to row properly, and they both got into the dinghy and cast off. Tony and I were not surprised to notice, when we had time to look, that the rowing lesson had somehow brought them alongside Smuggler, and a brief conversation was seen to take place. 'So, how did it go then?' I enquired when they returned. 'John was doing quite well.' 'Yes, we saw that, and what about the rowing lesson?' 'Yes, well, we asked them over for supper, but they declined.' 'Unbelievable, and did you tell them what you are going to cook us for supper, John?' John said, 'Well, I thought we would have sausages and beans.' 'And you told them that?' John looked thoughtful, 'Was that a mistake, do you think?' Tony said, 'Don't worry. It wouldn't have made any difference if you'd said you were fixing up oysters and champagne, they just don't look that hungry.' 'Well, they were quite friendly,' said John, defensively, 'And they said they would race us tomorrow; they are going to Hickling, wherever that is.' 'Looks like Hickling for us too then,' I said, 'So lets have these sausages and beans, shall we, it would be a pity to waste them.'

Several yachts and motor cruisers had come to rest in the broad by then, and soon cooking smells, suggesting variations on the same theme as our sausages, were drifting round. The sun had finally gone down on a beautiful, calm evening and mist began to form over the still surface of the water. We ate our sausages and beans, and after a certain amount of bickering about who should be doing it, the washing up was done, and everything made reasonably tidy. Then we discovered then that the cabin light did not seem to be working properly, and was pretty dim. Nobody was too worried and all hands just lay about on the bunks talking, but I had a slightly uneasy feeling about it, because as far as I knew the same battery was probably supposed to start our engine. But I decided to worry about that in the morning and soon peace, broken by the odd snore, descended on Dragonfly for the night.

The following morning, as might have been expected after the brilliant evening, was dull and misty. When I, being the first awake, put my head out of the tent cover over our cockpit, the whole world seemed to be dripping wet; the air so laden with moisture you could have wrung it out. One or two craft were close enough to show up as dim shapes in the mist, but the rest of the world had disappeared, and Salhouse Broad itself with its boats and tree-lined edges had become a sort of fuzzy grey emptiness. My watch showed seven o'clock, and it was fairly obvious that my three companions, all still sleeping peacefully, were not going to want to make an early start; so I thought I would take out the dinghy to pass the time. It was not a very good idea; everything you touched was wet and cold, especially the dinghy and the gear in it, and a steady dripping that probably came from the invisible trees seemed to be the only noise. I did a brisk circuit of our part of the broad, past other boats that appeared silent and mysterious out of the all pervading greyness, and then as quietly disappeared into it again. It was so quiet that the normal creaks and splashes of dinghy being rowed round were quite embarrassingly loud; I felt that I must be waking everyone else up, but if so nobody showed any signs of it.

Back at Dragonfly however there was at last a sign of human activity, Tony's head emerged from the cockpit cover as I came alongside, and he had his camera. 'Very suitable for some picturesque early morning Mist on the River sort of shots, is it?' He enquired. It was in fact beginning to lighten up now, the grey much brighter above our heads, and odd masts and tree tops appearing round about. So we did the circuit again, taking photographs. This time, when we got back the whole picture was changing rapidly, more boats visible including the girls' Smuggler, the mist broken up into patches on the surface of the water, and even bits of pale blue appearing above.

We clambered aboard, noisily, to wake people up, and Tony started to get the cockpit cover off and stowed while I boiled some water and found the tea pot. Moans and complaints about being woken in the middle of the night came from the other two, but they managed to accept cups of tea. I told them that the girls were up and getting their boat ready to leave, which was untrue, but helped them to get out of their bunks, and after a decent interval John was seen to look round for the frying pan in a very sleepy way. It seemed to take a long time to find almost anything that was needed, but with all hands helping a breakfast of sausages, again, was prepared and eaten.

By then the scene had changed once more. There was still mist on the water, but the sun was up and the suggestion of a fitful breeze stirred a pennant here and there on yachts' masts. The girls' boat came to life and immediately, taking us by surprise; the sails were hoisted, and the mooring rope was seen to be hauled in. 'Don't worry,' I said in answer to the startled looks around me. 'They'll never sail in a wind like this, they won't even move.' But they had clearly worked that one out; the quant was heaved off their cabin top, and away they went, punting surprisingly swiftly back the way we had all come into the broad, and out into the river. They disappeared to general consternation aboard Dragonfly. I thought quickly, 'Look, I was thinking we had better try the engine, I'm not to happy about the state of the battery, perhaps we had better run it a bit to charge up.' This was deemed a good idea, so while Tony supervised the crew and our ship was got ready for sailing, I had a go at getting the engine started. The battery was as I had feared, pretty flat, but with a little coaxing the motor did start, and we hoisted up our mud-weight anchor, circled round, and chugged out of the broad after the other boat.

The girls had already vanished round the next bend along the misty river, so we continued to motor; after all it was necessary to charge up the battery. After a time, we began to see other boats on the river, as others finished their breakfasts and got under way, and as we were not sure which was which and we didn't want to come up with them obviously under power, we cut the engine and tried sailing. There was so little wind that our progress owed more to the current than anything else, and we got out the quant and started punting too. After half an hour we at last caught up with the yacht we thought we were chasing, and then found it was the wrong one; so feeling slightly foolish, we pressed on. The breeze woke up a bit, and we passed another similar looking craft, but still no girls; but at last as we approached the next riverside village, there they were, filling their water tank. What a good idea, we all said, and drew up to the quay side too. There was also a village shop, and of course by then we had a list of things we had forgotten to bring, apart from needing a bit more than beans and sausages in the galley.

The crew of Smuggler had a smart water can which we, since we didn't seem to have such a basic essential, could borrow, and which of course lead to a certain amount of chat and general fraternisation. They were quite friendly, in a guarded sort of way, as girls might be who had seen boats full of young men before, but they made it clear that the race to Hickling was still on. We gallantly waved them on ahead of us again while waiting for John to reappear from the pub; and then on his return, cast off and made him jump for it. He said that was uncalled for because he had brought us a bottle of beer. But what was the use of one bottle of beer, everyone wanted to know, and John sulkily said he would sit in the dinghy again; but that was not allowed as it would cause drag, and we were racing. John went below. Perhaps he has gone to cook us a lovely lunch, we thought.

There was a bit of a breeze getting up and we were soon sailing quite well, and would have passed the girls, when the tall, rather haughty looking one, who seemed to be the serious sailor amongst them, suddenly fell overboard. It was the last thing that anyone had expected, but John who must have been looking out of a porthole, rushed up on deck and tried to get into our dinghy. He obviously saw himself as one of nature's lifeboat men, ever ready to perform a gallant lifesaving act; but it is not easy to detach a dinghy from a yacht under sail, and John was immediately in trouble himself. By the time he, and the dinghy, were untangled, the haughty but now soaking wet girl was being hauled aboard Smuggler again. Of course, they had to luff up to get her aboard, and we got ahead of them briefly; but John, saved from himself but once more in his beloved dinghy, cast the painter off, shouting that he would have to go back and see if they were all right. Needless to say they were perfectly all right; it was by then a warm, agreeable sort of morning for falling in the river, and a minute later the girls overhauled us again and forged ahead. We on the other hand, had to tack back for John. Some were in favour of leaving him there, but we reckoned that we might need the dinghy.

With our brave lifeboat man aboard again, and the dinghy in its correct position trailing astern, we pushed on in jolly sailing weather, along our river to where it is joined by the Thurn, which we entered to sail up towards Hickling. There were plenty of boats about by now, so many in fact that though we thought we glimpsed Smuggler ahead of us now and then, we were never quite sure where the girls had got to. Opinion was divided; some said they had probably sneaked off down the Bure towards Yarmouth to avoid us, others reckoned that they were just better sailors and were way ahead. Anyhow, we pressed on towards Potter Heigham bridge, which had to be negotiated before we could enter the wild, open waters of Hickling and Horsey.

Old Heigham bridge is ancient and very low, like the entrance to a tunnel, and looks far too small a hole for big boats to pass through; except of course that broads craft are built to do just that, so we lowered sails and our mast, tidied everything down, and eased Dragonfly through. All went well, except that at a critical moment I foolishly put out my foot to stop the hull of our boat drifting against the stonework. It is a mistake you only make once, because you learn instantly that a big boat cannot easily be stopped by the human foot, and in this case my leg slipped down between hull and bridge, and was ground between both. I dragged what felt like a badly mangled limb back aboard, convinced that I needed a doctor and probably hospital, gingerly removed footwear expecting to see at the very least extensive bruising and a fair amount of blood, but found it looking quite normal. It still hurt, but in these circumstances, with nothing dramatic to show, you do not receive any sympathy. I spent the rest of the day doing everything on one foot, but in the meantime the life afloat takes no account of minor injuries, and we hoisted our mast and sails again, and pressed on, into the world of reed beds and expanses of wide but shallow water.

The scene changes completely here. The friendly landscape of woods, trees and meadows, grassy banks and grazing cows has been left behind. The sky becomes much bigger, the solid river banks disappear and the line between water and land becomes vague and uncertain. As you sail close to the reed beds that seem to mark the beginning of solid land, you realise that they do nothing of the sort; the reeds rise straight out of the water, and between their thin elegant stems there is just more glinting water, and no land at all. The expanses of water between these uncertain shores look very inviting for sailing, with no trees to break the wind, but the would-be navigator has to remember that though there are channels, there are also shallows hidden under the silvery grey surface.

The afternoon, as Dragonfly ventured into this new world, was doing a repeat of the day before. As the sun slid down behind us, the breeze fell lighter and lighter, and we were soon doing little more than drift gently on between the reed beds. The bustle of busy water craft of all sorts, that had filled the sunny afternoon, had ended. Upstream of Heigham bridge there were fewer craft anyhow, and those few soon seemed to have mostly called it a day. We ghosted on, passing one moored yacht after another, but none of them turned out to be Smuggler. Still, Hickling had been the agreed goal, and we were only in Heigham Sound, which is a sort of approach to the great broad. The wind had still not completely failed, so we kept on, slowly passing between the reed beds as the light faded. There were soon no other sails visible at all, and common sense suggested that we anchor for the night; but the idea that Smuggler was there somewhere just ahead kept us going, and of course we had said that we would race to Hickling Broad.

John and Allan had an idea, and it was the one they usually had; they would take the dinghy and scout ahead, to see if they could find Smuggler. Then of course, they said, they would report back to Tony and me, and we could sail on however slowly, pass the other boat by a couple of yards, and claim to have won the race. Off they went among the reed beds, the splashing of their oars soon fading into the distance, while we, and Dragonfly, continued our ponderous progress; parting the now dark water with hardly a ripple. The sky was still clear, and it became pretty cold. Mist began to form over the water as we just kept moving, up Heigham Sound, past the entrance to Horsey Mere, and then at last through the channel to Hickling Broad itself. There was no sign whatsoever of our dinghy, or any moving craft, on the wide dark waters in front of us. Wondering where they had got to, we gave a shout and listened, but there was no reply; John and Allan had disappeared. 'Bet your life they found the girls', said Tony.

Whether they had or not, we had to try to make contact again before it became completely dark, so we sailed slowly on into the broad. There seemed to be little chance of seeing them in the dinghy against the dark shore, whereas we should be reasonably visible out on the water, so we just kept moving on slowly in the rapidly gathering gloom, giving a shout every now and then. We ran aground once or twice in shallow water, but moving so slowly that it was easy to push off again; then just about when it became completely and finally night, we came yet again to rest on a patch of invisible mud, and knew we were there until the morning. The only light we could see was a pinpoint or two in the distance, probably at the far end of the broad, where I knew there was a pub.

We told each other that if they hadn't found the other boat, they would certainly find the pub sooner or later; then another light flickered, not far away, Tony shouted, and Allan shouted back, oars splashed, and they came alongside. It appeared that they had been rowing about lighting matches and shouting for quite a time, while we had heard and seen nothing. Perhaps it was the mist, by now quite thick again. No, they hadn't found Smuggler and her crew, and didn't really seem to mind whether they had or not. Everybody was freezing and wet with dew and mist, and the most important thing seemed to be hot food and drink; which problem, thanks to our shopping earlier in the day, was easily dealt with.

Monday morning, again fine but misty, revealed that when we went aground the night before we had done it in style. Stakes marking the main channel, invisible to us at the time, now showed that we had come to rest about twenty yards outside it, and pointing the wrong way. Investigation of the mud round about showed that we were in inches of water only, horrifying, until we remembered that the Broads are to some extent tidal; so obviously the tide had gone out during the night. What goes down, in this case, must come up, so we only had to wait.

By the time we had cooked and eaten breakfast, and pottered about a bit, the tide was very slowly rising again, and as soon as it looked as if it might be deep enough to float us it was all hands to the quant pole, oar, deck mop, or anything that could be used as a lever in the mud. There proved to be just enough water to get Dragonfly turned in her mud berth, after a lot of heaving and pushing; and then with some of the crew punting and others rowing madly with the dinghy, she was slowly towed and levered through the mud back to the main channel. There sail was set, and with the breeze was getting up again, we were soon off back through Heigham Sound, heading for good deep river water.

Somehow nobody seemed to want to explore Horsey or Hickling any further. We were busy discussing what had happened to Smuggler, when she appeared again sailing briskly in the now freshening breeze. A shouted conversation disclosed that, no, they had not reached Hickling last night, they had moored in Horsey Mere, and they were heading for Yarmouth now. A minute later, as we tacked past each other we had the pleasure of seeing them run aground and come to a juddering halt on some of the mud we had recently come to know so well. 'I reckon we won that round', said Tony, as we watched them getting their craft back into the channel again.

Yarmouth suited us very well as our next objective, so the race continued. We got back to Heigham Bridge first, and managed through it quite neatly without any more foot crushing, but had to stop there to get some advice from the boat yard. Our lighting system was down to the merest glimmer, and there seemed to be something seriously wrong with our electrical gear. A mechanic looked it over, and was inclined to agree that we had been sent out with a faulty battery. He said he would telephone ahead and arrange for us to pick up a new one at Acle, on the way to Yarmouth, and off we went again. We were well behind Smuggler again after all this, but caught sight of their sail every now and then as we tacked back down the river we had sailed up yesterday afternoon, to the junction with the Bure, and then down towards Yarmouth and the sea. At Acle we stopped at the boat yard to get the new battery, which took a long time for no particular reason, and then it was late afternoon again.

Enthusiasm for pressing on seemed to have waned; the crew had discovered that Acle is a large village with pubs, and the race to Yarmouth was somehow less important; after all, the girls would probably have gone somewhere else by the time we reached there. I could see that with the choice of an evening in a cosy, warm, pub, or sailing on into another cold, misty night on the river, the pursuit of Smuggler was less attractive than it had been. I was quietly relieved. The arrival at Yarmouth meant that the next step would be the crossing of Breydon Water, the wide open estuary where three river systems meet, the tides are always difficult, and it usually seems to be blowing a gale. For me, tomorrow would be quite soon enough. So we moored up tidily below Acle bridge, walked to the village, and had a mildly inebriated evening ashore. Morning found us with heads slightly the worse for wear, but up and about at a reasonable hour, and on our way down the river on the final stretch to Yarmouth.

As you sail down the river the landscape becomes more open, the river wider and deeper, and more serious; this is the bit that your keen sailor enjoys. Whatever wind there is, reaches you across the flat freshwater marshes that stretch away for miles on either side, free, untamed. That which might be a gentle, elusive breeze up stream amongst the trees and meadows, is a different sort of creature here; strong, steady, and possibly a touch frightening at times as clouds scud across the sky. Sails strain, masts creak, heavy hulls take on unexpected angles as they slice through the water. Thus we sailed down to Yarmouth, with the fresh wind largely astern, and gibing a tricky operation on some of the bends in the river.

By the time we reached the Yarmouth yacht station the wind was really strong and we had the river pretty well to ourselves; most of the other boats seemed to be moored up there, leaving very little space for us to slip into, if we had wanted to stop; so we kept going. It was obviously quite near low water, so we luffed up against the mud on the side of the main stream, got the mast down, which we were quite good at by now, motored through the bridges into Breydon water, and moored up head to wind against the mud there. Everything had gone well, so far. What we had to do now, was to sail the length of Breydon and enter the mouth of one of the other two rivers, the Yare or the Waveney, that meet there. I knew from past experience that this is easier to say than do.

The geographical layout of Breydon Water is that of an estuary running from south-west to north-east, where it enters the sea at Yarmouth. The rivers Yare and Waveney enter it at the south end, and the Bure joins it about three or four miles further downstream, just before Yarmouth and the sea. In theory you simply sail down the Bure, pass under the bridges as we had done, moor in the wide estuary at low water, raise your mast again and wait for the tide to flow; then simply sail up with it into one of the other rivers, depending on whether you intend to visit Norwich or Beccles. We had performed the first half of the manoeuvre pretty well, and moored head to wind and waited confidently for the tide to flow. Precisely on time, it did. Thinking how neatly we had performed what can be a tricky operation, we got the sails up and pushed off from the mud into the deep, but still quite narrow channel. As the stiff breeze filled the sails Dragonfly should soon have been sailing again, and on her way up Breydon Water, but she wasn't.

The main sail filled all right, but the jib had somehow become tangled and was immediately trying to flog itself to pieces. Tony tried to free it but could not, John went forward to help, but they had to give up and hauled the sail down again in a tangle of flailing ropes. All this time I was juggling with the tiller trying to hold Dragonfly in the centre of the channel, but with the rig unbalanced, the strong gusty wind, and all this happening on the fore deck, we were getting nearer and nearer to the mud on the leeward side. There was a last desperate effort to get the jib sail up and behaving properly, but it was too late, there was no room left to tack, we bumped onto the mud, and Dragonfly was aground on the wrong side of the channel. There was no chance whatsoever of sailing her off from that position, and the wind was blowing her further on the mud as the tide rose, so we did the only thing possible; got the sails down, and started the engine. Even so she was being blown hard on the mud by what now felt like a full gale; but we got her off with a lot of heaving and pushing, motored back across the rapidly widening channel to the windward side again, once more raised the sails, getting it right this time, and sailed on up Breydon Water.

With the rapidly rising tide the channel was by now a wide stretch of grey, choppy water and the sailing was exhilarating, or so we were telling ourselves. We foamed along with spray flying, almost the full length of the estuary, three miles or more, and were approaching the mouth of the Waveney river when what looked like a buoy, or possibly merely a stick with a scrap of red material fluttering from it, appeared ahead. There was no way of knowing what it indicated, but some sort of hazard to navigation seemed a fair bet, which meant that we should give it a wide berth. But which side should we pass it on? I had to do something quickly, so made a decision and chose the right hand side; we should have gone left.

On the mud once more, we lowered the sails yet again, and prepared to wait for the tide to rise a bit further. We were in a more sheltered situation now, and the world round about was less of a wild, grey sort of blur, then we noticed that there was a small rowing boat coming towards us from the shore; it was the first craft of any sort that we had seen afloat since Yarmouth. There were a man and a boy in the boat, the boy rowing with casual ease and confidence as the little craft danced about in the tideway. The man, sitting in the stern, addressed us, shouting through the wind. 'We see you stuck on the mud. We'll haul you off and give you a tow up to St.Olaves.' 'Thank you,' I said, 'We don't want a tow, we're just waiting for the tide to flow a bit more,' trying to sound as if we always did that, at this particular point. The boy continued rowing slowly, holding his position against the current. They both looked at us, trying to work out if we knew what we were talking about. I had realised by now that they probably made a good business of 'rescuing' holiday makers. 'We're waiting for the tide,' I said again, 'It will rise a good bit yet.' 'Ah, you may think so,' said the man, glumly 'Chuck us your rope.' We all looked at each other for another minute or two. I began to think perhaps we should take him up on the offer, he must know a lot more about the tide than I did. Then he said something to the boy at the oars, who looked over his shoulder past us and started to row briskly again. A couple of hundred yards astern a motor cruiser had come up behind us, seemed to have also taken avoiding action on sighting the red flag, and had also gone aground. Our erstwhile rescuers had found a better prey and was soon alongside them; and then a good deal of arm waving could be seen going on, as they no doubt discussed suitable towing and rescuing fees.

By now our own boat was beginning to stir on the soft mud and showed signs of coming unstuck, and with a little more of our usual heaving and shoving, we were away again, and soon in the mouth of the Waveney river. From there, in much more sheltered conditions we sailed on to St. Olaves, and then Somerleyton, where we deemed it a good days work, and stopped. We had all had enough of sailing for the moment, so the sailing members of the crew, that is Tony and I, said we would do some cooking, while Allan and John went off in the dinghy to find a pub. They managed that quite well, and even brought some beer back, but not without getting soaked and covered in mud when they tried to tow the dinghy back along the bank rather than row it against the still brisk breeze.

The next day we planned to sail up the river to Beccles, but were defeated by the head wind, and never made it there. Friday morning saw us back in the lower reaches of the Bure again, having managed Breydon Water this time without further mishap. The wind had fallen a bit, but it hadn't finished with us and was soon increasing again, blowing hard from the north west out of a cold grey sky. As we tacked hard up towards Acle bridge again we had the river almost to ourselves, and all the fair weather craft had disappeared.

During these days of strong winds we had seen less and less of other boats, and for most of this morning we saw only one, and that passed us being sailed very briskly by an obvious professional from one of the boat yards. It looked as if it was probably being taken home after having been abandoned by its holiday crew. Others, we supposed, had gone home early, or were hopefully waiting somewhere for the weather to improve, and as we sailed on towards Wroxham we did find many boats moored up, so we thought we would do the same. There was not far to go in the morning, so we decided to call it a day and have an easy night. Tony and I were tired, but Allan and John, who had never shown much interest in learning the sailing art, and were thus noticeably less exhausted, went off in the dinghy again. They disappeared for several hours while Tony and I had a quiet time talking about our probable futures.

Having almost finished his time in the RAF, he had already made contact with a local paper who were going to give him a try as cub reporter. I still had no particular ideas about my future, but had come round to thinking about something overseas. By chance I had met someone who thought he might get me a job on a coffee estate in Africa, and there had also been advertisements in the papers recently about jobs in the Hong Kong police, or in Kenya Colony, and I was tempted to have a go in that direction. I think it was the thought of the possibility of lots of nice warm weather.

We had given up waiting for Allan and John to arrive back when they emerged with much splashing of inexpertly wielded oars, out of the blackness at about midnight. Yes, they had managed to find a pub, but were not sure where it had been and they did not seem to have much to say about it. I checked that they had attached the dinghy to the mother ship, and everyone turned in. It had been a hard week.

In the morning the weather had switched back to exactly what it had been when we had started out. Fine, misty, and hardly a breath of wind; and we found ourselves making our way back to Wroxham in a fleet of similarly becalmed sailing boats, all motoring back home for their Saturday change-over day. 'You'd think those girls in Smuggler must be somewhere amongst this lot,' I remarked, as we got our things together and made ready to leave our ship. 'Yes,' said Tony, 'There must have been a whole lot of boats moored around where we were yesterday.' Then looking at John as he pushed past with his battered suit case, 'I don't suppose you and Allan saw their boat anywhere when you were splashing around last night?' John and Allan looked at each other. 'It was pretty dark,' said John, and Allan just nodded in agreement as they busied themselves with getting their kit out on to the quay; but I noticed a sly look pass between them.

5
Africa

In 1954 the airport at Nairobi was still a simple and rather primitive sort of place; the smart buildings that eventually made it look like anywhere else in the world came much later. Then, it consisted merely of a few huts, hangers, and a control tower, set in a landscape of brown, burned grass. To a newcomer, who had just arrived via Rome, Cairo, Khartoum and Entebbe, nearly two days of flying in those days, it was somehow instantly what you had always imagined Kenya to be. The light was intense, dazzling, and it felt very dry; hot in a different sort of way to any summer day in England, not unpleasant, but different. Then there was the smell of East Africa, dry grass, and a sort of dustiness, a strange, sweet smell. The smell that I came to associate mainly with herds of cattle stirring up this African dust, and clouds of the same fine red dust hovering over long, long bumpy earth roads; just then I had no idea exactly what this smell was, but it was indubitably Africa.

There were half a dozen of us who emerged into that equatorial sunshine from the aircraft that had just rolled to a stop near the huts. All were young men in their twenties, fresh from the grey light of November in England, who had, for one reason or another, answered an advertisement in the British newspapers. This was the time of what came to be called the MauMau emergency in East Africa, and the government of Kenya was looking for suitable persons to work for them as Administrative Assistants; successful candidates were to be offered an initial two-year contract. It was not explained exactly what the job entailed, but it sounded vaguely Saunders of the River, and the pay was good; an attractive proposition to someone aged twenty-two, unemployed after four years in the RAF, and looking for something interesting to do.

My companions had all applied for much the same reasons as my own. Ex-service, unemployed or just with a dull job, and looking for wider horizons, but we were a strangely mixed lot. One was a civil servant from the north of England, two were standard issue wide boys from London, another one was a tall, dour Scotsman, who had been something in Insurance, and there was one who saw himself as future Foreign Office material. He had already confided in me that he reckoned that this was going to be his backdoor way into the colonial service. He had worked out that if you did your job and kept your nose clean, a two year contract would become four years, and so on. He said that it took longer, and an expensive education, and even then knowing all the right people, to get in by the usual route. As far as he was concerned, this was going to short-circuit the usual procedure. The remaining member of our group seemed to be mainly interested in cricket, and wanted to talk about whether there would be a good cricket club where we were going. I thought he was slightly mad, but it turned out that he probably knew more about it than I did; almost anywhere you went in Kenya there was a cricket club, a rugby club, perhaps a soccer club, even sometimes a sailing club.

All we knew about our future at that moment was that someone was supposed to meet us off the plane, and tell us what to do next. We'd had our interviews in an imposing office in London, waited while someone made up his mind about us, eventually received lots of information about inoculations and so on and a free ticket for Nairobi, and here we were. In fact, at that moment there was no one around who seemed interested in our arrival, and we were told to wait in one of the sheds, which we did. There were an assortment of rickety and unattractive chairs to sit on, and nothing else, so I wondered outside again to look at Africa. After all, we had flown thousands of miles to get here, and I at least was glad that I was not still hanging about under the dull winter skies at home; I wanted to absorb this new, bright, hot world, and stood there in the sun, enjoying the heat and taking it all in. The first thing I noticed was that no-one else was moving about out there. Oh well, mad dogs and Englishmen, I thought; being more or less midday, it was only to be expected that nothing much was in motion.

There were a few clouds low on the horizon, but otherwise a pale, sort of hazy blue sky was empty but for the sun overhead, almost pulsating with light. It was a sort of light that seemed to draw the colour out of every thing, leaving just muted shades of brown. Also on the horizon were low hills, or perhaps mountains far away, you couldn't tell which, then in the foreground a few buildings and acres and acres of that brown, scorched looking grass.

At last as I watched, along a track at the side of the airfield, something was moving; a vehicle hurried towards us trailing a plume of red dust. It came closer, turned out to be a long-wheelbase Landrover, and came to a halt outside our hut. A tall, thin, tanned and dusty looking young man climbed out, and regarded us quizzically as the other members of our little group emerged to see what was happening. I was startled to see that he was wearing a large revolver in a holster on his belt. 'You're the ones I'm supposed to collect, are you?' He said, 'Have you got all your stuff, luggage and so on, I mean?' We indicated that we were, probably, the ones he was looking for. He pulled a piece of paper out of his pocket and checked a list of names. Yes, it was us. 'Get it all aboard then, and I'll take you into town.' We climbed into the back of the Landrover with our bags and were soon bumping at speed along the track, back the way he had come. The canvas cover of the truck was open at the sides, but closed tightly at the back, and it didn't take long to work out that this was because of the cloud of dust that arose and followed behind us; even with the canvas cover arranged as it was, we were instantly covered with a fine layer of that red dust that seemed to be everywhere.

Our driver, who was friendly in an off hand sort of way, explained that he was KPR, which meant Kenya Police Reserve, though he did not seem to be wearing any sort of uniform. He was just doing odd jobs today, he told us, and this particular odd job was to collect us from the airport and deliver us to our various destinations. None of us had any idea where we were supposed to be going, but the list indicated that we were supposed to be helping at different government departments. He said that accommodation had been arranged for us at hotels, and he would drop us off there, and explain where we should go to in the morning when we had sorted out our living arrangements. By the time he had explained this, shouting over his shoulder, we were on a tarmac road and heading into Nairobi; first through what would have been described in a travelogue as the colourful native quarter, all little shops with open fronts, dark caves under dazzling, sun reflecting corrugated iron roofs; then on and into the surprisingly smart centre of the city. White buildings, wide tree-lined streets busy with traffic and shoppers; none of whom, also surprisingly, seemed to be wearing the sort of clothes that you could describe as tropical kit. One of my last actions before leaving London had been to buy a white suit of the type you used to see in films of hot, sweaty places, and I could see at once that I had wasted my money. There were a lot of people on the streets of Nairobi, but none of them was wearing anything like that; most people seemed to be wearing exactly the same as you would see on a summers day in London. No wonder that white suit had been hard to find, I was probably fifty years out of date.

The truck left the wide main boulevard, turned into a side street, and jerked to a halt outside a small hotel. Our driver got out his list again and said he had booked a room for two of us here; myself and the ex-civil servant from Manchester. whose name appeared to be Derek. 'I think you'll find it's all right, do you like Greek food? Anyhow it will do for a day or two while you get your bearings. Nothing else for you to do today. Come to the KPR building tomorrow morning. Just walk down to the bottom of Delamere Avenue, and it's opposite the post office. Have you got all your stuff? Right, see you in the morning at eight-thirty.' Off he went again, at high speed, which seemed to be his normal way of driving, leaving us standing on the pavement with our few bits of luggage. 'What did he mean, Greek food?', said Derek.

Through the glass door of the hotel was a sort of small restaurant room with a few chairs and tables, and a desk at one side beside which the only person visible was standing. He was short and stout, of undeniably eastern Mediterranean appearance, and probably the proprietor. 'Perhaps its a Greek hotel,' I said, 'Do they have Greek hotels in Kenya? 'Nobody said anything to me about eating Greek food,' said Derek, with the air of one beginning to wonder what he was doing standing outside a Greek hotel in the middle of Africa. We went in, to see what would happen next, and the stout, swarthy man smiled pleasantly and inquired if we were the two gentlemen who had booked accommodation? We said we were. 'Please to sign the book, and I will attend to your every convenience.' He turned towards a door at the back of the room and shouted, 'Boy', followed by a few completely incomprehensible words. A thin black youth, dressed in a white, night-gown like garment and a grubby pillbox hat, appeared. He muttered something, of which I only caught the word 'Bwana', somehow managed to gather all our bags together under his arms, and went out through the door again. 'I will be pleased to show you the accommodation, please to follow me,' said our host, and we all trooped through the door, out into a sort of inner courtyard, and up some stairs to a first floor balcony.

Our room opened from this, and the black youth dumped our belongings on the floor, and departed. While I was wondering if we were supposed to tip someone, our host also left with a slight bow, leaving us in charge of a large, rather bare room, with two beds and a hand-basin, a piece or two of furniture, and a view of the street below. 'Right home from home, this is going to be,' remarked Derek, bleakly, as we made a perfunctory effort at putting our gear away. 'I could really do with something to drink, do you think we can get anything in the middle of the afternoon?' 'Lets try them for some tea,' I said, 'you never know. This is a British colony, there must be tea about somewhere.'

We went down to the ground floor room again, and this time found a stout, dark, lady, most probably the consort of the dark, stout man we had dealt with so far. She conveyed our request for tea by shouting something that began with 'Boy!' into another room, and waved us to sit at one of the small tables. After an interval the same skinny black youth appeared again, this time carrying a tray with two cups of tea on it. 'Can we have something to eat, lad?' asked Derek. 'Bwana?' said the lad, looking worried. The dark lady, now sitting behind the desk, said something, as usual incomprehensible to us, and he went back into the nether regions, and returned with a small packet of biscuits on a plate. This was not at all what somebody from Manchester expected at tea time, but it was clearly all we were going to get. Derek tried communicating on the subject of more food, but only received the information from behind the desk, that dinner would be at seven-thirty. We ate the biscuits and drank the tea glumly, beginning to realise we really were in a foreign country. Derek muttered that they had told him that language was no problem, and everyone understood English, but that had begun to look unlikely. I could see that if we were going to make any real contact with people here, we would have to learn the local language. For the moment there was nothing else to do until this promised meal turned up at seven-thirty in the evening, so we went for a walk round the town, to get our bearings.

Back in the wide main street, where its modern white buildings, bright flowering trees and busy traffic were all still bathed in the hot afternoon sun, we turned left and walked along to see if we could find the post office. Walking was pretty hot, with the sun reflected from baking pavements and walls, but after a few hundred yards or so, we came to it; and opposite it across the road, a long low, older looking building with people in khaki coming and going, and a large sign with a crest on it. The people looking busy around it were mostly white men wearing khaki bush shirts and shorts, with blue stockings and, sometimes, a dark blue peaked cap. They all seemed to be armed with pistols. There were also Africans, mostly wearing similar shorts and stockings, dark blue jerseys, and carrying army rifles. 'Well, there it is,' I said, 'Our office at eight thirty in the morning. At least we haven't got to walk very far. Lets keep on going, and have a good look round the town.'

Beyond this point the wide main street seemed to peter out, and there was open land, and then trees and houses. Just ordinary looking dark green trees. It looked quite suburban, and but for the blazing light and temperature could have been in the home counties; not particularly interesting, so we turned back towards what seemed to be the town centre, and then up a busy side street. There was a big hotel on the corner, then one or two other large buildings, and then we were abruptly back in the region of small shops. Able now to look at them in a more leisurely manner than when we were being driven past at breakneck speed, we could see that each one consisted of a single square room, open on to the pavement. Each had a set of wooden, screen-like doors, that folded back against the walls, and presumably closed across the front when business closed down for the night. But it was the contents of these little shops that fascinated us, for many seemed to be selling spices, but not spices in the little pots and tins we were used to in English shops. Large sacks, open at the top, lined the space available; and the contents, shades of brown, yellow, and red, filed the air with the most amazing spicy perfumes. At home the idea of a shop smelling of anything in particular would have seemed odd, but these little stores filled the air with such a mixture of scents that your head swam.

The people running the shops were clearly mainly Indian, with a few Africans among them, and unlike the crowds in the main streets, there were few white faces here. Next we came to a big covered market, with lines of stalls piled high with fruit and vegetables, all colours and shapes, and most of which neither of us had ever seen before. Bananas were recognisable, but instead of being just the individual yellow bananas we were used to, these were sometimes yellow, but also green and often red, and they were being sold as great branches of fruit, of two or three dozens or more. I thought I could recognise mangoes, and lemons, and some ordinary English looking cabbages and green beans, but what were these other bright green fruits the size and shape of oranges? Again the scents and smells were overpowering; why had no one ever told us that Africa smelt like this? I badly wanted to buy some fruit, but had no idea how to set about it; in any case we had no local money until we had visited a bank, and changed our pounds for the shillings and cents that were apparently used here.

We made our way back to our hotel again, as the sun began to go down lower in the sky, and the heat and intensity of the light faded; and we discovered that it had now lost its rather deserted look and there were more people about. Two or three groups were sitting at the little tables having an evening drink, so we tried asking for a glass of beer, with complete success; the thin lad at least knew what beer was. The bottles had an elephant on the label, and Derek professed to find it poor stuff compared to the nectar served in Manchester pubs, but it wasn't that bad. Two of the others in our group from the airport came in and joined us; they were at another hotel just down the road, and had also been having a look round. We sat and chattered, and began to feel a bit more comfortable in our surroundings, and then we realised with a shock that it was suddenly dark in the street outside. 'The equatorial night fell with a sudden crash', someone remarked facetiously. The truth was we were all slightly startled by the speed with which the day had abruptly changed to night. You knew, in theory, that this is what happens on the equator, but it still came as a surprise. Bright afternoon sunlight, changing a bit towards sunset, and then suddenly the light turned off as by a switch, and dark. No twilight. People were eating in the little restaurant by now, and when our food arrived, promptly at seven thirty as promised, it turned out to be very good. We didn't know exactly what it was, but it tasted fine; if this was the Greek cuisine, we would survive.

Morning, I discovered next day after quite a good night's sleep, came just as abruptly as the night had fallen. Between six and six thirty dawn seemed to burst over the horizon, and just as promptly the skinny black boy in his white night-shirt arrived with two cups of tea. 'Jambo, bwana', he said, putting it down on a little table between our two beds. 'Er, jambo, um, thanks', said I. Derek struggled up in his bed, and sipped his tea. 'It's a bit early isn't it?' he muttered. 'They don't intend us to be late for work, do they'. But there were already sounds of traffic and general movement outside in the streets; this was obviously a land where people got going early in the day.

To be on the safe side, and to give the right impression on our first day, we walked down to the KPR building at eight o'clock. As I had suspected people were already there, arriving for work, so we went into the building too. There were several of the black policemen in dark blue sweaters and a lot of mainly very young looking white men and two or three girls, mostly in vaguely military looking khaki. What struck us both at once was that they were all armed, with an assortment of revolvers and pistols or rifles. The inside of the building seemed to be mainly one long, low room, filled with desks and tables and chairs in a random, untidy sort of way, and at one end a door led through to what seemed to be an inner office. As we looked round wondering what to do or who to introduce ourselves to, a somewhat older man strode out from there, very dapper and military looking, talking to someone behind him. I turned towards him, assuming that he was probably the boss, but he went straight towards the door, strapping a Luger pistol in a very shiny leather holster round his waist. He spoke to one of the young men, who jumped up and went with him, and two of the African police followed. They all got into one of the several Landrovers standing outside, and drove off at high speed down the street.

Derek and I glanced at each other a bit uneasily. We were aware that there was something a bit tricky, called the MauMau emergency, going on in Kenya; that was why we had been offered jobs here. But perhaps we hadn't really taken all that seriously. Now here were heavily armed people, rushing about in a determined sort of way, and looking as if perhaps this emergency thing really was quite serious. Another older man appeared from the inner office, less smart, more relaxed, and seemed to notice us. He came across to where we were standing, and we explained who we were; he obviously had no idea what to do with us, but took us into the office and told us to sit down while he telephoned someone else, who, it seemed, did know about our arrival. He put the telephone down and gave us a wry look. 'So you've come to help with the emergency, have you?' We indicated, sheepishly, that we had. 'Do you know anything about it?' 'No'. 'That's honest', he said, 'I like that. So we know where we are'.

'Well', he went on, 'There is plenty of work to do, so we can use any help there is.' He paused, obviously wondering where to start in explaining the job we would be doing. 'Let's start from the beginning. We are all KPR here, and you know what that means, anyhow?' We nodded. 'We are all civilians, called up because of the emergency. I'm a butcher, as a matter of fact, and my wife is running the business for the time being. There are all sorts here, farmer's sons and daughters mainly, I suppose. In theory we might be doing any police duties, but in fact we are stuck with this thing called Pass Book Control, which has been dreamed up by someone to control the movement of members of the Kikuyu tribe.

Its the Kikuyu who are involved in MauMau. Its a sort of tribal secret society, very nasty, but only the Kikuyu are involved, so the idea is that if we keep tabs on their movements we can cramp their style a bit. Pass books are like passports, which they have to use if they come out of their own tribal area. We are issuing them, and dealing with movement passes and work passes.' He gave us a rather humourless smile, 'Not very exciting, you are thinking. Well, that's true, but it's necessary, and there is a lot of work to do. There's an awful lot of Kikuyus in Nairobi.' Struck by a nasty thought, I said, ' We will be working in Nairobi all the time?' 'To start with, yes. But don't worry, you'll be getting up country sooner or later; and when you get to some of the places you're likely to go,' treating us to another glum smile, ' you'll soon be wishing you were back here again.'

He spent a bit more time explaining things, and then went to the door of the office and called, 'Ken, these two young gentlemen from England are going to work with pass book control. Show them the ropes, will you.' Ken, one of the several very youthful looking policemen in the main office, took charge of us and showed us what was going on. By this time a large crowd of black faces were congregated outside, and he explained that these were mainly Kikuyu living in and around the town who were changing jobs, or travelling, or for some other reason wanted stamps and signatures in their pass books.

The other people in the office, some white, some black, were all dealing with this crowd, and it seemed to me to be an impossible task for Derek and me to help with. What language were we supposed to speak, to start with? Kikuyu? Ken said not to worry, nearly everybody spoke a few words of Swahili, and there were always Kikuyu speakers in the teams that were doing this work. To start with we could help a lot by doing work that did not involve talking to the customers. Thrown in at the deep end, we just began to help with this and that in the office, until after an hour or two Ken suggested a break for a cup of coffee, and he took us up the street to a coffee bar.

This at least was familiar ground; it was just like any other coffee bar, apart from the smiling dark face behind the counter; then we were taken to an Indian shop next door for a snack called a samosa, which turned out to be something like a very small Cornish pasty filled with curry. Delicious, I discovered, but Derek said he wouldn't bother. 'Gippy tummy, that's what you'll get from that sort of thing'. The place where we purchased these was called a duka, apparently, so I added it to my small repertoire of local words. It was quite obvious that though English might well be the official language here, everybody used odd words of Swahili all the time. I'd already realised that a car was called a garri, and funga mlango, usually shouted, meant shut the door. The first item on my itinerary had suddenly become to learn something of the language that everybody spoke about here, I was not going to be mistaken for a tourist if I could help it.

Our other problem was that we looked like being stuck in Nairobi for some time to come, and this was depressing. Various police vehicles came and went all the time, and we constantly heard the names of interesting sounding places out there in Africa somewhere; Nyeri, Fort Hall, Nakuru, Athi River; sometimes in connection with an incident of some sort, or perhaps just some routine journey. I even noticed my first Swahili joke, - Nyeri yet safari, - indicating that at one hundred miles exactly that town was considered just far enough away from Nairobi to count as a real journey. I would have loved to go to any of these places, but we were stuck in this city in the middle of Africa, and seeing nothing of the great continent at all. I was talking to our new friend Ken about this, after we had been working in the office for a few days, and he took pity on us and said that as soon as he got the chance he would take us for a drive round. The chance came at the weekend, when Ken picked us up at our little hotel, and we set off at last in his rather rickety Land Rover to see what happened outside Nairobi.

He had seemed a bit uneasy at our hotel, and as we drove away down Delamere Avenue, quiet and relatively empty of traffic on a Sunday, he gave us a rather questioning look. 'That place is all right is it? Funny place to have put you in. It is European, is it?' 'Oh, yes,' I said, 'It's European all right, Greek, in fact.' I was pulling his leg slightly, having learned already that in Kenya 'European' meant 'white', not Continental, as it did at home. 'Still,' I added, 'We are probably going to move to the Queens soon, they say it's very good.' We had seen the Queens Hotel on our walk to work every day, and it looked a much better place to live than our rather stark little hotel. It was a big, old fashioned looking colonial building, with basket chairs on cool verandas and lots of potted palms, and we had enquired of a very attractive looking Indian girl at the reception desk about rooms, found that the prices were within our modest budgets, and arranged to move. 'Ha', said Ken, sounding relieved, 'Yes, the Queens is quite good, I believe.' We went on for a few minutes in silence as he drove at high speed down the main street, did a racing gear change where it crossed another road, just beyond our office, and sped on up the hill beyond, where we had thought it looked all Home Counties and suburban, then he gave us his full attention again.

'Full of lovely popsies, isn't it?' 'Popsies?' 'Yes', he said, 'Dozens of popsies, didn't you know?' Derek and I looked at each other, what was it we didn't know? Ken glanced round and caught our expressions. 'It's the army, you see. They bring their wives and daughters out here, and park them in the Queens while they go and make a nuisance of themselves up in the forest, chasing the MauMau. They seem to like the Queens. It's very popular with the British army.' 'Bloody hell!' groaned Derek. 'What have we done? We've booked ourselves into a hotel full of officers' wives.' It did not sound very good news to me either, but Ken was sure we were on to a good thing. 'Lovely popsies', he muttered to himself again as we drove on.

We had left the city now, and were driving through suburban scenery that could indeed almost have been between London and the south coast of England. Many big houses, half hidden amongst trees and shrubs, even green lawns, which must have taken a lot of watering in that climate. All just slightly too exotic for home though, with flowering trees making vivid splashes of colour, and some really unfamiliar looking plants such as the thing like a sort of cactus, with a great flowering head growing out of it as tall as a telegraph pole. 'That's sisal,' explained Ken, 'You'll see masses of it up country, it's just a crop. They make rope out of the leaf fibres.' Yes. of course, sisal, - ropes and sacks, and stuff like that. Learned about it at school, funny to think that it looked so strange.

Beyond the suburbs of Nairobi at last, we turned off the tarmac road, and headed along a narrow, bumpy, dusty track; the country open now, no houses or gardens, just a sort of wide, dry, moorland, dotted here and there with flat topped trees. Ken drove on at much the same breakneck speed that he seemed to go in for all the time, and soon the usual cloud of fine, red dust, was swirling along behind. From the town it had been possible to see a line of jagged peaks on the horizon, called, we had been told, the Ngong Hills, and now we were fast approaching them, and were soon among them. No longer a piece of flat, distant scenery, but a series of rolling hills that became steeper as our track wound among them. The slopes were all the same brownish colour of very dry grass, but in gullies between them there were patches of bright green where streams trickled, and everywhere flat topped trees dotted the landscape. Moving specks that we saw on a ridge as we approached it, turned out to be a herd of goats, all different colours and shapes; and as they lifted their heads to look at us, simple iron bells on some of their necks jingled and rattled.

A young child wearing a long shapeless shirt and carrying a stick, sat on a rock. I hadn't noticed him until we were very close, as he and his shirt and the hillside were all about the same colour. He, like the goats, just looked up at us with mild interest as the Land Rover bounced and rattled by, then he vanished in our trailing red cloud. 'That was a Masai toto looking after some of his families' goats,' said Ken, 'that's what the youngest ones do. As they get older they get to guard the cattle. There you are, look over there.' The track had dipped and entered one of the gullies, and there a small group of thin looking cattle were drinking, while two tall, slender youths watched them.

Ken stopped his vehicle with the air of someone showing guests an interesting feature in the garden, and we goggled a bit at the theatricality of the scene. The two young Masai wore short tan coloured tunics in the manner, you might imagine, of Ancient Greek youths; their hair was plastered down with what looked like red lacquer, they wore short swords in bright red sheathes, and they leaned nonchalantly on long spears. They turned, and regarded us with mild disdain. Ken glanced down at my camera that I had brought with some idea of sending pictures home, but so far had merely been clutching protectively as we bumped along. 'Like to take a picture?' He said. It seemed to me a bit cheeky to drive up and start pointing cameras at the local residents, but he said they wouldn't mind. 'It's quite a local industry, posing for tourists.' He leaned out and engaged them in a brief, shouted conversation, they smirked a bit, and did not sound as fierce as they looked. 'They say they want senti simuni, sounds a bit steep to me, what do you think?' 'That's about sixpence, isn't it?' said Derek, 'I don't mind investing that much to impress the girls at home.' He got out and went over to the two now grinning warriors, held out the little silver coin, and took up position beside them. He had put on a white shirt and shorts for the outing and somehow managed to look very fat and unhealthily pallid beside the thin brown youths, and it made a ludicrous picture. I took the photograph, then one or two more of the scenery, and we moved on, looking at the countryside, and catching sight of more Masai and their cattle here and there, and once a glimpse of one of their villages.

As we drove along I asked Ken if people from Nairobi came out there much; the hills looked inviting for climbing or walking, and it seemed surprising that so near the town we had seen nobody at all but our herdsmen. I wondered if it was because of the MauMau emergency. Ken said it had nothing to do with that. 'This is all Masai country, and they would have any Kikuyu for breakfast, if they happened to catch them here. In the old days their favourite occupation was having fights with the Kikuyu, which they always won. No, it is just that Nairobi people don't come out of the town much; there are ticks in the grass, and snakes and so on. They are much more likely to be riding round the game park in their motor cars, and we had better move on too, time is passing, and you'd like to have a look round, wouldn't you?' We said yes, we would like to see the game park; the truth being that we were happy to be doing anything away from hot paved streets.

Ken drove on and we left the hills, and were in flat country again. We came to a tall wire fence, the first we had seen that day, and before we passed through to the other side we stopped and pulled the canvas cover down firmly on all sides, Ken explaining that it was a rule before going into the game park, and kept baboons and things out. Soon we saw other cars, mostly full of family parties, and then under a group of trees several such cars stopped, while children fed a chattering army of monkeys. 'Really stupid, that,' said Ken, 'They'll be lucky not to have their wing mirrors pulled off. They just can't believe that these really are wild animals.' We drove on, and began to see quite an assortment of wild life. Herds in the distance that Ken said were wildebeest, a lot of small deer-like creatures, and once a tiny buck, smaller than a dog, that appeared for a moment on the track and promptly disappeared again into the tall dry grass. Some long horned orabi, unbelievably graceful, leaped ridiculously high over the track in front of us; then Ken stopped his truck and said, 'Would you like to see some lions?

'Are there really lions about here, near Nairobi?' said Derek, 'I mean, real wild ones, not just put here for the tourists?' 'Oh, they're real wild ones all right,' grinned Ken, 'So don't start trying to feed them. Look over there.' We looked where he seemed to be looking, ahead and to the right of the track, and saw more brown, dry grass, bits of light grey rock outcropping in the middle distance, and far away more trees. I spotted a tall bird, stepping delicately through the grass a hundred yards away. 'That's a secretary bird, isn't it?' I said. 'Yes, but much closer, say thirty yards, near a bit of rock.' He pointed, 'Watch while we move.' His Land Rover jolted forward a couple of yards, and at the same instant something twitched in the grass where he had been pointing. In that moment I was suddenly aware of a lion, exactly the same colour as the grass, moving his head to look at us. Once you had seen it, it was quite obvious, and he just lay there at ease, watching us; then he yawned and put his head down again. Ken began to drive further forward, off the track towards the lion. 'Hang about,' said Derek, 'We don't need to go any nearer.' 'It's perfectly safe', Ken kept going forward, 'I am pretty sure there are some more lions there, a family group probably; keep watching where that one is.' At that moment one wheel of the Land Rover went into a hole and the chassis crashed down very noisily on the rocky ground. In front of us, almost within touching distance it seemed, another lion leaped to its feet and others sat up and looked at us, perhaps not very happy about having their afternoon snooze interrupted. 'OK, we've seen the lions, lets go and disturb something smaller,' said Derek.

Ken was trying to reverse out of the hole, juggling with the gears and the four-wheel drive, but we seemed to be firmly aground on a piece of rock. He stopped revving the engine, then switched it off. 'I think we have a problem,' he said, 'But don't worry.' 'I'll try', remarked Derek, dryly.

'No, there's nothing to worry about', repeated Ken, looking worried, 'We'll just wait for them to move off, then we can get out and lift the old buggy out of the hole. They're bound to move off, soon'. We sat there for several minutes, looking at the lions, and they looked back at us. Then they seemed to decide that the annoyance was over, and prepared to lie down again. It did not look as if they were going away. I seemed to remember hearing that when lions have had a good meal, they sometimes just settle down somewhere comfortable, and stay there for a day or two. I had also just noticed that the sun was getting low in the sky.

'Look', I said, 'Say we all got out of the other side very quietly, and lifted the wheel out of the hole'. 'Don't even think about doing that ', said Ken,' They look sleepy, but don't be fooled, they would still eat you, just to pass the time. I'll have another go.' He started the engine, put it in gear, and we bucked and heaved again as he tried, first one way, then the other, to get out of the hole. The lions looked up, but with less interest this time, and then settled down once more; they had already seen this show. The Land Rover came to rest again too. Ken switched off the engine and said 'Bugger it.'

I looked vaguely round about the place we were stuck in, wondering what we could do about our predicament; then I noticed that a plume of red dust had appeared away to the left, so at least there was someone else about. We watched it coming closer, then Ken said, 'Thank the lord for that. It's the game warden.' The other truck pulled up beside us, and the driver opened his window and shook his head at us. 'It's your lucky day. Someone going home saw you stuck here and told me. You're in a right old mess, aren't you. Just stay exactly where you are, put your gear in neutral, and I'll get a chain on you and pull you out.' He spoke with the weariness of someone who had seen it all many times before. We sat there, feeling very foolish, while he manoeuvred his vehicle round behind, and we heard a chain clanking, then we began to move slowly backwards as his truck heaved us very slowly out of our hole in the ground.

Half an hour later Ken had delivered us back to our little Greek hotel. As we came back into Nairobi the sun had done its final dramatic dip towards the horizon, where a thin strip of cloud went orange and then dark red, and then the equatorial night rushed in on us. 'They say that if you watch closely, at the exact moment the sun disappears it goes green', said Derek. 'What goes green?' 'The sun. Or perhaps the sky, or something.' 'I didn't see anything. Did you see that, Ken?' 'Can't say I did,' said Ken. 'Sorry about the bad driving and getting stuck in the hole and everything.' 'You're a bloody good driver,' said Derek, 'Anyone can get stuck in a hole. I know plenty of people who've get stuck in pot holes in Manchester. Never seen again, some of them.' 'You don't know how good it was just to get out of Nairobi for an hour or two,' I said. We'll do it all again any time you like, including the hole.'

As Ken drove away into the rapidly deepening dusk after dropping us at our little hotel we stood on the pavement watching him go, at top speed as usual. 'Grand lad that,' said Derek, for once without cynicism. It sounded as if it was meant to be high praise, and I added, 'Yes, he's a nice chap. He told me that he is hoping to go to university in England soon, he seems really keen on it; but I don't know, I think he's going to find the Old Country a bit dull.'

6
Safari

Soon after that Derek and I moved into the Queen's Hotel with our piece or two of luggage, and settled down there for a time. It made a much better base than the first little hotel, and turned out to be quite a pleasant place to live in. Ken's idea of wall to wall lovely popsies turned out to be much exaggerated of course. It was true that there were plenty of British army uniforms to be seen about, but the women folk who seemed to go with these military men did not cause the blood to pound, being mostly drab, pale, and worried looking. Much more exciting seemed the dark young lady we had met at the reception desk. She came from Goa, I discovered, and moved about the hotel with a sort of exotic, glowing vitality, dressed but not very adequately covered, in an assortment of brightly coloured diaphanous garments.

I soon noticed that she always had her lunch alone at a table for two in the restaurant, and taking advantage of the fact that it was very busy one day soon after we arrived, I pretended that I could not see anywhere to sit and asked if I could join her. She smiled charmingly, and we had a pleasant meal and a jolly conversation, and I discovered that she was the daughter of the hotel housekeeper. It all seemed very promising, but it was not to last. The next day, when I tried the same ploy again, she smiled just as charmingly, but pointed out that the restaurant was only half full, with plenty of empty tables.

I was not sure what to do next, being used to English girls who you took to the pictures, or possibly the annual Young Conservative's Dance, and neither of these alternatives seemed very appropriate. Derek was no help, his advice always being to leave dark, foreign girls alone; also he said, her mother was watching me closely. I decided to adopt a casual man-of-the-world attitude, play it cool, and see what developed. But nothing did, even though I took to chatting to her mother whenever we met in the hotel. In retrospect, I would say that the girl, and I, and her mother, were all rather puzzled by each other.

Meanwhile life went on just the same at the police H.Q. in Delamere Avenue, while we went through the daily routine of dealing with pass books, watched with increasing boredom the endless line of applicants emerge from the apparently unchanging crowd outside, and took countless photographs and fingerprints. Weeks went by, and there was talk of teams being sent up-country, and eventually some of the young men from H.Q. were issued with camping equipment, and departed to set up their tents at a place called Thika, north of Nairobi. But I seemed doomed to stay where I was and in the end, when even Derek had also departed for Thika, I was the last of the new boys from England still there.

Then I began to notice that others were assuming that I was a fixture there, and at last became really worried one day, when someone congratulated me on having carved out a cosy little job for myself for the duration of the emergency. I was flattered to be taken for a Kenyan, but a nice little job in an office in Nairobi was not what I had come to Africa for. The trouble was that I had made the mistake of becoming useful, and so there I was, stuck; so I decided one day that if they were not going to send me up country, I would have to get out of town under my own steam, and get a car. If I had a car at least I would be able to move out of the town centre into one of the many small hotels that existed in the band of semi-suburban African countryside that surrounded Nairobi. I had discovered that most of the young Kenyans doing their emergency service seemed to live in one or other of these little hotels, and they all sounded a lot more fun than where I was in the middle of the town; so, impecunious as I was, a car it had to be.

I began haunting the used car lots, of which there were several, and eventually found an old MG two-seater which I could, by scraping together every penny I had, just afford to buy. The owner of the used car lot, a Mr. Patel, described it as a lovely little car in really tip-top order, which was not quite true, because it had only the tattered remains of a hood, and a cloud of smoke came out of the exhaust pipe when it was started. But a glance under its bright blue painted bonnet showed that the basic essentials were all there, and it had wheels, it moved and thus represented freedom, and it was cheap. Common sense suggested that it was not the most sensible sort of vehicle for travelling about Africa, but common sense was on a loser. It had a Uganda number plate, and I reasoned that it must be tough enough to have travelled from there to here, at least once. I also said to myself that plenty of people were to be seen driving about Nairobi in small cars; this was true, but the reasoning here was not so good, as their owners probably never took them far outside the town. I had not quite realized then that living in Nairobi and living in Africa were not always quite the same thing. Many people hardly went beyond their houses in the suburbs, and the Nairobi whites, as a tribe, seldom ventured far afield. Ken told me that he knew a man who had in fact driven his baby Fiat, a thing about the size of a pram, to Mombassa and back, but I suspect that was just to encourage me.

Anyhow, I bought the bright blue MG and drove it happily away down the street, and immediately discovered that as well as its more obvious defects, its brakes did not work. I found this out when a car stopped in front of me suddenly and I jammed my foot on the brake pedal and nothing happened . This was in a busy street, full of traffic, but luckily where the car in front of me stopped there was a space on the side of the street, a little forecourt with lumps of white- washed stone marking it off from the road. I had little choice but to swerve towards it, hauling on my hand brake, go over one of the white painted rocks, and come to rest there. Having done that, I looked around me and realized that we were in the yard of a police station.

But as it happened no-one was looking out of its windows, or at any rate no-one came out to see what was happening. I pondered briefly the wisdom of trying to explain the situation to a Swahili- speaking constable, but then noticed that the road had cleared again and was now empty. I let the clutch in, swerved back out over the stones, and headed back to Mr. Patel. He showed no surprise at seeing me again so soon, perhaps this often happened with his customers. 'Most regrettable' he said, 'The mechanic fellow did not check the brake fluid, I will speak to him.' I watched the reservoir being topped up, hoping that the fluid was not running out somewhere else at the same time, got back in and drove away again. There did not seem much point in saying anything to Mr. Patel about letting people drive off into a city street without any brake fluid in their car.

This time I drove along more soberly, prodding at the brake pedal every now and then, but all seemed to be in order this time; so pausing only to get some petrol, I zoomed off out of town. It was a wonderful feeling to be able to get away from the city streets. Being in Africa, yet unable to see any of it apart from the odd tantalising glimpse had been very frustrating. Now I intended to see the lot. I drove around the outskirts of Nairobi until it got dark, and as soon I had finished my work the next day, which was Saturday, I took the road to Thika, to visit the lads who were camped there.

The camp, when I found it, was almost deserted. Every one except Derek had gone off for the weekend, and I discovered him lying in his tent reading. He said that if I found being stuck in Nairobi boring, I should try Thika. I showed him my newly acquired transport and suggested it might be less boring to take a trip round about and see a bit of the country. A weekend safari, in fact. Derek looked thoughtfully at the bright blue, but now rather dusty looking little two seater. 'Why has it got bicycle wheels?' he said. 'Probably something to do with racing, special design,' I replied, wishing that the whole thing did look a bit less flimsy. Derek did not seem to find that idea particularly reassuring, but soon made up his mind. 'Must be better than spending the weekend alone in this camp,' he said, 'Let's go.'

We decided to head for Nakuru, which was about a hundred miles west of Nairobi, on what we had been told was the best road in East Africa. It was actually tarmac, unlike the more usual gravel surface, and had allegedly been built by Italian prisoners during the war, so it sounded a good idea for a first long run in the MG. We had to go back to Nairobi first, to get on this road, so back we sped. On the first sharp right hand turn the passenger side door flew open, and I had to grab Derek to stop him falling out, but he soon learned not to lean on it, and in half an hour we were back in the city again. There we filled up with petrol, and checked the oil, which seemed surprisingly low, so we put plenty in.

My first idea had been to camp somewhere, but Derek said he'd had enough of that sort of thing, and fancied a comfortable bed in a good hotel and some decent food, so there did not seem to be any point in taking much with us. There must be hotels in Nakuru, so we just took a jacket each, so that we could look respectable. We thought we might take a bite of food with us in case we felt peckish on the way, but most of the shops seemed to be shut by then, except a few back street ones that we judged a bit dodgy to buy food from. In the end we bought just a loaf of bread, and then a big juicy looking pineapple from someone by the roadside. 'Lets get on,' I said, 'We don't want to waste any more time. There are bound to be shops somewhere, so we won't starve. Next stop Nakuru.'

I knew the direction to take, the little car was happy on the smooth tarmac, and we were soon well away from the town, bowling through open country which I had been told was part of Kikuyuland. It was heavily cultivated in a haphazard sort of way, with market-garden crops that you might have seen in England, plus irregular areas of maize, and some completely unfamiliar plants; and children and chickens everywhere. Then after a few miles the patches of cultivation petered out, and there were only trees beside the road. Not the steaming jungle that you might have imagined on the equator, but just regular dark forest, of the Hansel and Gretel variety, that could have just as well been in central Europe.

The road had been climbing through this forest for some time, and we were shouting to each other above the noise of the engine that it didn't seem like Africa at all, when we turned a corner, and suddenly there it all was, the whole continent of Africa apparently spread out before us. Driving along we had been too shut in by the dark trees to see more than a few yards on other side, then suddenly there were no trees in front at all, and it was like coming out of a dark cave into the full light of day. I stopped the MG at the side of the road, and we sat there in the brilliant afternoon sunlight and gazed at the view.

The land fell away in front like a cliff, while the road we were on turned to the right and made its way, with many twists and turns down a steep escarpment. This must be the edge of the Great Rift Valley, and Nakuru was there down in the bottom of it somewhere, that much we knew. We were on its eastern edge, which ran like a great wall north and south, its upper edge fringed with forest and outcrops of rock. Smaller trees and rocks covered the higher slopes, while lower down there were bushes and more occasional outcrops, and the slopes gradually levelled out into the sort of East African bush country dotted with thorn trees that we were already familiar with. This plain stretched out into the far distance, with a conical hill, like a volcano with one side broken down, in front of us, and other strange shaped hills further away. Everything was below our level, and set out before us like a plaster model in a geography class room at school. It was probably the most dramatic scene either of us had ever seen, and we just sat and looked at it. Derek said, 'Well, that must be the Rift Valley, but if so, where is the other side of it?'

The truth was, it was not easy to make sense of the great panorama before us. Valleys have sides, and we were obviously on one side of it, but where the other side should have been, the tree studded plain and the low hills seemed to fade into the haze of a remote distance. There was simply nothing out there that you could identify as the far side of a valley, and with nothing familiar for the eye to rest on, it was very difficult to grasp the scale of the scene. Still trying to work out the mystifying geography, we started the car again and continued to drive along our road, that now descended the side of the escarpment to the right, and which we could see then ran on along the floor of the valley, a distant strip of ribbon reflecting the sunlight.

It had been quite cool in the forest at the top, but now with the rays of the late afternoon sun lying almost horizontally on us and the cliffs close on our right hand side, it was hot again. Then I realised that it was not only hot, but there was a distinct smell of burning. I stopped the car, and turned to Derek, 'Can you smell anything?' He looked suspiciously round the inside of the car, sniffing, 'There's something on fire, it may be us,' he said, looking ready to jump out, 'No, wait a minute, it's the scenery, look !' A short way ahead of us, below the road, only just visible in the glare of the sunlight, a band of low flames were burning their way steadily up the side of the valley. These flames disappeared into high scrub, but further ahead, seemingly right across the road, we could now see that there was a band of smoke. 'I think we have found ourselves a bush fire,' I said, 'I wonder what we do now?' ' I don't know,' said Derek 'But I wouldn't count on the fire brigade coming.'

We had seen very little sign of human life since we left the Kikuyu area way back along the road, so what were we going to do now?. Report a fire across the road to someone? Who? How? Meanwhile the fire below us was moving quickly up the slope. The flames still almost invisible, but now we could clearly hear it crackling through the dry grass and bushes, and the smoke ahead was getting thicker. 'I don't know what we should do either, ' I said, 'But we aren't stopping here. Do we go forwards, or back?'

The only sensible thing seemed to turn back. I could already imagine a voice saying, 'Of course the bloody young fools drove straight into it.' But to turn round and go back to Nairobi again seemed such a feeble end to my first safari. Then through the noise of crackling flames we heard the sound of a car somewhere down below us, invisible, but obviously revving hard as it came up the hill; and a minute later it appeared through the smoke, and sped on up the road towards us. It was an ordinary looking saloon car, with an ordinary looking family inside it, and no one looked in the least excited about the situation as they drove past us.

'Come on,' I said, 'If they can do it so can we'. 'They were inside with the windows shut,' said Derek, as we pulled out onto the tarmac again. 'We can hold our breath, I suppose,' I suggested, 'Anyhow, we can go a lot faster going down than they could coming up. Hold tight.' Derek got out his handkerchief and carefully knotted it round his face. I accelerated down the road towards the bank of smoke, now very solid-looking, grey and white, with yellow shafts where the strong sunlight pierced it. In a moment we were in it and could barely see the road, and there seemed no air to breath, just the strong acrid reek of burning grass and brush. I just had time to wonder what on earth I was doing, then it thinned again, and the sunlit world reappeared.

Tears were streaming down my face as I blinked to get my eyes clear, and Derek emerged from behind his handkerchief, spluttering, 'That will be quite enough excitement for today, now we will just find that hotel and have a nice cup of tea, and with a bit of luck, a quiet evening.' The excitement did indeed seem to be over for the moment. The road was perfectly clear again, and the bush fire was now only a faint smell of burning hanging in the air, as with a bit of coughing and sniffing we continued down to the valley floor; but he was going to have to wait a bit longer for his cup of tea.

Down here, with the fire now only a few puffs of smoke, way up the escarpment and well behind us, we went on our way towards the distant town of Nakuru. The road stretched on almost dead straight before us, keeping all the time quite close to the escarpment we had just descended. On that side the same jagged scenery of rocks and scrub and outcropping cliff went on as far as we could see, while on the other side was the plain; rough grass and thorn trees, and those same strange shaped hills in the distance. The road went on straight and featureless, with telegraph posts along the side that cast regularly spaced shadows across it as the sun crept down the sky. Every now and then one of these posts was the perch of hawk of some sort, that seemed to be sitting there watching the road, perhaps waiting to scavenge any unfortunate creature that happened to get run over. The country was much the same as we had driven through with Ken, in the game park near Nairobi, but without the herds of animals we had seen there.

It went on and on for many miles. An occasional car passed us going towards Nairobi, but otherwise we had it all to ourselves, with the plain on the left and the escarpment on the right; tedious after a time, and it was getting late. Then on the left hand side of the road, suddenly there was a signpost, the first we had seen. A narrow road went off towards the setting sun, and the signpost said to Narok. There was no indication of how far it was, and of course we had no idea what sort of place Narok was, but we both thought we had heard of it as somewhere important, so there must be a hotel. 'Come on,' I said, 'Let's go down here. It's still a long way to Nakuru, and we could stop at Narok for the night, and go on to Nakuru in the morning.' We were beginning to feel pretty hungry.

But we were never to find out what Narok was like, or even how far away it was. We turned off to go down the narrow road and followed it along for what seemed a fair distance, but the surface was just dry earth and rock which got worse the further we went, and eventually deteriorated into twin wheel ruts filled with sand and dust; and after slithering and sliding along it for a bit, we came to a halt with our wheels spinning.   Whatever vehicles had made the ruts must have been a good deal more rugged than our MG, and we were obviously out of our class. It didn't look as if we were going any further across the plain that way; and then we found that we couldn't easily turn round and go back the way we had come, either.

As the sun finally disappeared over the plain and beyond those hills we were still struggling to get our car out of the deep ruts, and facing back the way we had come. By the time we had accomplished that, it was to all intents and purposes dark, and it was going to be a tricky job, in the dark, getting back to the main road; with an excellent chance of running on to a rock or otherwise damaging our only means of transport. Common sense decreed that we stay where we were until the morning, but then we began to notice the cold.

It had seemed hot enough heaving and pulling and man handling the MG, but as soon as we stopped all that strenuous activity the air struck very chill indeed. The sky above us was clear and bright with the millions of stars that are supposed to make the tropical night enchanting, but it felt as though all the heat of the earth had suddenly been sucked up there towards those stars, and dispersed into the freezing vacuum of space. It did not slowly cool off, it went in a matter of minutes from the warmth of the late afternoon to the frigidity of a polar plateau. We put our jackets on, and began to think about the night ahead; it was not going to be cosy.

It would not have been so bad if we'd had any proper provisions with us. We could have made a fire of some sort, and cooked up some food, and it could have been quite pleasant; but you cannot create much of a culinary triumph with a loaf of bread and a pineapple. At least, I thought, we won't be thirsty with a juicy pineapple to eat, but even that did not work very well. After a slice or two the acid began to burn our mouths, and as an accompaniment a loaf of dry bread left a lot to be desired.

We spent most of that night sleepless, hungry and cold, and waiting for the dawn; it was a very long night. Derek passed it huddled down into the passenger seat, alternately dozing and grumbling. I dozed a bit, but then found that I was not only cold and hungry, but also very bored; so I passed the time as best I could by walking up and down the track. I didn't go far; the car was invisible from a few yards away, and walking in the dark meant stumbling and tripping over ruts and rocks and bushes. My imagination began to sketch out a scenario of getting lost in the African night, or breaking my ankle, or both; so I ended up just sitting in the car too, and waiting for the dawn. After a long, long time, and innumerable looks at my watch, it came, and as soon as we could see what we were doing we emerged into the cold grey light, and resumed our journey back the way we had come.

With the car manhandled into a position where the wheels were not going to immediately sink back into the ruts again, I gingerly started the engine, an appalling noise in the stillness, and cautiously headed back towards the main road. In the way of such things, the track that had seemed so difficult the night before, now seemed easy, and we were soon back on the tarmac road again. I turned back onto the smooth surface with enormous relief, and we once more bowled along in the direction of Nakuru. It was soon broad daylight, but still piercingly cold as we sped along in the open MG; and then, miraculously, a notice saying Hotel appeared on the side of the road. We looked at it, scarcely believing it was real, then pulled off the road, into a driveway up to a low, rambling wooden building.

'Dear God,' groaned Derek, 'Food. Warmth. It must be a mirage.' The hotel looked old and a bit tatty, but solid. It had a long veranda all along the front, with steps leading up to it. The roof was corrugated iron painted faded green with rusty spots. There was a large dry looking lawn, and a lot of colourful flowering shrubs. When our engine stopped there was complete silence at first, then we heard the noise of something going on round the back, like a pail rattling, and then the clucking of chickens being fed. So there was life. It seemed a bit unlikely that anything was actually happening inside the hotel so early on a Sunday morning, but we climbed up the steps to the veranda and tried the front door. It was open, and we went inside and found a large, old fashioned entrance hall with a hat stand and a desk, everything polished wood, and animal skins on the floor. The heads of several beasts that might well have once owned the skins were hanging on the walls. Open doors off the hall gave us a view of shabby Edwardian comfort in the surrounding rooms, and from one of these a man emerged.

Tall, very English looking and of vaguely military type, he matched the hotel perfectly, and did not seem even slightly surprised to see us. We asked, a bit hesitantly, about the possibility of breakfast, and he said, yes, of course, what would we like? Well, eggs and bacon, and that sort of thing, we suggested. 'I'll just see if there's anybody about in the kitchen,' he said; went out through one of the doors, and immediately returned. 'Be ready in a jiffy,' he said, 'Dining room's through there,' indicating another of the doors. More polished wood, tables with white tablecloths, faded water colours on the walls. A young Kikuyu, buttoning his white kanzu, came in and indicated where we should sit. 'Jambo, bwana, habari gani?' He enquired politely. 'Mzuri tu.' I replied, glad that I knew what to say, but hoping that the conversation would not go much further. I was learning a few words of Swahili, but knew it wouldn't stretch very far. My best hope of appearing in command of the language lay in being taken for the strong silent type.

We sat down and he departed again, saying he would bring coffee, which he immediately did. Drinking it, we began to feel human once more as we thawed out and relaxed, luxuriating in the warm coffee and the delicious scent of bacon being prepared in the kitchen. Soon two heaped plates of bacon and eggs and tomatoes arrived, followed by a rack of toast, refilled twice, and more coffee. Life felt good again. The hotel owner reappeared, and offered the use of a bath room to spruce up a bit; and a glance in the mirror told us what had put that idea into his head. We looked terrible; palled, unkempt, and bleary eyed. But he did not show any curiosity about our appearance, and I hoped that he had taken us for a pair of intrepid transcontinental travellers; 'Across three Continents in an MG' or something like that, and we did feel as if we had been travelling for months. In fact or course we were on the main road from Nairobi to Nakuru, and he probably assumed that we were just another pair of something pretty unimportant in the army, on their way back to camp after a rough Saturday night out.

Back on the road again after that, clean, well fed, and feeling very much better, we resumed our journey. The sun was well up by now, the chill had gone from the air and adventure beckoned once more. We caught a glimpse of water glittering over the plain to the left; one of the Rift Valley lakes, no doubt, and we passed the township of Naivasha. The tarmac road went on and on as before, to be honest a bit dull, and I was just beginning to think that now we'd had our breakfast there would be little to do in Nakuru on a Sunday morning, when we came to another sign post. Such things had been very rare along our route so far, so it was automatically an object of interest, and we studied it. The escarpment that had been on our right hand all this way had now fallen back further away from the road and was less a distinct cliff, but more like a broken range of hills, and into these hills the sign post was pointing. It was a very old sign post, which had lost a lot of its paint, but we could make out the name Thomsons Falls, and the figure six. The road it indicated was not tarmac, but was at least broad and well made, unlike the one we had tried the night before, and it was tempting. We agreed that it would be quite nice to see the falls, after all the dry bush country, and so off we went again leaving the tarmac behind.

This road was obviously important and well used, and engineered in the gravel-like murram that was the usual road surface in East Africa. It soon began to go up into the hills, and as it wound about and we climbed higher and higher the flat plain of the valley floor disappeared, and we were once more in completely different country. Now the world was greener again, and we were amongst a jumble of tree clad hills. After six miles or so we still had not come to the waterfall, but with all the climbing it seemed a good idea to stop and see how the engine was coping, so when we came to a level bit, I pulled on to the side. There were no boiling noises from the radiator, and no hot smells, so all seemed well. We got out to stretch our legs, and I thought I would just check the oil level before we went on, opened the bonnet, and pulled out the dipstick. It showed only half full.

This was worrying. It had been over full, if anything, when we left Nairobi, so we must have used up a lot of oil in travelling less than a hundred miles. Derek noticed that I had found something I was not very happy about. 'What's trouble?' he asked. I said, 'Don't know, but the oil seems low. Perhaps we're not standing level here, I'll look at it again when we stop next.' The trouble was, I knew all too well what was wrong; with all that smoke coming out of the exhaust we were burning oil up at a rate of knots, and I hadn't thought to bring a spare can with us. There was nothing else to do but to drive on, Thompsons Falls could not be far away, and there might be a garage. We drove on and on, and it became obvious that however you measured it, we had gone a lot more than six miles.

We could not have missed the place, there was no other road going this way, just this one, and we were on it. 'Well,' I said, 'It couldn't have been six on that sign, it must have been sixteen, but anyhow it can't be far now,' and on we went again along this road that just wound on and on into the hills, and arrived nowhere. But the character of the countryside was changing again now and becoming less rugged, and we began to see cultivated land alongside the road. We also saw, for the first time since we had started this long climb, the occasional African along the road. We stopped and asked one how far it was to Thompsons Falls, but he either didn't understand our question, or we didn't understand his answer.

At last a vehicle appeared coming towards us, the first we had seen since yesterday. It was a well-used looking Landrover with no doors, and rattled past us trailing the usual cloud of red dust, its driver in the dress of the up-country farmer: shirt sleeves, shorts, and slouch hat. The dust had hardly cleared when another car appeared. It was big old American saloon, travelling very fast, and as I pulled cautiously into the side of the road, it suddenly veered across in front of us, hit the bank, bounced off, and stopped. I also drew up and a young man leaped out, looked at his front wheels, shrugged, glanced at us and said, 'Blow out, man,' in the clipped tones of South Africa. Then he pulled a rusty old jack out from under his driving seat, threw it down in the road beside his car in a bored sort of way, and kicked it in place underneath. He did not say anything else, so I politely enquired if we could help with his tyre. 'No, man,' he said, which seemed to be the end of that conversation, so I asked him how far it was to Thompsons Falls. 'Not far, man,' he said without looking round as he went on with removing the wheel, 'About thirty.'

Thirty miles ! That battered old road sign must have originally said sixty. Feeling slightly stunned we drove away, and as we left him the young South African straightened up, grinned and shouted after us, 'You'll never get there in that thing, man'. 'Surly bastard,' muttered Derek. 'Oh, I don't know,' I said, 'That was probably a sort of Yarpie joke. I expect he thought he was being particularly charming to foreigners.' But I couldn't help thinking that he might be nearer the truth than he knew, and sure enough when we stopped to check the oil again, it was now even lower. 'This is the last time I drive anywhere without a can of oil in the back,' I said, 'But there isn't anything we can do about it except hope for the best.' My vision of sparkling waterfalls was now entirely superseded by thoughts of a refreshing can of oil, as we went on carefully and at a modest speed, to use as little as possible. I knew that sooner or later, when the oil level fell too low, the lubrication system would begin to break down and we would be in real trouble, and there was no way of knowing when that might happen. I had an idea at the back of my mind that someone had once told me that an MG would run on an almost empty sump, or was that some other car?

We pressed on a few more miles, and stopped to check the oil again, and this time it hardly seemed to touch the dipstick. 'OK,' I said, 'This is now serious. Next time we see a car we'll have to stop it and see if we can beg or borrow some oil.' But then we didn't see another vehicle of any sort for miles. We were in real farming country now, and wild Africa had disappeared apart from the red murram road we drove on. There were rolling green hills in the background, but now along the roadside it was all fields of wheat, and here and there pastures with very English-looking dairy cattle. Once or twice we caught glimpses of farm buildings far off, and there were tracks with farm names on notice boards, which suggested the possibility of homesteads with farm machinery, and probably oil; but the tracks looked pretty tough going, and there was no telling how long they were.

So we just drove on, listening to the engine and waiting for the dreaded sound of the thump and rattle of a big-end running dry. We had even begun to discuss the ways and means of getting back to Nairobi if the engine did die, when at last another sign post appeared. Nine miles to Thompsons Falls. 'OK,' I said, 'We've got to be able to get there now. Hang on, and exert maximum willpower.' Through his gritted teeth Derek said, 'I've been holding this lot together by the power of prayer for at least twenty miles. Just hope that my faith doesn't falter.'

Soon scattered African buildings along the sides of the road showed that we were approaching the township. Chickens, children and wobbling bicycles were reassuring hazards along the way; and then abruptly we were there. It wasn't much of a town, but there was a sort of general store with a petrol pump outside, and that was all we needed to see. A sign above the door said, Thompsons Falls Suitable Emporium H. Patel, and the dark interior of the store, with a great conglomeration of sacks and boxes of every size, seemed to contain everything from tractor parts to dog food. Above all these things stacked on the floor rose shelves along every wall, also filled with smaller boxes and bottles; and from somewhere in the back regions of the shop a middle aged Indian advanced to meet us. I was wondering what language to attempt but he said, 'Good morning sir, how can I help you?' I explained that I would like to purchase a large can of oil, and fill up with petrol; and he called, also from the back of the shop somewhere, a dirty, ragged looking African and told him, 'Petroli kwa bwana, boy'.

While the car was filled with petrol, he sold me a gallon can of oil, a bottle of lemonade and a packet of biscuits, and Derek purchased a hat. It was a rather odd looking trilby, made from some sort of waterproof material, and could not honestly be described as smart, but he said it would protect him from the sun, and he proved to be wiser than me there. I was determined at the time to acquire a rugged up-country sort of tan as soon as possible, and so was doggedly going round everywhere without a hat, but the only result of that was that at the end of our safari I had merely burnt all the skin off my nose.

While Mr. Patel was totting up our bill, I asked him if he sold road maps. There were none visible, but he seemed to sell everything else, and he duly produced a Shell road map of East Africa from a drawer. It did not show much detail, but for the first time we could at least see roughly where we were in relation to the rest of Kenya, and we decided that there was little point in retracing our path to the Rift Valley again, and pursuing our original plan of going on to Nakuru. By the time we got there, we would just have to drive straight back to Nairobi. But on the other hand we could see from the map that there was a road going on from where we were at Thompsons Falls, in a north easterly direction, round the Aberdare Mountains to Nyeri. We knew that from Nyeri there was a good road back to Nairobi, and Derek had been there and said it was not too far from their camp at Thika; so that sounded a reasonable route back home again, and we would a have done a sort of circuit of a large chunk of Kenya. It sounded more adventurous than just doubling back the way we had come again, and the road ahead looked as though it was an important one, and so should be all right.

We bade farewell to Mr. Patel and Thompsons Falls and drove on. Just as we left the township we realized that we still had not seen the actual falls, but didn't feel like going back and looking for them. 'Ah, don't bother,' said Derek, 'Keep going. It's a long way home, and who cares about some water running over a rock, anyway? You'll see it another day.' It seemed good advice so we just pressed on, and on. Miles and miles of red, rutted murram roads passed under the bouncing wheels of the little MG as we followed the map in the direction of somewhere called

Mweiga, which was on the way to Nyeri. The car was going well now, full of oil and with plenty more in the can, and I was once more full of confidence in its ability to get us home. It was true that it rattled more and more alarmingly as time went on, and we danced across Africa on spindly wheels that were never meant for this sort of terrain, but nothing fell off, and we didn't even get a puncture.

As time went on we were treated to yet more changes of scenery. At first after we left the township the surrounding landscape remained almost like British countryside, except that the fields contained more maize then we were used to seeing at home. As we went there was always high land and hills on the right hand, that could have been in Scotland; scenery of moor land rising in layers of rounded hills to what we supposed must be the Aberdare Mountains, with the tops shrouded in cloud. To the left the land fell away slowly again towards distant plains, and as our road followed a generally downward course towards them we realized by degrees that we were in Africa again. The mild, summery sort of climate with cloud dappled skies above became dryer feeling and much hotter, and the breeze whistling through our little open sports car became less refreshing and more like the proverbial blast from an open oven.

Soon the sky was a hard, cloudless blue above what had now become typical cattle country of sparse grassland studded with thorn trees; no more fields and hedges. Yet, glancing back over your right shoulder the gentle, cloud dappled sky was still there, and further over there those high hills were completely shrouded in clouds. Climate in Africa, I was learning, depended on altitude; up there, cool and European, but down below, hot and dry. There would be plenty of times in the future, when my work took me up even higher in those hills, into the cold murk and drizzle, when I would remember what it looked like from down in the plains; all jolly white clouds in the blue sky. Those same jolly white clouds, seen from immediately below or even inside, meant dripping trees and bleak moors.

So on we went, and eventually by mid afternoon, came to the next township, Mweiga. Hardly a township at all really, just a few sheds and shacks and a police post beside the road, but there was a sign post that told us that we were within striking distance of Nyeri.

The final stretch of road climbed up again to the eastern edge of the

Aberdares, through some forest, and there we had the slightly unbelievable experience of turning a corner and seeing an elephant crossing the road ahead of us. We stopped in our tracks, and the enormous grey elephant just kept on going, and that was that. We sat there and looked at each other; a wild elephant, seen close to from the seat of an open sports car, looks very big indeed. 'You wouldn't want to run over one of those would you?' said Derek, and we agreed that running over elephants was not a good idea. We stayed where we were for a minute or two, watching the waving undergrowth where this one had disappeared, and just waiting to see that there were none of his friends or relations wishing to also cross the road in front of us. The sight of an elephant in the middle of the road was made even more surprising by the fact that in all our driving that day we had seen hardly any wild life at all, not even a rabbit. But then, most of the time we had been in farming country, where there probably wouldn't be much wildlife about in daylight. The elephant was less surprising, I realized later, when I had worked out that at that point on our safari we could not have been far from the famous Treetops Hotel, just outside Nyeri. It was closed down then because of MauMau, but it was where all the well heeled visitors used to go to see the wildlife, so we reckoned we had seen a bit of that, free.

Shortly after that we came to Nyeri, and after a brief stop there, went on to Thika, and Derek's camp. From there back to Nairobi seemed nothing after our three hundred plus mile journey, and I parked the little blue MG with a great feeling of having at last experienced something of the real Africa. I had also learned a lesson or two about making proper preparations before going on safari, and the inadequacy of a loaf of bread and a pineapple for a really good and satisfying meal. My nose was also beginning to smart a bit, and in the next day or two, as the skin came off it, I came to realize exactly why everyone up country seemed to wear a hat.

7
Up Country

Months went by, other people came and went in the KPR headquarters at the bottom of Delamere Avenue, but I felt doomed to remained there for ever. I learned a lot about this new world I was living in, about how our little backwater of the Kenya Police worked, and about the mostly very young people who made up the KPR. They came mainly in two sorts: those of fairly recent British extraction, who were much the same as us, if with a bit of an unusual accent, and the Yarpies, who were of South African origin.

Yarpie appeared to be a mildly derogatory name, applied to them by the 'British' Kenyans, which just meant a farmer, or cowboy. These young South Africans seemed to us to be a strange crew; virtually all the sons of farmers, usually from the remoter parts of the country, where their grandparents had arrived by ox-wagon soon after the Boer War. They all apparently shared a deep dislike and distrust of anything British, and sometimes seemed hardly aware that the war fought between their ancestors and the British army, in what they invariably referred to as The Union, was actually over. They seldom bothered to wear correct police dress, usually affecting a broad brimmed hat and vaguely cowboy clothes, with a bit of police uniform here and there. They spoke in a mixture of English and Afrikaans, usually very loudly, addressed you as 'Hey, man.......', always referred to Africans as munts or kaffirs, and swaggered about rather a lot. But their bark was worse than their bite, and they were good hard workers, if they approved of what they were doing. And that was just the two main white tribes.

Then there were the Indians, of course. Relatively few of them were in the police, but in the business world they seemed to be involved in nearly everything, and most of them appeared to be called Patel. They ran most things, from shops and businesses of all types, up to the various government offices and the railway. If you had a tooth problem you went to see Mr. Patel the dentist, and if you had to visit your bank for some reason or other, you would usually find yourself talking to a clerk called Mr. Patel. They had all come to East Africa originally, it was said, to work on that big new colonial project, a railway from the coast to Lake Victoria. In those days the British Raj in India apparently stretched across the sea to Africa, when convenient, and even the original currency in Kenya was the Rupee. One of the first East African Patels, who was a railway guard, acquired a sort of posthumous fame by being dragged out of his guard's van and eaten by a lion.

We also started to understand that there was no such thing as a race that could be called The Africans. The two local tribes, living roughly on opposite sides of Nairobi, were the Kikuyu and the Masai, either of whom would have been horrified to think that anyone could possibly mistake one for the other. Further away lived other tribes such as the Kipsigis and the Luo, equally unlike each other, and usually mutually hostile. In our office we worked mainly with Kikuyu clerks, for the good and simple reason that they could speak the language of our customers. It used to seem strange to us at first that members of this tribe, in which the MauMau originated, seemed quite happy working with us; then we came to realise that most of them had been educated at Christian missions and did not see themselves as having anything to do with a heathen secret society. A few might have had some sneaking regard for their fellow tribesmen in the forest and just kept quiet about it, but many feared and hated the MauMau.

We learned too, something about the complexity of this MauMau business. From England it had appeared to be one of these anti-colonial movements that had sprung up all over the old Empire, a sort of vaguely democratic popular left-wing sort of thing. Close to, it was not like that at all, and it was not even particularly anti-settlers. True, there had been a few horrible and rather bizarre cases of white people being murdered on lonely farms, but there had been far, far more cases of MauMau gangs attacking Kikuyu villages. So it had little to do with race or politics, but a lot to do with a power struggle within the tribe. The occasional white victims were usually people who were living close to, and on good terms with the Kikuyu; like a member of the well known Leakey family, recently murdered when we arrived, who was actually a tribal blood-brother and very highly regarded among them. He himself, since he was something of a father figure and adviser, was probably seen as a rival for power within the Kikuyu tribe.

Our boring work in Nairobi, of issuing pass books and permits of one sort or another, went on steadily until we began at last to hear whispers that soon we would be wanted to do the same work on the many farms where Kikuyu workers were employed up country. Magic words! Up Country! To get away from hot Nairobi streets and hotels, of which I had tried several by now, and to see different parts of the country. Derek had gone, of course, but didn't get beyond the KPR camp beside the Thika river, about fifty miles from Nairobi, and there he seemed to stick. I went to see him every now and then, but as on that first occasion, he always professed to be very bored. There was nothing to do, except to sit in his tent, he said, and read a book or listen to the Yarpies playing Jim Reeves records. Derek didn't like Jim Reeves songs, especially the one about Rose Maree, but they certainly did. One of them had an old wind-up gramophone, which they wound up a lot and played day and night, said Derek. Then there were the insects, especially the large flying things called sausage flies, that zoomed about during the evening, crashing into the lamp in your tent and falling into your hair. He wished he was back in Nairobi.

I just wished I had the chance to be encamped at Thika, even with Jim Reeves day and night and the horrible sausage flies. These insects I had met, once or twice, and they were indeed all too like a flying, blundering, sausage with wings; and there were mosquitoes, and even snakes, one supposed. You could see that there were some advantages to living in the town, where such things were rare; still, I was very ready to swap any possible town advantage for any and all up-country hazards; but my work went on at headquarters. Eventually I found myself inhabiting that inner office, and unofficially second in command of the place, in spite of having no police rank whatsoever. This was all very well, but it was also worrying; I still did not want to be in charge of an office, I wanted to be living in a tent up country somewhere. So I complained a lot, and was told as usual that I would soon want to be back in the comfort of town again. But then the powers that be relented, and I was told that I would soon be taking a team to Timau, on the slopes of Mount Kenya.

This was it, at last. Not just up country, but Mount Kenya ! I went out and bought myself a leather jacket, because it was going to be cold on the mountain slopes, and chose a large military revolver of first world war vintage, to wear on my belt. There were to be seven of us, three whites, and four Kikuyu clerks, all to be packed with our equipment into a long wheel-base Landrover. Why up a mountain, was the obvious question. There could not be many people there, surely? The answer was that no, there weren't very many, probably, but our job was to locate, issue pass books to, and keep tabs on all Kikuyu; and there were several small farms and homesteads run by settlers up there, probably with some Kikuyu employees.

Equipment was simple. We were issued with camp beds, and mosquito nets that nobody ever seemed to use. We had to carry all our office gear, including a camera for producing passport style photographs; but otherwise were left to our own devices about our personal luggage, and in the end carried little. The Kikuyu clerks seemed to carry everything they needed wrapped up in a small bundle, and we three Europeans managed with a few spare items of clothing in a bag, and a blanket for bedding. Our first destination, Timau, would be a very small township of a type that soon became familiar. There was a general store, run by someone called Patel of course, three or four African shops, and a post office. These shed-like buildings were clustered beside the road, on the other side of which stood a police post, equally simple, consisting of a few huts surrounded by a wire fence. That was it.

Our first step on the road there was by way of the now well known camp at Thika, and we waited a few days there, for final instructions. Although there was nothing much for us to do at the camp I was happy just to be outside the town at long last, and actually using my official camp bed in an actual tent. The bed, a sort of wire frame with canvas stretched across it, was surprisingly comfortable, and the tent, though shared with a wide selection of insect life, was OK by me.

Having nothing else to do I explored the neighbourhood, and one day walked a fair way along the Thika river. Poking about in the shallows at one point I came upon a rusty old tobacco tin, which seemed a slightly unexpected sort of thing to find on a lonely stretch of an African stream. Puzzled and intrigued, I fished it out and looked at it; its lid was still on, and something inside rattled. Interesting. So the lid was soon prized open, and the contents revealed; a dozen or so small coloured stones. I couldn't believe it. Coloured stones, in a rusty tobacco tin? It could only by some old prospector's hoard! I took my treasure back to camp, and cleaned up the stones. Some were green, some red; emeralds, rubies? There were lots of stories of lone prospectors in the early days in East Africa, so such a find was not impossible; but no, there had to be a catch somewhere.

Needless to say, there was. On thoughtful closer inspection the gems turned out to be coloured glass. But it was still very odd; where on earth had they come from, and why should they be in a tobacco tin in the Thika river? They were odd little bits of water worn glass such as you often find on the beach, and the answer to the riddle suddenly came to me. Some way upstream of our camp, on the road from Nairobi to Nyeri, was a waterfall and a well known old inn or hotel. The connection became obvious. Roistering travellers at the inn, wine or beer bottles thrown into the waterfall, pieces of broken glass grinding among the rocks. All became clear. But who had collected the little bits of coloured glass must remain a mystery.

Our short stay at Thika over, we were at last told that we were wanted at Timau, and to get on our way there and do some useful work. We accordingly loaded our bits and pieces in the long wheel-base Landrover, and were off on our way along the long and sometimes rough road to Mt. Kenya, by way of Nyeri and Nanyuki. The first part, quite familiar by now, was on the road over the plain north of Nairobi, a land of coffee plantations; and then through wilder country with the rolling green hills of Kikuyuland , rising up towards the forests of the Aberdare Mountains, on the left. After that the road left the plains and rose slowly towards Nyeri, a largish sort of township on the slopes of the same hills, just where the edges of the highland forest reached down towards the plains, and where Derek and I had seen our elephant. After the town of Nyeri we left the foot hills of the Aberdares and set our course over the plains again, towards Mount Kenya, many miles away to the north east. The road was fair enough by Kenya standards; well made up of murram, at the beginning, but very rough indeed towards the end. By then it was mainly lumps of rock, small lumps if you were lucky. This, I soon learned, was to make it still passable when all else was mud, during the occasional heavy rain that suddenly converted dry, dusty roads into rivers.

African rain was another thing we had been learning about. Just when we had got used to the apparently eternal sun that blazed down on Nairobi day after day, we found that some days great heavy clouds would build up all the morning, and then suddenly split asunder while rain bucketed down out of them. Then the clouds dispersed, the sun came out, and in minutes all was dry and dusty again. You could almost watch the puddles evaporating, but during the downpour it was like being under water. Cars that had been progressing serenely along a well made up murram road would suddenly lose their grip on the instantly muddy surface, and slither inelegantly to the ditch at the side; there to churn about until they eventually came to a halt probably facing the wrong way. On this particular journey we were spared the rain and mud, but it was rough going as we eventually passed the next township, Nanuyki, and approached Mount Kenya itself.

This great glittering pinnacle of rock and ice, rising so high above the African plain, makes an unbelievably dramatic sight when you see it in its entirety; but its higher slopes are more often invisible in great billowing banks of white cloud. As we bumped and juddered over the plain towards it on this occasion, all we saw in front of us at first was this bank of cloud on the horizon, with a vague blue-green landscape of rising ground below it; then as we got closer this landscape became wooded ridges and gullies. The road was climbing again towards the mountain now, and by degrees came under its cloud cover, so that the country we travelled through was no longer bathed in the full glare of the equatorial sun, but dappled with light and shade like Yorkshire dales. Exactly the same sort of countryside as we had seen in the Aberdare foothills on our Thompsons Falls safari. Near the mountain the sky was not clear, hard blue any longer, but more and more cloudy; then quite suddenly we were in this higher country, in an instantly different climate; quite cool under the cloud filled sky, and with the dry, hot plain behind and below us. The road wound on and up and down, and round little steep valleys, now filled with forest, while moor-like ridges rose above.

This went on until we came to the police post at Timau, on the edge of the Mount Kenya forest. There had never been any problem with finding our way there, because there was usually only one road linking the very few townships, so you simply followed whatever road there was. Beyond Timau the same rough track led on north and then east round Mount Kenya to Embu and Meru, but this was as far as we were going. We had been told to make a base camp here in the forest, a short distance up a side road from the police post, where there was alleged to be a sort of guest house, run by an elderly lady. It seemed wildly unlikely that there should be a place like this, in remote forest country, and during the course of the MauMau emergency, run by a lone English lady and two or three African servants; but there it was.

The lady in charge turned out to be in fact, a very tough and stringy looking retired nurse from Nairobi, who had been running a nice little business here for climbers and walkers on the mountain, before the Emergency started. Now of course, there were no holidays on the mountain, no walkers, and no climbers. But she was still here, and was delighted to have a little unexpected business thrown her way by the Kenya police. It seemed very odd that she was there at all, at least still theoretically running her guest house; but as she said, no one had told her to leave, so there they still were. Behind her own house there was a barn-like building with a primitive bathroom and Elsan toilet, and some other outbuildings; so we could set up shop there, while we looked at the farms, or whatever employers of Kikuyu labour there were round about.

We soon found that there was not very much for us to do. There were a few sheep farms up on the mountain, and cattle farms further down where it was warmer, but none of them had many employees of any sort, and very few Kikuyu. The few we found we issued pass books to, as required by law, and so we spent a couple of weeks. Up here, well away from Nairobi, nobody seemed very interested in what officialdom had decreed down in the capital. People were friendly, but were inclined to regard us as a bit of a nuisance, with our strange rules and regulations. The local view was that if there was any MauMau nonsense amongst Kikuyu here, why not just throw the whole lot out? Every one was ready to have a good old natter about the political situation, and to put forward their own solutions, but the Government idea of controlling a tribal secret society with the issue of pass books was just regarded as a waste of time.

I liked Timau. I was away from the big city at last, and enjoying the completely different environment; the farms we visited were usually run by hardy characters who had little regard for officialdom, or us as representatives of it, but it was not personal. We were always offered drinks and meals; and once I was taken on a wild boar hunt by a grizzled farmer who ran several thousand sheep over the high moors. I borrowed a police rifle and had a shot at a pig, without much effect; but this was the life, I thought, and at long last we were in the real Africa. But since there was not much work for us to do there, a message soon arrived for me to move on. I was to leave my team at Timau, to finish up what work there was, while I packed my few belongings and took to the road again, to go and set up another team at a place called Mweiga, which I vaguely remembered driving by on our Thompsons Falls journey.

Mweiga was yet another little township, consisting of the usual few dukas, or shed-like shops, police post, and apparently an office for me in an empty shop that had been set up by the local District Officer. This was going to be the pass book control centre for keeping tabs on the Kikuyu tribe in the whole area. The township was on the lower northern slopes of the Aberdare mountains, perhaps fifty miles to the west of Timau, and the 'district' we were supposed to control stretched from small farms high up in the foothills, to great cattle ranches that occupied wide semi- desert spaces on the plains to the north. My orders were to go and find Mweiga, and then look for the District Officer, apparently called John, who would pass on any further instructions.

Dusty and hot after the long drive across the plain between the two mountain ranges, I eventually arrived at the Mweiga police post, and found a tall, fair haired young man standing beside another Landrover and talking to someone inside it. 'This has to be John', I said to myself, he just looked too much like a young District Officer to be anybody else. I was right, and having introduced ourselves to each other, he gestured towards a young woman sitting in the vehicle. 'My sister Kay,' he said, 'She is going to run the pass office we are setting up here. She keeps house for me,' he added, as if to explain her presence. Kay, also very fair, and not bad looking, smiled and nodded; and I suddenly felt that things were looking up. Life at Mweiga could be interesting; was I going to be invited to share the D.O.'s official residence? But apparently not.

John went on, 'We have been told to look for somewhere for you to live, and of course somewhere for the pass book team you are going to set up. There's a farm house up the valley, it's empty at the moment, the owner has gone down to Nairobi because of the Emergency. There's plenty of space, and I believe it's even got electricity. Kay will take you up there and show you in the morning. I expect you'd like a bath and a meal.' I said I would indeed be grateful for both. 'You had better stay at our place tonight. You can just follow us up to the boma.'

I knew that District Officers usually inhabited a 'boma', which meant a local government centre of some sort, and I duly followed along behind them a short distance to a smallish, bungalow type of house, with one or two other buildings around it. Two or three police askaris armed with army rifles stood about, apparently on guard, and that seemed to be it. There was however the inevitable government rest house, just an extra room really, separate from the main building, and there I was invited to spend the night. It didn't look as if I was going to get very near the D.O.'s sister. John's almost friendly, but still formal, manner made that clear; still I was invited to have dinner with them, and Kay said that she would show me round the neighbourhood in the morning.

Mweiga stands on a sort of invisible boundary between two completely different climate zones; to the north wide open plains, that soon become semi-desert scrub land that goes on and on for hundreds of miles, merely getting more and more desert-like as it goes; but to the south the foothills, and as the land rises, the cool forest country of the Aberdares. The vacated house that it seemed we were going to use for our team was somewhere up in the hills to the south, and after breakfast Kay said we had better go and look at it.

That seemed a reasonably sensible starting point, and off we went down to the police post and the main road again, then we turned south off the main road and drove along a winding cart-track of a road that meandered up into the hills. The country was much the same as it had been on the Mt. Kenya slopes; ridges that climbed up to join the great bulk of the Aberdares, fairly bare and open along the tops, but divided from each other by gullies that were full of forest and looked pretty impenetrable. Two or three miles along our track Kay pointed down into the valley on our left. It was more open than some of the gullies, and there were bits of cultivated land in the valley bottom; there was also the corrugated iron roof of a small house glinting amongst the trees below us. 'That's it,' said Kay. 'I'll drive you down and you can look at it. It's supposed to be quite nice.'

'But the owner's just left it, and gone to Nairobi?' I said. 'Well,' she said, 'Plenty of people have, in the Aberdares, don't worry, it's probably quite safe.' 'You mean, safe from the MauMau?' I was beginning to wonder about being expected to go and live in a lonely house that had been deserted by its owner, presumably for reasons of self preservation. 'You mean, there are MauMau in this valley?' 'Oh, I shouldn't think so,' she said, 'The army have been mortaring it a lot. There won't be any of them about here now.' 'You mean....' I started again. 'Well', she said, 'they live up in the forest. Kikuyuland is only over the other side of those ridges. They've come down to steal food and stuff from farm houses on this side. People got a bit nervous about it, but the army have been up here making so much noise that they've all gone off back up into the forests again, where they know they are perfectly safe.'

Kay had turned off the track we were on, to an even worse one that led down towards the house, through scrub and the odd bit of cultivated ground. We came to an open space a hundred yards from the building, which seen close to was bigger than it had looked from above, built of wood and corrugated iron, and with a wide veranda. 'There you are,' she said, 'Have a good look round and see if you need anything.' She showed no inclination to go any closer herself, and added, 'I'll stay here and turn the car round, take your time, there's no hurry'. I got out and walked towards the house, wondering whether she preferred to stay outside on account of being alone with a stranger, or because of what might be inside. I couldn't quite make up my mind about Kay. Was she very hard boiled, or was she just putting on a bit of an act to support brother John? I was also wondering what she knew about the house, or its past, that she wasn't telling me.

In fact there was nothing untoward inside, no sign of MauMau, or even vandalism; the house was a bit damp and musty, but seemed to be otherwise exactly as the owner had left it. There was a dining room, and big sitting room, nicely furnished, with a big fire place; two or three bed rooms, an office, a kitchen. One or two other farm buildings. All,

I noticed, with electric light bulbs dangling from wires here and there. Thick electric cables, strung from poles, ran from the rear of the house alongside a footpath, which led steeply down into a small gorge; and from somewhere down there arose the sound of tumbling water. We seemed to have some sort of miniature hydro-electric scheme here, so I followed the path down a rocky, muddy slope to see exactly what was at the bottom. This was revealed to be a rushing mountain stream, with a shed built beside it from which emerged the electric cable. There was also a water wheel, driving a shaft, and a simple wooden lever had been arranged to connect this shaft with a drive belt, which disappeared into the shed. Curious to see if it actually worked, I pushed the lever over and after a certain amount of slipping, for everything was very damp, the belt began to turn and mechanical noises started up inside the shed. To my complete surprise a bulb hanging above the door suddenly flickered into life; so we really did have electric power.

I went back and told Kay that everything seemed to be fine, and the house was perfectly all right for us to camp in. She still showed no inclination to look inside the house herself, but said she would introduce me to some of the people round about. This was intriguing, as I had not seen a living soul so far, but we drove back on to the road and further up the ridge, and after a few more miles came to quite a big farm. This had none of the Mary Celeste qualities of the place I had just seen, and was obviously fully occupied and busy with a normal day's work. The owner was in a big, well equipped work shop, doing some welding, and stopped to talk and offer us a cup of coffee. He obviously knew my companion well, and we chatted about this and that. Eventually he said, 'So you are going to live on old Jack's farm, are you? Well, it's all right now, isn't it, Kay? The army went through that valley like a dose of salts.'

Back on the road my driver said she would show me another part of the district, and we went up and down a succession of steep tracks, and further round the hills to the west, to more open country on the edge of the plains. She probably assumed by this time, not unnaturally, that I was getting a bit jumpy about the MauMau, and said she would introduce me to someone who had no truck with them in spite of having her farm raided several times. This formidable lady was a widow, it seemed, who ran a big cattle farm, she and her husband had come out to this place in an ox wagon in the early days. He had died, but she still ran the place they had built up, all by herself. 'You'll have to come and visit her, anyhow, because she employs quite a lot of Kikuyu, and won't get rid of them.'

When we eventually bumped up another long farm track, and stopped at her house I fully expected to see an Annie Oakely figure, hung round with guns, but she turned out to be another thin, slightly elderly lady, rather like the ex-nurse at Timau. Her face and hands were brown and lined, the rest of her covered by nondescript shirt and trousers, and a large floppy hat. She was surrounded by Boxer dogs, in fact the whole place seemed to be alive with Boxers; they leaped round our car, and in the way of that breed, tried to lick you to death when you got out. This lone lady farmer was friendly in an ever so slightly grand way, assumed we would be staying to lunch, and produced large glasses of gin and tonic. This was brought by a servant, who even I could now recognise as a Kikuyu, and there were several others about. Our hostess seemed worried that my job might be to round them all up and send them away, so I was able to reassure that this was not our function.

As we drove away, after a lunch that no-one seemed to have any difficulty about producing at the drop of a hat, Kay explained why some people had tried to persuade her to get rid of her Kikuyu servants. It was assumed that they could have all sorts of tribal pressure put on them by the MauMau with murderous intent, as had been known in other cases; but she was determined to keep them all. Having spent most of her life, she said, in training up some decent servants, she wasn't going to let them go as easily as that. 'But how does she survive then?' I asked. An old lady, living alone, with valuable cattle, and goodness knows what else, on the edge of the forest.' 'It's the dogs,' said Kay. 'Boxers?' I said, ' They might give you a nasty licking, but serious guard dogs?' Kay laughed. 'Well, you or I might think that, but all Africans seem to be quite convinced that they are hounds from hell. I don't know why, but that's what they think. And it's a fact, that the MauMau have raided that farm and stolen the odd cow, but they have never tried to get into the house. They're terrified of Boxers. Funny, isn't it?'

Back at Mweiga, the news was that my new team was supposed to be arriving tomorrow, and John seemed to be assuming that I would want to get back to the farmhouse to get it ready. Not feeling very keen about spending the night there alone, I asked John, seriously, was it safe? I pointed out that if attacked, I had only my rather ancient army revolver. He paused, contemplating the situation, and I thought he was bound to invite me to stay another night with him and his sister. But he had thought of something else, and said that he would arrange for me to be issued with a rifle and ammunition from the police post. Feeling that that seemed to have dealt with the problem of me hanging about when not particularly wanted, I went along with him and collected my rifle. Kay, unbending slightly, offered advice on getting some supplies from the shops, including kerosene, that most basic up-country necessity. Away from the bright lights of Nairobi everything seemed to depend on it; lighting, heating, cooking, even refrigerators. So I loaded my Landrover up with a four gallon can, plus some basic foodstuffs, and set off again into the hills.

The farmhouse looked quiet and peaceful in the late afternoon sun, and on the second time of driving there it didn't seem all that far away from Mweiga. I found some lamps for my kerosene and decided not to try the electricity. It might not be reliable and there was something daunting about the possibility of all the lights going out suddenly in the pitch dark of the African night. With two or three kerosene lamps dotted about the house, they couldn't all go out at once, could they? Also, though I had apparently discovered how to get the dynamo by the river to start up, how was I going to stop it again, without climbing up and down that steep slippery path in the dark? Lamps seemed simpler.

There was also a small kerosene stove in a sort of pantry, separate from the main kitchen with its big, wood fired range, so I would use that. The taps worked, and water came out of them, from a reservoir somewhere I supposed; so all the basic requirements were there. I would cook myself a steak and chips from the stuff I had brought with me, and that would be fine. Mind you, it did seem a bit quiet. As it got dark it seemed even quieter; then, looking outside I saw that on the far side of this valley, over the stream, there were other lights. There was a house over there that I had not noticed in daylight; it must be amongst trees; but at least there was a house there, no doubt with people inside it, and that was quite comforting. I crawled into my sleeping bag with my rifle and revolver, and blew out my lamp, at least slightly cheered by the thought that there were other people around, and that they at any rate had not fled the MauMau. Life could be not too bad here, I thought. The team would arrive tomorrow, and that would liven things up, I might even, having acquired a rifle, go out and shoot a buck or something. Free food, I thought.

From a peaceful sleep I suddenly awoke. Something had wakened me and I lay there in the darkness wondering what it had been, but the house seemed peaceful enough; then I heard the noise again. Far away, up the valley somewhere, was a distant thump-thump noise, pause, then thump-thump again. I had never heard a mortar fired in anger up till then, but there was no doubt what it was; the army was up there, blasting away at the MauMau who, I had been assured, were no longer around. Well, someone thought they were still there. As I lay in my bed, wondering exactly what was really going on in my valley, the double thumps went on intermittently. My mind wondered on to the assorted horror stories that I had heard.

The MauMau did not seem to go in for straight forward murder; their actions, in the cases where white-owned farms had been attacked, seemed always to be connected with bizarre tribal rites, or even witchcraft. Victims never seemed to have died quickly, but at the end of long rituals, and always of many slashes with the long panga knives that were the favourite weapon. Had something of this sort happened here? In the morning, I told myself, I would go and see who ever it was living on the other side of the valley. They must know if there was something about this house that I had not been told.

I tried to cheer myself with the thought that these attacks always seem to have been connected with white people who were well known to the Kikuyu, for one reason or another; and no one could possibly know who I was, or even that I was there at all. The mortaring went on and on, up the valley somewhere, for hours; then it must have stopped, or perhaps I just got used to it and went to sleep. In the morning everything was bright and cheerful outside and all seemed normal again. I made myself some breakfast, then set off down to the river with the intention of finding a crossing place, and climbing up the other side of the steep little valley to find out who's lights I had been looking at.

The path I had followed down to the electricity hut and the

waterwheel ended there, in the deep gully below my house; but there was also a sort of farm track that left the house in the general direction of the river. I followed it along, and it descended by a gentler slope to a place two or three hundred yards upstream where there was a rough ford, and a similar track that continued on the other side. Surprisingly, on that track on the other side of the stream an old Chevrolet station wagon was standing, and its driver shouted, 'Halloo! Are you staying on the Cuthbert's farm?' I said I was. 'We saw a light last night, and were coming over to see what was going on, but I think there's too much water in the river.' By this time he had left his vehicle and walked down to the waters edge, followed by a young woman and a dog. From there we could converse reasonably well above the noise of the stream, and I explained what I was doing here, and learned that the people I was talking to were George and his wife Elizabeth, who farmed the opposite side of the valley. 'This is the short cut between us,' said George, 'When you can use it. But there is a better road round by Mweiga. Mind you, that's eight miles instead of half a mile. Have you had any breakfast?' I said I hadn't got round to that. Elizabeth smiled. 'If you can get across you had better come and have some with us.' That was easy enough with a bit of leaping from stone to stone, and I joined them on the their side of the water.

They had two dogs, a large shaggy thing that might have had Labrador and sheep-dog in its ancestry, and a strange little creature like a very short legged spaniel that had to be helped up into the back of the station wagon. 'Beauty travels steerage,' remarked Elizabeth, 'the other one can run.' We all, apart from the big shaggy dog, got into the old station wagon and bumped and rattled up the track, with great whining of gears. Their house was much the same as the one I was camping at, except that this one was obviously well lived in, and there were encouraging smells of breakfast being cooked somewhere. There was also a small crowd of Africans standing round a tractor, and taking turns at swinging its starting handle. Elizabeth pointed to a packet of cigarettes standing on top of it. 'It's a bit difficult to start', she said, by way of explanation, 'George isn't very good at engines. The one who gets it going, gets the cigarettes.'

Over breakfast we talked about the local situation, and much was explained that had seemed mysterious. Yes, there had been a lot of

MauMau activity about, and the army were still around, but those mortar shells last night were way up on the edge of the forest, much further away than they sounded. Yes, there had been a very nasty attack on a farm, and a whole family including young children had died; but it was not very near here. The Cuthberts farm had not been attacked at all, but they were quite elderly, and had been persuaded to leave their place for a time. George thought that the whole situation was getting better and nothing much had happened recently. I went back to my deserted house, with an invitation to come over whenever I felt like it, and in the weeks that I remained there, I often did that.

The team duly arrived and we got on with our work; but when we were not very busy with our pass books, which was quite often, I used to go and help on the farm across the stream; especially with the machinery, which as Elizabeth had said, George was not very good at. What with that, and of course continually meeting other farmers and ranchers, when travelling round with our team, I got to see a lot of farming in that part of Kenya; and I began to realise how much I liked this new and strange sort of world. From the first I'd had a sort of idea that I wanted to stay in Africa, and this idea came to solidify round one quite specific ambition. I liked Kenya farmers; I wanted to be a Kenya farmer too. How on earth that could be brought about, and how I might acquire a piece of Africa for myself was quite a problem, but something might turn up. I still had a year or so of my contract with the Kenya government to work out, so there was plenty of time.

8
Learning Swahili

By the end of my first year in Africa our work with the Kenya Police was running out of steam. The main job of registering the people of the Kikuyu tribe and issuing pass books to them all had been completed, leaving just routine work for a few clerks in offices here and there. Already one of our little gang who had emerged from that aeroplane at Nairobi airport a year ago had managed to leave the Government service and get himself a job in the outside world, and I reasoned that I should begin to work towards my plan of becoming a Kenya farmer. As a first move it could be a good idea to get myself moved from the Police to the Department of Agriculture; I had met two or three agriculture officers up country, they always seemed very busy doing interesting things, so if there wasn't much work left for me with the K.P.R., why not try for a transfer?

The moment came when I was back in Nairobi again, virtually unemployed for a week or two, and one day I just walked along to the appropriate government office, which was only a couple of hundred yards away, to see what the possibilities were. At that stage I did not even know if a transfer could be arranged, but the people I spoke to seemed quite relaxed about the idea and I soon found myself talking to someone at the Ministry of Agriculture. It was all very promising, but there was a snag. How is your Swahili, my interviewer wanted to know? Well, it wasn't very good. I had picked up a few words here and there, but mostly to do with asking for a cup of tea, or telling someone where to sign one of our forms. Anyone with any real knowledge of the language could have seen through my very superficial grasp of it in seconds.

Luckily my kindly interviewer did not pursue what could have been a rather embarrassing line of questioning, but asked me if I would like to do a Swahili course at the government language school? I said that I would love to do that, and surprisingly he said there and then that he would arrange it, and his department was in fact short of an assistant at Fort Hall. This was far better than I had really hoped for. The Kenya police department did not seem to be very worried about letting me go, and only a few weeks later there I was with a dozen or so other young civil servants from various departments, starting a course in the Swahili language.

It was again necessary to live in Nairobi, at least for the duration of the course, but this was not a problem. Unlike in the bad old days when I had been stuck in a hotel in the town, this time it was possible to join in with two or three others in like circumstances and hire a house well away from the city streets. We all had various types of transport, mostly vehicles acquired because they were very cheap, and so could live anywhere within reasonable distance of the language school. I still had the old bright blue MG, which had been left behind in Nairobi when I went off up country with my official Landrover; a bit older and more battered now, but still going strong.

The house which I joined a half dozen other young men in was virtually a small mansion, cheap to hire as its owners had left it because of the Emergency, in the Karen district just outside Nairobi. It stood in forest, looking towards the Ngong Hills over a narrow river gorge, in what must have been considered a very romantic spot by its builders, but that was in the old Happy Valley days of the thirties, long before MauMau was thought of. No one wanted to live there now, except a few impecunious young men, as the whole area was considered unsafe. Why it had this reputation no one seemed to know and nothing untoward ever happened while we lived there; anyhow I suppose I had been hardened up a bit by the casual attitude of the people I had met up-country. The nearer Nairobi people lived, the more nervous they usually seemed to be. We neither saw nor heard anything of the MauMau while we lived there, and the most exciting thing that happened to me, was when I got stuck half way up a cliff in the gorge below the house.

At the bottom of this gorge ran a swift, clear stream, amongst a jumble of loose rocks. It was mostly only a foot or so deep, but with some deep holes, and we reckoned that if we did a bit of rock moving a bathing pool could be cleared out. One or two of us worked on this at odd times, then one day I happened to be down there alone. We normally climbed up and down the gorge quite easily by a rough path, but immediately above our pool the rock was sheer for about twenty feet or so. On this occasion the thought just happened to drift into my mind that this rock presented an interesting challenge and I might try climbing straight up it. There was a bit of a ledge about half way, which I reckoned I could easily reach, and I had soon scrambled up to it. However, once perched there, rather precariously, the way beyond that point proved to be less obvious close to, than it had looked from below. Having spent some time spread-eagled on this very narrow ledge, trying to see where to go next, I decided I did not like it there very much and the only thing was to go back down again. Like many another in this position, I then discovered that climbing down is harder than climbing up; in fact I had forgotten how I did get up there in the first place. Time passed while I tried to work out a way of going up, down, or sideways; while at the back of my mind lurked the thought that nobody had the slightest idea where I was, and of course it was supposed to be MauMau country.

Stuck there on my ledge I was already getting cramp, so something had to be done, and downwards seemed the only way to go. There was the pool below, but I knew all too well that our work hadn't made it very deep yet, so there was going to be no graceful dive into the sparkling waters. Anyhow, I was not Tarzan. In the end I just let go and slithered, hoping to avoid hitting anything too hard and sharp on the way. I was lucky, up to a point. I did hit the pool, and not a rock first, but the pool was just about three feet deep, the optimum depth to completely soak anything falling in to it. It was the first time that any of us had actually tried out our new bathing pool and it was unbelievably cold. I extricated myself, climbed up the usual path to the house and crept in soaking wet, very relieved to find that there was no one at home; so at least I was spared the ignominy of having to explain what had happened.

Once the course in Swahili started, I had more to do than behave foolishly in gorges, so the bathing pool project was never finished. Apart from most of my time being taken up with the language school, which was run on a strictly nine to five basis, fate arranged that I should have something else to occupy my mind. I was walking along a Nairobi street one day, when I girl I had met before, during my first long spell in that town, appeared before me. It was quite a surprise, as the last I had heard of her she was several thousand miles away from Kenya. Her name was

Judy, and her father was one of the British army officers billeted with their families in Nairobi when we had arrived there. In fact she must have been an example of the 'lovely popsies' that our friend Ken used to talk about in those early days.

Judy and I had met in some casual way, at one of the hotels I had lived in then, and had been on quite cosy terms when dad had been posted home to England for some reason; and of course his wife and daughter, went too. I had been only slightly sad about it at the time. Judy was all right, except that her name always made me think of the line, 'The Colonel's Lady and Judy O'Grady'; but her family were openly unenthusiastic about me. Mum in particular made it quite plain that when it came to young men hanging about round her daughter, she would really prefer someone with a few more pips on his shoulder. Still, in spite of or possible because of this parental disapproval, Judy and I had quite liked each other, and had indulged in quite a warm parting when she left for the home country. Now surprisingly, here she was again, shopping in Delamare Avenue. So what had happened? Apparently dad, for some inscrutable army reason, had been posted back to East Africa again, this time on a more permanent basis. Life in hotels was over, it seemed, and they now had a house in the suburbs. 'You must come and see us, Mummy will be pleased to see you,' said Judy. I honestly doubted that, but life at the Karen house was pretty dull in the evenings, and I became a fairly regular visitor.

Judy and I resumed our warm, if rather vague relationship, and I was invited to little social events of one sort or another at her parents' house. It was all quite cosy, but nothing that went on there seemed in any way related to Africa; and slowly I came to realise that this must be an exact mirror of army family life at Aldershot. We often had to watch home movies of weddings, with various happy couples ducking under arches of extended swords carried by regimental buddies. It was pretty heavy going, but made worth while by other occasions when Judy and I had the house to ourselves, and I could pass the time exploring her underwear. We both enjoyed this sort of really rather innocent activity and it would have gone on indefinitely, I suppose, but Mummy had other ideas. One day, without any preamble, she took me aside and asked point blank what my intentions were. Completely surprised, as I hadn't realised that mothers actually said things like this in real life, and as I had never seen myself as a serious suitor for her daughter's hand, I could only say truthfully that I did not have any intentions whatsoever. This did not seem to be the right answer, so I briefly sketched in my present undesirability as a son in law; my uncertain future, no particular prospects, etc., but not forgetting my warm regard for Judy, and my great respect for her family. But none of this was what Mummy was looking for, and I began to realise that perhaps she would quite like to get her daughter off her hands. Well, I was genuinely not in a position to do anything about that; anyhow my time in Nairobi was drawing to an end again, and I was due to go off to Fort Hall, to be an assistant agriculture officer amongst the Kikuyu. Judy and I eventually parted good friends, as far as I could tell; but the next time I met her, again by chance a year or so later, she was safely married to a young man in a suitable uniform. So one way or another, Mummy had at least got that problem sorted out.

In the meantime I had, as required, been learning Swahili. At the school this particular course was run by an elderly gentleman who seemed to have spent most of his life in Africa, and was a great expert on East African tribes and their languages. He had written books on the subject, and loved talking about; as I also found this interesting and liked talking about it to, we became good friends, and he even gave me a signed copy of one of his books. At the same time I worked hard and learned quite a lot about the language that I discovered should be correctly called Kiswahili. It was an unexpectedly fascinating subject, because it transpired that this language was not the simple, rough and ready, primitive jargon I had expected; but an elegant inflected language rather like the Latin I had grappled with at school, but much more interesting. After all, Latin had just been tricky stuff to confuse boys in the classroom, but this was practical and useful.

Kiswahili, our tutor informed us, was closely related to Arabic, though luckily for us, was written in familiar European script, and was pronounced like Italian. The grammar was intricate but logical, and the use of many prefixes and suffixes made it very precise. It was used originally by the Swahili tribe who live on the coast of Kenya; and had been brought into the interior over hundreds of years by the Arab traders, who were busy buying and selling goods and slaves in Africa when the British hardly knew the place existed. It was all very interesting stuff.

It was true of course, that few people, white or black, spoke the correct language we were being taught. But almost anyone on the eastern side of the continent, from the Red Sea in the north to the Zambese river in the south would know enough words to converse with. Having spent by then the best part of a year struggling to make myself understood by the thousands of non-English speakers surrounding us on all sides, that was a wonderful thought. One of the first things we had all learned about Kenya was that though the language was officially English, that meant nothing, but everybody spoke Swahili in one way or another. Usually quite badly, but still people understood each other. So in future we would be understood and be able to understand others too.

At the end of the two months course I packed my modest belongings into the back of the bright blue MG, said farewell to Nairobi and Nairobi people again, and set off on the long, dusty road to Fort Hall. I was on my own this time, no KPR team, no tough official Land Rover, just me and my fragile and unlikely vehicle that jumped and skittered along the corrugated murram road. These roads, when reasonably smooth, were usually 'corrugated' because they always developed a curious surface that was like the ridged sand on a tidal beach. The ridges were perfectly regular and several inches apart; the effect of driving over this can be imagined, and less firmly attached pieces of car body frequently fell off. Discussions about the best way to deal with the corrugations were common, and most people agreed that the secret seemed to lie in the exact speed of your vehicle. Slow driving merely induced a sort of seasickness, while really high speed tended to end in complete loss of control, especially with a car like mine. The optimum speed was reckoned to be forty miles per hour; the theory being that the wheels of your car then simply jumped from the top of one corrugation to the next, and the overall effect could be described as uncomfortable but bearable.

Not for the first time, as I drove along, I reflected on the necessity of getting a more suitable mode of transport; but the little MG had been on several quite long safaris by now, and had managed fairly well. In any case I had no choice with this journey, I had simply been told to report to the district agricultural officer at Fort Hall, and there wasn't any other way of getting there. I had never been anywhere near Fort Hall before, all my journeyings had been in the 'white' highlands, but this was in

Kikuyuland, a wide area to the north west of Nairobi that was reserved for that tribe. However, there was as usual no difficulty in finding the place. Roads were so few that you simply drove out to the north along the well known route to Nyeri for about fifty miles, until you came to a road that branched to the west and a signpost that said Fort Hall. Then you drove along that road as far as it went, and you were there. It was that hilly country that travellers saw but seldom visited, rising up towards the Aberdare Mountains, when driving to and from Nyeri. Now, as I took that road towards the distant Aberdares, I found a wide, green country of rolling hills with fast, rocky streams between them, sometimes bridged, sometimes forded. Unlike the European farmed areas of cattle and sheep where we had been working, this was market garden land. Everywhere along the road there were patches of fruit and vegetables, some recognisable, ordinary sort of crops that would have been at home in a English garden, some more exotic looking. There was no forest here at lower levels, it had probably all been cleared; but far ahead on the higher slopes you could see it stretching, dark blue-green, up to the bare moorland peaks. There was more traffic on the road than I had expected; mostly ancient looking, dilapidated lorries, well overloaded with assorted produce, probably on their way down to the Nairobi markets.

Fort Hall proved to be a good sized township with a large group of government offices and an assortment of Indian and African shops. I found the department of agriculture and introduced myself, and explained that there was supposed to be a job for me. The district agricultural officer looked at me doubtfully and asked what sort of transport I had. It was standing outside the window of his office, and I pointed the little blue car out to him, looking highly out of place amongst a collection of rugged trucks and Land Rovers. I had the feeling that he couldn't quite believe his eyes, but he made an effort, and merely remarked that the department could probably find up something more useful for me to use. 'Do you know where Kangema is?' he asked. I had to admit I did not. 'No, I suppose you wouldn't,' he said, and you could see that he was thinking that this was just about the level of ignorance you would expect from anybody sent out from Nairobi. 'Well, its about twenty miles up in the hills, near the forest; the A.O. there, Jenkins, is doing some work introducing improved breeding stock, pigs and dairy cows. He says he could do with an assistant. You had better go and see him. I'll lend you an askari to show you the way.' He glanced out of the window again and added that he would have something different for me to drive, in a day or two.

The police askari who was to show me the way was also a bit surprised when he saw the vehicle he would be travelling in, but I moved some of my luggage out of the passenger seat and pointed out where he would be sitting. He climbed hesitantly over the low door, and sat down, crouched with rifle grasped between a pair of bony knees. It was obviously the most dangerous assignment that had come his way so far, and I searched my recently acquired knowledge of Swahili for something reassuring, yet wise and amusing, to say. Nothing came, but I managed to mutter 'Gari mzuri tu' meaning roughly 'The car's not as bad as you think'. 'Ndio, bwana' he replied. Neither of us was having much of a stab at conversational kiswahili. His instructions for the route consisted mainly of 'Kwenda, kwenda', 'just keep going'; this road again being the only one, as we left Fort Hall and went on climbing up into the hills.

The country remained much the same, except that the climbs up and descents down became steadily more precipitous and river crossings more rocky. I was going to need a different sort of vehicle all right, but the little MG made it, and at last we climbed out of our last river valley up on to a ridge, and Kangema was in front of us. It was a group of basic African style thatched houses, whitewashed, plus a few square ones with corrugated iron roofs, all pretty small. Slightly apart stood a group of three round ones, connected to make one dwelling, beyond that some more huts that looked like a police post, and beyond that again more huts inside a barbed wire compound. This last, I soon discovered. was a camp for MauMau prisoners, about a hundred of them, who were taken out every morning to do useful work round about, guarded by half a dozen African askaris. The police post held two or three white police officers, and the little group of connected round huts was a sort of medical centre, inhabited by an Irish nurse called Jean. The agriculture officer I was going to work with lived in the first group of square, whitewashed buildings which had a rather incongruous rose garden in front of them. Bob Jenkins, it immediately became obvious, was very proud of these roses, and no sooner had we met than he was showing them to me and asking my opinion. My knowledge of roses was zero, so I just tried to look as if I did know something, and complimented him. It seemed to be the right thing to say, and luckily we moved on to his office, there to be introduced to the other love of his life, a Persian cat of sulky expression, that occupied his chair or was carried about on his shoulder.

He showed me which was going to be my hut, very neat and decent, with two rooms and a proper bed, and then took me round to meet the various police officers and Jean the nurse. The police officers were regulars, very military in style, and I could see we were not going to have a lot in common. Jean was another of these tough women of no particular age who seemed to crop up like rocks in the Kenya landscape; this one was obviously the school matron. It was plain that this was a tight little community who were used to each other, and not that much interested in the outside world, and I wondered how I would fit in. It was obvious at any rate that they were all busy with their various jobs, and that either I was going to immediately become a busy assistant agricultural officer, or there wasn't going to be much else to do at all. I asked Bob about the work, and was told, 'Oh, there is plenty to do. It's a big district, Kangema, goes right up to the edge of the forest. I'll keep you moving, all right.' This sounded a bit vague, 'What about this stock breeding project they told me about at Fort Hall?' 'Yes, they do make these things sound very cut and dried, don't they? Well, we've got a very nice dairying project going on a few miles further up towards the forest, I'll show you that when I go up to get my supply of cream. We are going to build a pig centre, it's only on paper at the moment, look, here you are.' He pulled out a sheet of paper amongst many others strewn on his desk; a plan of a long shed, divided into pig-sized divisions. 'We haven't really got it going yet. You could do that.'

Trying to sound as if I knew something about pig breeding, I said, 'That sounds really interesting. Terrific.' This cheered him up, and he quickly added that he had been thinking about breeding better chickens too. 'You could do that. What do you know about hens?' Funnily enough, I could easily think up one or two things to say about poultry, because Dad had always kept chickens on a fairly business like basis, and Rhode Islands and Leghorns had been part of everyday life at home. Bob liked this even more, and I began to sense that he was not really very interested in stock breeding himself, if he could find someone else to do it. I remembered the carefully tended rose beds outside his house; this was not Bob the Stockman. He thought for a moment, while the large, white, very furry cat, which had been pacing back and forth on his desk, got bored with that and climbed up on to his shoulder. 'OK, right, ' he said, I've got a bit of machinery to take up to the dairy farm. We'll go up there first thing in the morning. You'll find it very interesting.' I went to bed that night wondering what on earth I had got myself into.

In the morning, hoping that I was not going to make a fool of myself on my first day as an Agricultural Officer, I got up at dawn to have a walk round and at least see where we were geographically. In the late afternoon when I had arrived at Kangema the sky had been cloudy and there had seemed nothing particularly unusual about our surroundings, just the same hilly country that I had been driving through most of the day. We were on a high ridge, with similar green ridges stretching away to the south, and up to the Aberdare peaks to the west. Now, at dawn, with the sky clear of the clouds which were a permanent feature of these hilly regions most of the time, a fantastic view was revealed to the north east. The green ridges on that side fell away, down and down to the plains, brown and shadowy; and then beyond them, perhaps fifty miles away, rose Mount Kenya. From most places theoretically in sight of it, you hardly ever get a clear view of this mountain; in fact it has an almost mystical reputation for being invisible, hidden in the clouds. But from here, in the clear air of very early morning, the sacred mountain of the Kikuyu, which they call Karenyagga, was revealed. From the distant flat plain a massive pyramid arose on the horizon, its lower slopes, like the plain itself, dull and subdued browns and greyish dark greens; then near the top of the pyramid, uplands glinted as they caught the early sun, and above that a few strands of white cloud. The eye rested on these horizontal clouds, registering this as the top of the picture for a moment, but then as the eye moved on above them, you saw, somehow detached from the earth, that unbelievable pinnacle of glistening snow and ice. The same brilliant white as the clouds in the morning sun, but hard edged and vertical like a handful of shining knives pointing upwards.

I had glimpsed this peak once or twice before, but never like this. I stood and gazed at this strange mountain, so high, somehow too high, in the blue sky. No wonder early explorers had been disbelieved when they reported the sight; even as you stood looking at it you wondered if it was really there. Ice and snow, high in the sky above the equator? That could only be a traveller's tale. I walked on, meaning to have a better look at it and perhaps take a photograph when I came back to that spot again, and quickly paced round our little boma, exchanging a morning ' Jambo' with the sentry at the MauMau compound. No one else was up and about, and it did not take long, but by the time I had completed my little walk, the peak had done its usual vanishing trick as clouds formed round it. The great pyramid was still there, rising from the plain, but topped only by the usual mass of white clouds. Karenyagga had hidden herself again.

At breakfast later with Bob, I said what a splendid sight it had been. 'Yes. you do get a good view from here,' he said. 'Now, we'll go up and look at the dairy. See if we can catch them still in bed. If you bring a clean bottle you'll be able to get some very good cream.' Leaving my weary MG where I had stopped it the day before, and from where it seldom moved again while I was at Kangama, I got in to Bob's official truck and off we went. The road went up and down the ridges as before, but always ascending towards the far peaks of the Aberdares, until we came to a big village with a high fortified fence and watch towers guarding it. This was very near the edge of the forest where the MauMau lived, and whence they were likely to come down at night, raiding and stealing food and supplies.

In the early days of the MauMau, gangs had often descended on Kikuyu villages and held forced oathing ceremonies. These were in effect press gangs sent to enrol recruits, for no one in the tribe would dare resist once the oaths had been administered with all the power of the ancient tribal religion. Those who resisted and refused to take the oath of allegiance were killed, usually being slashed to pieces with pangas. Many hundreds, especially Christians, had died like this, while white Kenyans living outside the Kikuyu areas were hardly aware of what was happening; but eventually the emergency was officially declared, and the forces of law and order began to take the situation seriously. Then the many small villages, often mere collections of a few family huts, were grouped together, and high, strong fences and watch towers built. This village, with its fortified walls and tall watch towers, looked like some ancient mediaeval city, and I wondered what would happen when we came to the gate. Would we be allowed in? Was there a password? Would the guard turn out and salute? But in fact it all seemed very relaxed. The gate stood open, and some women were just walking out to their vegetable plots, others were coming in carrying loads of firewood on their backs; women usually seemed to be doing most of the physical work in tribal Africa. We drove on up a track to a large mud-brick and thatched building which was the dairy, and went in. All was whitewashed and spotless inside, and a cream separator was whirring away; milking was obviously finished, so no one had been caught in bed today at any rate. Bob addressed the man in charge, 'Jambo Mwangi, habari gani leo?' 'Jambo Bwana, habari mzuri tu.' I could just about follow this; Mwangi, the dairy manager, was saying that the news was good today. I had already come to realise that as a greeting, the news was always good, followed by 'lakini', meaning 'but', if it wasn't. On this particular morning it was pretty good though, with a record amount of cream separated, and all the cows looking healthy. Bob carried on a conversation about cattle , which I could follow in parts, and then told Mwangi that I would take a bottle of cream for testing, as well as the usual one, and off we went again.

Mwangi had also said something about MauMau, which I could not follow, so I brought the conversation round to that, as we drove back towards Kangema. 'Oh, yes,' said Bob, 'Mwangi said that he'd heard that two had been caught at Itterri, near the bridge. We can go that way.' I didn't know what to expect when we got to Itterri. Would we have to take a couple of MauMau prisoners back with us? No, I supposed, the local police askaris, however relaxed, must be around, even if it was still early in the morning. We had descended into another valley by now, and came to yet another stream and a bridge. Two or three men stood about, one dressed more formally than the others with an official looking pith helmet and shiny brass badge, instead of the more usual rough and ready European clothes most wore. A local headman, I guessed. Bob addressed him, and they exchanged a few words; I couldn't follow what they were saying, but he moved away and Bob went with him. I walked along behind, wondering what they were talking about, and they stopped on the edge of a small pit and stood looking into it. I moved forward and looked too. The pit was only two or three feet deep, and there seemed to have been some branches lying over it; in it were two bodies, almost naked, slightly bloated, shiny black. They looked big men, perhaps because they were already swollen up, and they each had several deep wounds, dark red against the black skin. I found myself with nothing to say. Bob and the chief said a few more words to each other, and we walked back to the truck, got in, and drove away. 'They seem to have caught them in the hole, a sort of hideout, I suppose, and speared them to death,' said Bob. ' They were probably planning some sort of raid, or they wouldn't have been so far from the forest.'

Back at Kangema there were some MauMau prisoners working round the huts, doing some sort of cleaning up job, watched casually by a couple of guards. I looked at them more thoughtfully than before, but they looked a very unexciting lot, dressed in old army greatcoats and the like; just a scruffy lot of dull looking men doing a dull job. I reflected that they were probably lucky to have come into the hands of the police.

I continued going the rounds with Bob for a couple of days, and getting to know the people round about, then a message came from Fort Hall that a suitable vehicle was ready for me, so we went down to collect it. This vehicle turned out to be a very early version of the short wheel-base Land Rover, and was probably being offered to me because nobody else wanted it. It had little practical use, being virtually an open two seater, with no hood and room for only about two sacks of cement and a bucket in the back, but it enabled me to scoot around in a cloud of dust and get on with my newly appointed job building a pig breeding centre. I discovered straight away that if the windscreen was lowered flat on the bonnet the slipstream actually swept the dust away before it could settle on the driver, if driven at a certain speed. It was extraordinarily uncomfortable to drive, jumping about even more than the MG, and with the driver's seat apparently made of a piece of lightly padded wood, but also gave the impression of being pretty tough.

We soon built the new pig house, with the help of two of the Indian 'fundis', or craftsmen, that always seemed to be available anywhere in Kenya, and then the high-class Large White pigs arrived, as had already been arranged with the veterinary department. There was also a Kikuyu livestock officer to look after the animals, so there was not much else for me to do then, but wait for them to start producing the piglets that would then, hopefully, be used to improve the local stock. When I pointed out my lack of employment to Bob, he merely moved his large furry cat from one shoulder to the other and said, 'Well, what about the chickens, then?' 'Right,' I said, for I was quite getting into this livestock business, and with my immediate superior clearly not very interested, I could see myself building up a nice little empire. I had already noticed that if you seemed to be busy doing something useful the people at the Fort Hall headquarters seemed happy to leave you alone. 'Where will we get the stock from?' Bob said he didn't know, but try the veterinary department, so I bumped and rattled down to Fort Hall and tried to find out who might supply breeding fowls. Nobody there appeared to have gone into this at all, but seemed to think that I had come up with an interesting idea, and should get on with it. Slightly taken aback, I wondered what to do next, then I thought of simply looking in the Nairobi papers; there might be a section about poultry in the small ads. Sure enough there was, just like there would have been in any local paper back home, and someone was advertising day-old Leghorns. A conversation on the telephone soon established that there would be some available in a week or so, and my department would provide the modest amount of money necessary.

The immediate problem then was to find a suitable place to rear the chicks, and one of the as yet unoccupied sties in our new pig unit would do for that. I knew how to make a brooder, which is basically a draught-proof area with a lamp to provide warmth, so that was soon attended to, and then I was on my way back to Nairobi again to collect the chicks. Bob loaned me his truck for the journey, it being more suitable than the vehicle I normally used, and at the end of a days travelling I, and several boxes of day-old chicks, were back at Kangema, ready to start serious chicken breeding. It was the one aspect of livestock that I actually knew something about, and we soon got the whole thing going nicely. The simple brooder I had contrived worked very well, suitable food was organized, and we soon had a healthy population of young chickens growing up happily in the pig sties They would eventually have to go and live somewhere else, and I decided to use the moveable ark system, so plans were drawn, another suitable Indian fundi contacted, and construction put in hand.

Things had gone so well thus far that I was again looking round for something else to do, to enhance what I hoped was my growing fame as a young, up and coming agriculture officer. As it happened, at Kangema there was no water, apart from the domestic supply pumped up from a well, but I had noticed that there was a small but steady stream running in a shallow valley just below the houses. Why not build a dam, I thought to myself? There was no earth moving machinery available, but who needed machinery when there were a hundred more or less unemployed MauMau prisoners nearby? I put my plan to the District Officer, who had the final say in most of what went on locally, and he agreed to let me give the prisoners some useful employment. It gave their guards something more interesting to do as well, and soon we were marking out plans, with a stick, on the ground in the bottom of the valley. I knew nothing about dams beyond what might be suggested by common sense, but we cut a foundation trench across the valley, and began to move earth. It proved to be popular work with guards and prisoners alike; I suppose it gave them something different to talk about. My boss seemed happy about it too; his idea of an assistant was someone who did useful things without being told, and kept out of his way. He preferred to stay in his office, with his cat, and shuffle papers about. I discovered eventually that he was at the end of a government contract, which either they or he did not want to renew, and he intended to work out his remaining months as quietly as possible. He could see my dam from his window, and that was as near as he approached it.

In fact at this stage I was not sure whether I was still working for him, or the District Officer, it was all a bit vague. But the dam went ahead very well, apart from minor problems with leaks, and soon looked quite impressive as it filled with water. Some local Kikuyu farmers began to bring their cattle to drink at it and I was very pleased with myself; I was quite the local benefactor. Perhaps the day might come when a modest plaque would decorate the spot where I had built the Kangema Dam, and also introduced the Leghorn chicken to the Kikuyu people. Then one day when I had been elsewhere, rattling round in my bone shaking Land Rover, I saw as I drove back up to our ridge, a line of official looking vehicles parked alongside my dam, and several important looking persons busy inspecting it. Fame already, I thought, and was a bit piqued to think that I had not been invited to the official inspection. But the D.O. had done me a good turn really, in not arranging for me to be present, and saved me quite a lot of embarrassment. As he told me afterwards, he had begun to wonder where the copious supply of water that filled the dam was actually coming from, and thought he would get the experts to look at it. They had, and had been quite impressed by our workmanship; but then they analysed the water and came to the conclusion that most of it was coming from the houses above. In fact its main source was our bath water, and also everything else from the Kangema sewage system. So much for my dam.

The chickens were not a great success either. The arks looked great when built to my carefully worked out design, but I'd had this bright idea of having them thatched, which would make them light and easy to carry, and also beautiful to look at. Unfortunately I had not thought of the fact that a determined animal, such as a mongoose, could easily dig its way through thatch. Also I did not even know that after dark the countryside was in fact alive with mongooses, all looking for something juicy to eat; such as a chicken. My young poultry in their smart, but not mongoose-proof, arks could not last long, and they didn't. One morning we found that most of them were dead. It was all a bit depressing, and I was almost relieved when one day soon after this, word came through that my original Government employers would like to have me back, because there was some more work coming up in the near future. The political scene was moving on in East Africa, and soon the first elections for a new multi-racial government would be held. Someone in Nairobi, or possibly London, had worked out that all spare hands would now be required to help in producing a new register of electors, to include everybody of whatever race living in Kenya. It was apparent that very junior agricultural officers, who did things like building useless dams and chicken coops might be regarded as spare hands, so I was sent off back to Nairobi again, leaving Kangema and its Agriculture Officer, and his cat, in peace.

Nairobi: My MG on Delamare Avenue (town centre)

One of the Kikuyu fortified villages during the Mau Mau emergency

Askari (African policeman) on guard in the Aberdare Mountains during the Mau Mau emergency

Steamers Lake Victoria

An African police post during the Mau Mau emergency

Kikuyu men with donkey 'transport' in Aberdare Mountains

Fishing boats on Lake Victoria

Cattle herdsman at Kitale (it can be quite cold at 6,000 feet)

A typical simple farm house and out buildings

Some of the Kipsigis who worked with the cattle at Fort Ternan

My Foxhound at Fort Ternan

Me with my half-bred Somali pony at Fort Ternan

School master and Headman at Fort Ternan

One of the Indian Sahiwal bulls, bought from Veterinary department

Sahiwal bull and Arap Langat on the ranch at Fort Ternan

Rodeo at Nakuru

9
Settlers

The new job that I now found myself doing for the government of Kenya involved yet another change of scene. This time it was far to the west of the areas I had been in before; in the hills that end in the wide, flat plain that stretches to Lake Victoria. It was a district of relatively small mixed farms and dairying, which was made possible by the railway that runs across Kenya from the coast to Kisumu on the great lake. A railway means regular transport, and therefore access to the markets, and so any farm within a few miles of it could do a regular business sending off milk or cream and other produce every day. The climate in this western area of Kenya seemed milder, less extreme, with neither very hot dry plains, nor the bleak uplands I had found myself living in before; it was also far from the Kikuyu part of Kenya, and there had never been any serious MauMau activity here. It felt quite different.

The work I was doing this time was back to the clerk's world of making lists of names and addresses; producing the first register of electors for the nation-wide elections that were to take place in the near future Dull work, but it promised visiting many farms, in a different part of the country, and that could be interesting and contribute to my long term aim of becoming a Kenya farmer. To start with I had some of my own visiting to do. My route to western Kenya would be via Nakuru, in the Rift Valley, and I had heard that my friends George and Elizabeth, from the farm next door at Mweiga, were now living there. They had invited me to call if I was ever in that area, and here unexpectedly, was the chance. My instructions from the government department that was directing me were to find my way to the district headquarters at Kericho, the tea growing capital of west Kenya, and thence to wherever they wanted me to go. There seemed to be no hurry, so I got in touch with George by a faint and crackling telephone line, and announced that I was coming to see them.

The first thing they asked, apprehensively, was if I was still driving about in an MG. I could reassure them on that point, because during my stay at Kangema I had managed to swap it for an old Peugeot police car, a slow but rugged station-wagon sort of vehicle with a stout roof rack and a spotlight mounted on it. I had reckoned it would be more useful to me as a farmer than the MG. 'That will be great', they said, 'Provided you can find your way here', and proceeded to give a string of very involved directions. 'See you tonight,' I said. 'We'll put a light in the window', said they. But by the time I found my way there, late in the afternoon, I was beginning to feel that we might really need that light in the window. The road down from Nairobi presented no problem, I had driven along it several times since that first safari with Derek and a loaf of bread and a pineapple, and knew the way to Nakuru well enough. According to my directions the turn-off to the farm was a few miles short of Nakuru itself, and I was well warned that it was a rugged cart track of a road. It went off in much the same direction as the well remembered route to Thompsons Falls, and climbed up through the same rocky, wooded hills, winding about and dividing itself several times as other farm tracks met or departed from it.

I followed it as it climbed and became even more rugged and less like a road, until I began to wonder if I had left it accidentally and was driving along the dry bed of some mountain stream. I had passed the last farm turn off, indicated by the usual finger post, a mile or so back, and was seriously thinking that I might be completely lost, when my labouring and overheated Peugeot topped a ridge, and there was a little cluster of farm buildings across the next valley. It was late afternoon, daylight still and too light to detect a lamp in the window, but something told me that we had arrived. I had got to know George and Elizabeth well enough to understand that they really liked remote places, and this was remote.

At the house I found Elizabeth, and the funny little dog they called Beauty, looking just the same. 'You got here in good time', she said, 'but I had the lamp all ready.' I said I was very glad I had arrived in daylight, and would probably never have found them at all in the dark. She agreed that it was not much of a road, 'but you get used to it'. George it seemed was working on the pyrethrum dryer, which was not operating properly; they were still, obviously, not having any luck with anything mechanical.

The pyrethrum flower, used by the chemical industry to make insecticides, was a popular crop in the highlands of Kenya; it grew well at high altitudes, and was easy to grow and harvest with unskilled labour, but had to be dried before going to market. This involved using a mechanical dryer of some sort and was just the sort of thing that George would be having problems with. 'Come in and have some tea,' said Elizabeth. 'He will either get it going or he won't. In either case he'll be back for a cup of tea himself soon.' She told me the story of how they had moved from Mweiga, up on the Aberdares, to this place in the hills above the Rift Valley. It seemed that they had not owned the farm at Mweiga, but had it on some sort of long lease that was supposed to be more or less permanent, but which the owner suddenly decided to end. George thought they had been virtually cheated out of the lease, and was all for fighting it, but it was all very complicated, and they had decided to leave with good grace. This land had been available on a government lease, and they had taken it and moved here. It was good land for cattle, Elizabeth said, and they were going to build up a dairy herd. The existing pyrethrum crop was useful, because it would bring in cash in the meantime; well, that was the theory, she added, somewhat ruefully.

George appeared, as expected, and after our cup of tea we all went and looked at the pyrethrum dryer. It was working now, to my relief. It was getting late too, so we went back to the house, had a more alcoholic drink and some food, and discussed the new farm well into the night. It seemed to have great possibilities. There was good land, and their few cattle were doing very well. They seemed to be pushed for capital, but prospects looked good; for my part, I would have a little money to invest at the end of my government contract. Conversation drifted round to the possibility of taking on a partner, and I wanting to get into farming; was this the chance I was looking for? The next morning I set out again on my way to Kericho with all sorts of vague plans going round in my head. Could I raise some more capital? Was it a good idea? Could I really work with the charming but desperately impractical George? I was forced to admit to myself that though an attractive idea, it would be a doomed venture, and I put that possibility firmly out of my mind.

It was pouring with rain when we parted, and the road down to Nakuru was even more like the bed of a mountain stream than it had been the day before, now that it had water in it. But being down hill most of the way helped, and then the last few miles into the town were tarmac again. Nakuru was bigger than the usual little Kenya townships, and was everybody's idea of a nineteenth century frontier town, with shops and all sorts of other buildings spread out on both sides of the wide road that ran straight through the middle of it. As a concession to the twentieth century it had tarmac, but this finally ended where the town ended, and then it was the usual murram surface; which in this steady rain meant mud. Some way beyond Nakuru the road begins to climb up the far side of the Rift Valley, and this stretch was a nightmare of slippery mud and sliding vehicles, grinding and slithering their way towards the top. People were sliding about on the road also, pushing vehicles through particularly bad bits; but by luck or judgement my old Peugeot police wagon managed it, though not without a helpful push here and there. Then after that the road was running through highlands again, rough but passable all the fifty miles or so to Kericho.

This was a complete change of scene. A smart little town, centre of the tea growing industry, and surrounded by a rolling landscape of the bright green tea bushes. It was high, but more like open downland, without the brooding, dark forests of the Aberdares. This was the tribal land of the Kipsigis, a tribe completely different to the Kikuyu, and it had none of the market garden look of the Fort Hall district. Their lifestyle was involved with cattle, not growing crops, and the only cultivation much in evidence was on the land used by the big tea companies. It was not an area of white farmers either, and the town itself was a place that had been created simply for and by officials and administrators, as a regional government centre. It was a bit lacking in the casual, rather scruffy charm of most up country townships, and even the round, grass thatched native houses that dotted the landscape elsewhere were not to be seen much here. The big company-run tea estates had everywhere built rows of neat concrete and corrugated iron houses for their workers. I drove in to the centre of the town, located the District Commissioner's office, and presented myself. Nobody seemed to have heard of me, or had expected me to arrive; but they thought that I was probably wanted at Kisumu. That was a hundred miles further on, not far from the Uganda border on Lake Victoria. Someone provided me with a bed for the night on his veranda, and some supper, and the following morning I set out again on my travels. Down hill this time, with the highlands of Kenya behind me, and the flat plain stretching ahead, all the way to Lake Victoria.

At Kisumu the District Officer hadn't heard of me either, and after some telephone conversations with other officials in various locations round the country, it was decided that I should be at Kericho after all. So back I went again. I didn't mind any of this driving round East Africa, since I was on official business and would get some travelling expenses eventually, and so I was simply seeing the country at someone else's expense. Kisumu was interesting too. The great lake is like an inland sea, and even the inlet on which the town stands, called the Gulf of Kavarondo, is a vast sheet of water. There were steamers coming and going, and brightly painted fishing boats unloading their catches, all very different to the Kenya I had known so far. I would have liked to have stayed there for a while, but it was back to Kericho I had to go. This time round they had found the bit of government paper that referred to my official position in the scheme of things; I was allocated a local man called Kipkoech to be my clerk, and told to go and get on with compiling a register of electors among the workers on the white owned and managed farms to the north. It was a relief not to have to stay in Kericho, working in some government office, so I was happy enough to load my clerk and his belongings in the back of the Peugeot, and set off yet again.

My base for this work was to be Muhoroni, a township on the railway at the bottom of the escarpment, where it left the White Highlands for the Lake Victoria plain. This had been a key point in the construction of the railway track, important in its day, where the line which had slowly climbed its way up several thousand feet from the coast, descended precipitously again from the cool highlands of Kenya into central Africa. This was also the end of European settlement; the land to the south was the home of the Kipsigis and Nandi, and to the west, the Luo. The farms I would be visiting to enrol the workers were scattered along this escarpment; at the bottom cultivating crops like maize and sugar cane, and at the top, cattle and dairying. The railway, which here negotiated a switchback of cliffs and rocky gorges on high trestle bridges, the like of which I had hitherto only seen in pictures of the Wild West, was the lifeblood of the whole area and from the commercial point of view made it possible for the farms to exist. Nakuru or Kisumu were not far away by rail, and even the important markets of Nairobi were less than a day's easy journey for the local livestock and dairy produce. Remote farmsteads at the back of beyond, up in the hills, were often only an hour or less away from these long trains, with their great engines, that climbed slowly and painfully up into the highlands towards Nairobi, or rattled their way down, with screeching breaks, towards Kisumu.

The creation of this railway at the end of the nineteenth century must have been a great feat of engineering by dedicated men, building bridges and laying sleepers and steel tracks into the unknown. Such feats always have their stories of heroes, and I soon heard of Muhoroni's own legend. This was the local Casey Jones, an engine driver in the early days who discovered, just as his train began the long descent from the highlands, that the brakes were not working properly. He could have jumped, but didn't. He told his crew to get off while the train was still only moving at walking pace, and then nursed it down miles of twisting turning track at ever increasing speed. He succeeded in bringing his train safely down almost to the bottom of the escarpment, after which it could have been allowed to coast on over the flat plain until it slowed down of its own accord. But at that point, as it rattled and roared its way over the last swaying viaduct it left the track, the great engine turning on its side, and gouging its way through rock and earth before it stopped. The driver died, but no-one else was hurt.

That drama was long ago, in the same era as the railwayman who was eaten by the lion, and there seemed to be little excitement on the railway or anywhere else in the Muhoroni area now. Apart from the station there were a couple of Indian shops, and a grubby, disused looking government rest house, and that was about that. I enquired at the station about the rest house, and was told by an obviously rather surprised Indian station master, that yes, I could stay there, he supposed. But he had the look of a man who hadn't been asked that question for a long time, and wasn't too sure where he had put the key. I didn't really fancy staying there, anyhow, so I decided to push on and see if there was accommodation of some sort on any of the farms. I had a list of the employers in the district, and the first farm along the road from the station was obviously a big estate with plenty going on, so there might be somewhere there where a passing official with his clerk could put up for the night.

The road from the station that I was following ran along the bottom of the escarpment, with hills rising up steeply on the right hand side, and the flat plain on the left. Where, I asked a tribesman who was walking along the road, was Kwoisos? That being the name of the first farm on my list. He gave me the look of a man who has been asked a stupidly obvious question, and pointed with his chin, out over the plain. This was surprising, as I had assumed that all the farms were in the hills, and that the plain stretching away on the left to Lake Victoria was Luo tribal land. My road was on a slight rise, and so there was a good view, and true enough there were cultivated fields in the distance; and there also, rising from the plain like an isolated island was a single hill, and on the hill, amongst trees, were several corrugated iron roofs, glinting in the sun. That must be the farm, and I could see that there was a dead straight track from it, over the flat land, that looked as if it must join our road somewhere ahead.

As we drove on I asked my official clerk what he knew about Kwoisos, but he, being Kipsigis did not admit to knowing anything about the land on that side of the road. That flat plain between us and the lake was Luo country, which was beneath the notice of the Kipsigis people who lived in the hills, and were cattle experts. The Luo, he implied, knew nothing about cattle, and merely made some sort of inferior living digging in the earth. 'Are they miners?', I asked, having heard some stories about gold in this general area. No, he said, they just dig their shambas and grow vegetables. He clearly did not want to discuss the ways of the Luo tribe. A mile or so further on along our road we came to the point where the straight track from Kwoisos joined it, so we turned away from the edge of the escarpment that we had been following and drove along this farm road, straight as an arrow over the flat land towards the isolated hill in the distance. As we approached it seemed even more like an island rising out of calm water, and I thought that perhaps, long ago, Lake Victoria had been bigger, and then this had actually been an island in the inland sea.

We came to the cultivated land and then the base of the hill, and the road we were on began to rise steeply up and round it. It was very rocky, and there were cattle pens on either side with rough dry-stone walls; the track became steeper and rougher, then we turned a last corner and came to a stop on a small plateau. A line of stables stood on the left, and on the right some sheds, and a short flight of rocky steps curved away up to a big, rambling bungalow perched on the very top of the hill. It had a veranda that stretched all along the front, several doors and windows, all covered with fly screens, and great round stone rainwater tanks to which pipes led from the rusty corrugated iron roof. On either side of the steps there was a sort of rough rock garden with prickly pears growing amongst the stones, and around the house were trees that were full of twittering bower-birds.

I got out of the car and looked around to see if anybody was about. There was no-one visible, but anyone around the house must have heard the noisy progress of my old police car up the rocky track, and sure enough after a moment a young white man dressed in greasy looking shirt and shorts appeared from the direction of the sheds. There was a large American truck parked there with its bonnet open, and he must have been working on it. He put down his tools and walked towards us, obviously wondering who we were, and asked what he could do for us. I started to explain about lists of future voters, but he said, 'Oh, yes, we have been told about it all. I am Struan Robinson. Do you want to see our books or anything like that?' I said, no, nothing so formal, but it would help to know roughly how many workers there were on the estate, so that we would have an idea of how many we would have to deal with when we started doing the actual registration. He seemed quite friendly, so I thought I would ask about accommodation while we did our work. 'Yes, I should think so,' he said, 'There's plenty of room. You'd better have a word with my mother.' He glanced towards the truck he had been working on, and changed the subject. 'Do you know anything about petrol engines? I'm working on a scheme to make this run on water. Well, partly on water.' He walked back towards it and pointed to a small tank mounted inside the bonnet. 'The idea is, once the motor is running you allow water to trickle into the carburettor at a certain speed, and it beaks down into hydrogen and oxygen and becomes fuel.' 'Does it work?', I said. 'Oh, yes. Just a matter of getting the ratio of water to petrol right. Mother is in her office.'

He led the way up the steps to the veranda, and ushered me through the screen door. At the end of the veranda was another similar door, and a small office crowded with shabby furniture, most of which was covered with an assortment of ledgers. A middle aged woman, with fair hair braided round her head in an old fashioned sort of way was sitting at a desk working on one of these books, and she looked up and smiled as I was introduced. 'Oh, yes', she said, echoing her son's words, 'We have plenty of room. Everybody stays here.' She had a distinct Scots accent, unlike Struan who, in spite of his name, had none. I explained that I had a Kipsigis clerk with me, but this was apparently no problem either. 'He can stay with the schoolmaster,' she said. Kwoisos was obviously big enough to have its own school, as the larger farms often did. 'Struan will show you round,' she added, then you'd better come and have something to eat with us, it's nearly lunch time.' She had the casual manner about unexpected visitors that the old settlers always seemed to have. It was automatically assumed that you were going to stay for a meal at least, and probably for a day or two.

At lunch as we chatted I asked how long the Robinson family had been there, for it somehow felt to me that it must have been a long time. 'Oh, yes, my husband was allocated this land after the Great War', my hostess said. 'We came up from the coast on the railway, and then an ox cart to Kwoisos. There was nothing here except the hill, and the little stream, and a lot of mosquitoes; and the first thing we discovered was that the stream, which was supposed to be a permanent water supply, wasn't.' 'That's why the big rainwater tanks are there?' 'Ah, yes, they cost a fortune to build. We don't rely on them now, we have a very good well.' I was wondering how they had come to such a strange place to farm, and said, 'It seems to be a very interesting sort of place, how did you chose it?' Struan laughed. 'I know what you mean. Father used to say always that no one knew anything about it really. It was just a place marked on a map as potentially agricultural land; the map was not very good, and they probably thought that this place was up in the hills, not stuck out here half way to Kisumu.' 'You must have been here a long time,' I said, 'So at least it was good land?' 'It's all right,' he said, 'But it's a bit hot for comfort and really only good for mealies and sugar cane, we grow a lot of that, and some oranges. Nobody much lived here then, so it was not easy to get farm workers; just a few who turned up to see if there was anything going for nothing. We've got some good regular staff these days, but it took a long time. My mother could tell you how hard it was to get started here.' 'It wasn't easy,' she joined in, 'But having come all the way here, there wasn't much choice but to get on and make the best of it. You couldn't just get on the next plane and go home again in those days. The journey took ages by ship and train.' 'And bullock cart?' I added. 'Don't laugh,' she said, 'There wasn't even a road up from Muhoroni station, it really was by bullock cart, until we got some horses. And there was no bridge over the stream, so you sometimes could not pass it at all. Of course we had to build a house, we had expected that, but it took a long time to do, because it was just as important to begin to farm the land, and get some cattle, and find labourers to do some of the work. We just built one room and lived in that, and then added another, and so on, as children came along. Now it is just Struan and me here at Kwoisos, and if anything the house is too big.'

The Robinsons seemed glad to have someone staying with them in the rambling and rather empty feeling house, and in the end we did most of our work from there. It seemed that the other children of the family that had once filled the large empty rooms, had moved on, but for Struan. He had a younger sister who was apparently at boarding school somewhere, and a twin sister who was married to a policeman elsewhere in East Africa. His father, who had been something of a leader in the community, had died suddenly a few years before, leaving his wife Margaret, and Struan, to run the estate and everything else. Between them they knew everybody who lived in the district so well that I could have done most of my work simply by questioning the two of them and writing down their answers. My clerk Kipkoech seemed happy enough staying with the schoolteacher, and the arrangement suited me perfectly. I had the use of one of the large airy rooms that had been added at one time or another, the primitive but adequate toilet arrangements that went with it, and family meals which they seemed to be assume I would share, when I was there.

In return, when I was not at my official, and not very demanding work, I sometimes helped on their farm as I had before at Mweiga. Struan also recruited me to play in the local hockey team. I protested that I was not any good at it, but admitted having played in my school days, and was therefore signed up. The first fixture was up at Kericho, and I put on a good show of aimless rushing about for the first ten minutes, but then realised that I hadn't taken the six thousand foot altitude into account. I suddenly ran out of air, and spent the rest of the match hobbling up and down the pitch, gasping. I was excused further matches. I also rashly offered to paint their roof. Someone happened to mention at our evening meal that it needed doing badly, which was true as rust was showing through previous paintings in many places; it seemed that some local painter was supposed to have done it, but had not turned up. Hoping to appear a useful, practical sort of person, I said, 'Well, that's all right. I can do it for you.' My hostess gave me a rather worried look, 'That would be very kind of you, but are you quite sure?' Struan was also regarding me uncertainly, and I was slightly stung. They obviously thought I was incapable of splashing on a bit of paint. 'Just show me where the paint is, and I'll do it in the morning.' I said.

Next morning Struan duly produced a drum full of white paint, and a large brush; 'You're quite sure about doing this?' I was beginning to feel that there was some problem here that I hadn't spotted. 'Yes, I'm fine,' I said, 'Well, it's not very high up, is it?' 'No,' said Struan, that's quite true, it isn't very high up at all. You can get up on to the roof easily at the back.' This I had noticed; there was a point where the corrugated iron of the roof came down to within five feet or so of the ground. Struan also produced some old overalls, which I put on; then I scrambled up, hoisting the drum of paint up behind me. The logical thing was to start at the top and work down, so I scrambled on, up the sloping corrugated iron to the top of the east gable end. As I did so I began to realise that the roof was much bigger than it had looked from below; also, because of the position of the house on the edge of the hill, when I reached the top of the ridge the view down the other side was quite different. It was horrifying. From where I crouched on the uncomfortably narrow ridge, the front of the roof seemed to plunge away into space, with nothing much between me and the plain below except a few tree tops.

There was no way I was going to paint that side of the roof, so I quickly decided to do the back first, and think of an excuse for not doing the front. I painted away, slapping on the new white paint. It seemed to take a long time. The sun rose higher in the sky, and then I understood what the other snag was; the sun was very bright, and the reflection of the sun from the white paint seemed even brighter. I painted on, squinting, and then using only one eye, and then trying to avoid looking at the paint at all. I scrambled down and got a pair of sun glasses out of my car, and tried again; but because of my essentially head-down attitude on the roof they kept falling off. Then they fell in the paint. At this point I seemed to have been struggling up there for hours, and had finished one side of one gable. That, I calculated, was about one tenth of the whole roof. Fortunately at that moment my hostess appeared below and shouted up, 'Would you like to come down for a moment to have a cup of coffee? I am sure it must be very hot up there.' With enormous relief I scrambled down, found my way into the blessedly dark and cool house, and had my coffee. No more painting of the roof was done that day; in fact roof painting was never mentioned again. I don't think they wanted to embarrass me, so I pretended to have forgotten about it too.

I lived there, off and on, for several weeks while my clerk and I visited all the farms round about; and I learned a lot about the old Kenya farming life. I also learned to ride a horse, not as a sport or pastime, but simply to get about. There were no roads on Kwoisos apart from the track that connected us to Muhoroni, and it was too hot to walk far, so if you wanted to leave the top of that hill you saddled up a horse. Being on horseback also enabled you to see where you were on that flat plain, that was dotted with low scrub and bushes so that a man on foot could never see more than a few yards. A horse was also good at getting you through marshy bits near the stream, but you had to be careful near the water, as there was nothing a hot horse liked more than lying down in it and having a good roll. That could be tricky.

Thus my education on the subject of East African farming continued, especially in the amazing variety of it on the farms I was visiting. Some parts of Kenya were almost regimented in their sameness, like the coffee plantations near Nairobi, or the tea estates of Kericho; but here on this western edge of the white highlands, each farm I visited was different to the last. They were all up in the hills, and thus cooler than Kwoisos, but few buildings were of the sturdy stone construction that was used on farms elsewhere in Kenya. Here wood and thatch seemed to be the preferred materials. One farmhouse I visited, another large and rambling bungalow, appeared to be constructed entirely of reeds and grass. The interior was comfortable and even luxurious, with fine furniture that the owners must have brought with them from Europe, but the exterior walls looked flimsy enough to walk through. They said that it was cool and waterproof, which I could believe. But what about rats and snakes? Well, I was told, you don't get rats, because the snakes eat them, and the snakes apparently might live in the walls, but don't like it inside the house. So that seemed to be that.

All sorts of crops were produced, from pineapples and other fruit, to cut flowers which were carefully packed and carried on the train to Kisumu or Nakuru in damp cardboard boxes. Every farm had some cattle, and sent cream and beef off on the train, or at least had enough to produce milk and some meat for their own use. Once away from the plain where Kwoisos lay, the country was all narrow valleys and forested ridges, so no two farms were ever in sight of each other. Yet everybody seemed to know everybody else, and usually everybody else's business. Partly no doubt, because of the local telephone system, which consisted of just one line running up from Muhoroni, on rickety posts or nailed to convenient trees. This was called a party line, not for any political reason, but because everyone used it. You just picked up the receiver and whirled a small handle attached to a box on the wall. A telephone bell then trilled in every house attached to the same line, and anyone might pick it up. The custom was to use a sort of code for ringing, according to how you twirled the little handle, but anyone might answer, and probably would, if the person you wished to contact was not at home. Several people could, and often did, join in on the telephone conversation at the same time. The only time they were likely to meet otherwise was perhaps collecting their mail at the station, or in the store at Muhoroni; or every now and then at the 'club'. This was a sort of approximation of a cross between a pub and the village hall at home in England. People met there to gossip, or have a drink, and usually three or four men might be leaning on the bar playing liar dice of an evening; or sometimes there was a film show.

The people running these remote, isolated farms, were a strangely mixed lot, with a preponderance of ex-military men who had come out to Kenya on various government settlement schemes. Amongst the ones I met were an ex-admiral and an ex-infantry corporal, who farmed adjacent pieces of wilderness, and who both had their ranks emblazoned on their respective gate posts. Farmers, in the old fashioned traditional sense were few, but the standard of farming seemed very high, if sometimes unconventional. One man I met had worked out his own device for converting cattle dung and farm waste into a domestic gas supply, and it worked pretty well. Wives were a very mixed lot too, ranging from the leather-skinned ones who strode about in grubby overalls running everything, to one I met who was apparently an ex-ballet dancer, and who always appeared in public dressed and made up as though on her way to a cocktail party. Once, when I chanced to be at the club, she caused a sensation by appearing in evening dress with a sort of gauzy skirt, into which a large spiky insect had crawled and managed to trap itself. The men left their game of liar-dice at the bar, and spent quite a long time extracting it, while she had hysterics.

Whatever their funny ways, these people were all at the very least interesting, and I liked being amongst them. I had quite definitely decided by now that up-country Kenya was where I would like to live, at least for the immediate future. Being virtually at the end of my Government service, I had begun to look round to see if there were any jobs going on farms for someone like me, and discovered that there was always at least short-term employment going for temporary managers. Most of the smaller farms and estates were run as one-man shows, with an assortment of very casual African workers, and if the boss and his wife had to go away for any reason, there was no one to take over. Also bigger farms and estates sometimes took on a junior assistant.

At the end of my Government two-year contract I soon found a job, which lead on to others; and I gradually acquired plenty of experience, managing farms for odd weeks, or even several months, while their owners had to be away for one reason or another. I was still looking for a chance to get a toe hold in a farm myself, perhaps in some sort of partnership, but none of the people I worked for wanted a permanent assistant even, much less a partner with virtually no capital to invest. Still, I told myself, if I just hung about, made myself useful, and learned as much as I could about being a farmer, something might turn up one day.

10
Kitale

The first proper paid job I did, after the end of my two year stint with the Government of Kenya, was on a farm in the Kitale district. It was a random choice, simply because I had been told that someone up there was looking for an assistant on his mixed farm. It was described as 'up there' because it was at a fairly high altitude, about 7,000ft., which was higher than most farms and also way up to the north west of the main settled areas, on the slopes of Mount Elgon. In Kenya everyone tended to talk in 'up and down' terms, rather than distance. If you were in Nairobi you always went 'up' country, and if you were anywhere else, except possibly at the coast, you always went 'down' to Nairobi.

Kitale was as far north as any white-owned farms existed, on the Eldoret plateau in Western Kenya, and beyond it was only bush, desert, Lake Rudolph, and the Sudan; so as well as being at a good altitude, it was well and truly up country. Yet this small enclave of farms was the least 'African' of any area I had been in. Because of its altitude it was cool, and most of the time the weather was much as you would have found in spring or summer in the south of England. The crops were cereals like wheat and maize, and the farm I was going to start my agricultural career on also had a dairy herd and pigs. It was owned by a youngish man called Jim Smart, who like many of his neighbours was ex-army; his wife was ex-army too, and they had acquired their land from the government, and settled in Kenya, at the end of the war. He and his wife ran the farm with a few African labourers, and were doing well enough for Jim to feel that they could now employ an assistant, which was to be me. There was a slight problem with accommodation, as their own house was too small to take in a lodger, being only a round thatched hut with a couple of extra rooms attached to it. A round hut like this was the basic unit of construction in East Africa, and I suppose some local fundi [odd job man] had put it up for them. It had served their purpose, but the new assistant would have to be fitted in somewhere else. I was pointed in the direction of a shed that was being used as an office cum storeroom, and told that they would put a bed and a bath in it, and I could convert it into a desirable pad in my spare time. I was more interested in getting into farming than arguing about where I slept, so readily agreed.

My two year contract with the Kenya government had included some paid leave, and a passage home by air; so I took my leave and went home for Christmas, it being that time of year, and spent a month with my slightly bemused parents. They were not sure what to make of my desire to become a White Settler, and somehow there did not seem to be much to say about it. Africa had worked its strange magic on me and I only wanted to get back there and get on with my new career, but it didn't seem possible to explain that to Mum; and Dad as usual was happy enough to let me got on with my own life. His life was centred as ever on the Norfolk coast and his beloved marshes, and though he tried to show a little interest in my goings on, he did not really want to talk about Africa very much. My old girl friend, who I used to take to the pictures and Young Conservatives meetings, was not that enthralled with Africa either; and though not averse to a little hanky-panky with me to pass the time, made it plain enough that she did not see her future as involving life with me on a primitive farm in the wilds of the dark continent.

So early in the new year I said my goodbyes to one and all, flew back to Nairobi again, at my own expense this time, drove the two hundred and fifty miles up to Kitale, and presented myself for duty. Jim Smart and his wife seemed slightly surprised to see me, and nothing appeared to have happened about my promised bachelor pad, which was not a very encouraging start. But a basic sort of bed and a tin bath were soon produced and installed in my shed, and I was invited to have my meals with them. I never quite knew if they had not expected me to come back, or were too disorganised to have done anything about it, but in any case I was not going to ruin my start as a settler by being too sensitive about little things like that.

All the same, with the best will in the world this did not seem to be the best farm I could have chosen to start my new career on. The Smarts were not very good at being employers, and I soon found that they were at loggerheads with most of their African staff. I also began to suspect that I was there mainly as a buffer, especially for Mrs. Smart, who was managing the dairy and the pigs. Her attitude towards every African working for them was that they were probably busy stealing milk and pig meal, and this did not make for a happy relationship. I also soon noticed that she did not have a very good relationship with Jim either, their discussions about running the farm often taking the form of muttered arguments in front of me or a shouting match not quite out of earshot.

Still, I was seeing all sides of farming in Kenya, and I told myself that I had better stick it out, and just get on with the job of improving my living accommodation. Being a bit of an odd job man myself at heart, I soon made it reasonably comfortable if basic, and after work used to lie in my tin bath full of hot water quite happily, listening to a record or two on my portable gramophone. This may not have been the ideal introduction to my new life, but at least it offered plenty of scope for learning about all the ins and outs of running a small farm. Jim spent most of his time on the arable part of the land, riding about on an enormous, bright green, John Deere tractor, far away from the hurly-burly of pigs, cows, staff problems, and his wife. This left me to deal with most of the minor incidents that occurred day by day and hour by hour, and was a baptism of fire. But on the other hand, his love for the big green tractor, and my general interest in mechanical things did bring about a certain rapport between us. I think he also became really quite impressed at my expertise with machinery the day the old farm pickup truck broke down, due to a chronic lack of oil, and I took the engine apart and installed new big-end bearings.

So I spent several months on that farm, making myself useful and remaining on a reasonably friendly level with everybody, but finding less and less to say to Mrs. Smart. She never actually accused me of stealing the milk or the pig food, but working with her became a very tricky relationship, and I often told myself to ignore her and get on with learning about my new life; and there was plenty of scope for that. All the time I was finding out new things about running a farm, and coping with unexpected details like the language problem with a very mixed labour force, none of whom were very happy with the rather smart Swahili that I had been learning. Then there was the fickleness of the weather up there on the plateau, where a sudden hail storm that lasted only a few minutes could destroy a crop that has taken months to grow. Or where a playful little tornado, not even big enough to be noticed a mile away, could lift the substantial wood and corrugated iron roof off a farm building, whirl it round, and bring it down again twenty five yards away..

I learned a little more about African insect life too. Up there nobody seemed to bother much about the malarial mosquitoes of which newcomers were always warned, perhaps the altitude was too high for them. But there were other hazards. In particular we had wild bees and a lot of very large wasps; such things did exist elsewhere, but Kitale seemed particularly blessed with them. One night as I was going to bed in my little shed I noticed a large dark sort of something in the corner of the room just under the roof. It looked like a big shaggy football stuck up there, and on closer investigation was a heaving swarm of bees. At home in England you would have just invited the nearest bee keeper to came and take them away, but I knew these were wild bees out of the forest and not the inhabitants of some domestic hive. Not having the slightest idea what to do I watched them for a time, wondering if you were supposed to put them in a box and take them outside, or back to the forest, or something. But they seemed to be settling down for the night, and it was a reasonable guess that they were not going to do anything until it was daylight again, so I went to bed too. In the morning they were still there when I got up and went down to the dairy, and when I came back they had gone; moved on to a convenient hollow tree, I suppose, so that was a relief. I had an even closer brush with the giant wasps.

Everybody just referred to them as hornets, but they were completely unlike any hornet I had ever seen before. These creatures were shiny black from end to end, no stripes, and a good two inches long. They did not make the usual sort of wasp nests, but lived in little groups of half a dozen or so, and they suspended their small individual nests under the eaves of all the buildings on the farm. There they seemed to spend their time dangling from these miniature nests at just above head-height, so that you were in permanent fear of walking into them. They were alleged to have terrible stings, and judging from the size of them, this seemed all too likely; so one day when I did accidentally manage to disturb a nest I thought my end had come. I was whitewashing a wall when several of these enormous insects zoomed out and attacked. I felt more than one of them strike at my head so I threw down my paintbrush and ran, then wondered what to do next. I had been stung, probably several times, so what were you supposed to do about it? Rush for the nearest doctor? Take some special antidote? There was no one around to ask, so I just walked home to my hut, lay down on the bed, and waited to see what would happen next, half expecting to pass out. Absolutely nothing happened. So I lay there for half an hour, poking gingerly at a largish, slightly sore bump on my forehead where one of the stings had gone in. Then, as I was obviously still alive, I went back, found my whitewash brush, and got on with the job.

I never found out why the stings did not seem to do me any harm, while everybody was convinced that these hornets packed a terrific punch. Perhaps the popular belief was based simply on the size of these insects, more than any actual evidence. Anyhow, all this was part of learning about life up-country, and that was why I was there. Then at last one day good luck did came my way. The owner of the next farm, a Mr. Hanlan, needed to go back to England for several months, and asked Jim if he could spare me to look after things for him while he was away. This gave us all a chance to end an uneasy relationship on good terms, and I moved down the road, and left the Smarts to continue their eternal fight between themselves and their farm workers in decent privacy.

I was vastly flattered to find that Mr. Hanlan, who I hardly knew, had decided that I was reliable enough to be left in sole charge of his farm, and this gave me a real chance to get into the farming scene. It was going to be a seriously responsible job, and if I brought it off successfully similar jobs would probably come along. I moved onto the Hanlon farm, a similar one to that which I had been working on, but bigger, and much more peaceful. Here there were no niggling disputes, everyone seemed to be on good terms with each other, and all got on with their work amicably. I was introduced to the headmen who supervised the various farm activities, and who clearly knew what they was doing without any interference from me, and a few days later the Hanlon family departed. I was suddenly, and much sooner than I had ever expected, in sole charge of a proper Kenya farm.

Left alone, my first reaction was, how had I the nerve to do this?

I did not have any real knowledge about this farm, so if it all began to go wrong, what would I do? But then I reasoned that as it was running perfectly smoothly, why should it not continue? My best course of action was going to be to do nothing new, and avoid interfering; after all, if I did not give myself away, no one else knew how ignorant I was. The one thing I did know about farming, of which there could be no dispute, was that true saying that the best manure is the farmer's footprint. So I got up early every morning, and walked round looking thoughtfully at the work going on, making the odd comment, and showing interest, but vague enough not to make a fool of myself. It seemed to work very well. Apprehension might be surging round inside, when I thought of all the things that could go wrong, as things do on any farm, but I just hoped that no one else was aware of that. So time passed quite peacefully and I began to get to know the place, I even met the owners of other farms round about, they seemed to accept me at face value, and I began to feel almost confident.

But something had to go wrong, of course, and one morning as I strolled round, there in the paddock not far from the house, one of Mr. Hanlon's horses lay, looking, well, kind of odd. It was lying down, which horses don't do very much, and very still. On closer inspection it was also stone cold with the early morning dew lying on it. My instructions for emergencies had not included dead horses so I called the local vet. He came and looked at it, also thought it was dead, and did not seem to have much else to say about it. The odd dead horse probably did not loom very large on his particular horizon. We discussed briefly what it might have died of, I trying to hide my complete lack of knowledge of equine health problems, or even what its diseases are called, and then he departed again, leaving me with the problem of what to do with the corpse. A large, dead, horse is quite a difficult thing to get rid of, so I called a conference with the farm headmen. I knew that a dead cow was often considered a suitable item for an impromptu feast on some farms, so was there anyone on this farm, I enquired, who might like to eat a horse? But apparently not, nobody wanted to eat it, so that easy option was out. Thinking hard I remembered something someone had said about an old well that was sometimes used for the disposal of large, unwanted items; so wanting to give a quick decisive judgement, I said we would throw it down the well. I thought I caught the odd uneasy glance, but everyone buckled to, and the carcass was dragged slowly the two or three hundred yards to the old well, the half rotten timbers that covered it were pulled aside, and the dead horse was tipped into the dark, deep hole. The body seemed to take quite a long time to reach the bottom, then a horrendous crash echoed up to us, the covering timbers were pushed back into place again, and that was that.

I wrote to Mr. O'Hanlon to explain the demise of his horse, as far as I could, and he took it in good part. But what I hadn't thought of was the inevitable result of the rotting remains lying there at the bottom of the well; and about a week later the carcass began to let us know that it was still there. And for the next month or so, depending on the direction of the wind, there was always a strong aroma of dead horse about the farm somewhere, and so I learned the hard way not to dispose of large dead animals down wells.

I also had a little trouble with dogs. The first problem was my employer's own dog, which luckily did not die, but frightened me to death one day when I suddenly discovered that its head, apparently, was full of maggots. This dog and I had hitherto lived parallel but separate lives. He lived in the farmer's house with me, but an employee from the dairy gave him his daily ration of milk and posho, maize porridge, and we rather ignored each other. So we were not in very close contact and I hardly noticed when he tore his ear on something, as dogs do. A few days later I was casually patting him on the head when I realised that there were maggots on my hand, and on a closer look his ear seemed to be heaving with them. Horrified, I quickly cleaned out around the torn ear expecting to find the animal on the point of death from a maggoty brain, but discovered, to my surprise, only a perfectly clean wound. I splashed on some insecticide to discourage the flies a bit, and bound his head up with a bandage. Of course the dog immediately removed the bandage again, but there was no further trouble. I had discovered by accident the interesting fact that maggots are very useful in cleaning up wounds. The second dog problem was a number of shenzies, that is semi-wild, apparently ownerless dogs that tended to hang around the district. No one took much notice of them, but one day I walked into what I though was an empty calf shed, and found a pack of them in there. They, thinking they were cornered no doubt, with me between them and the door, lunged at me and several teeth tore at my hands, arms, and my side. Luckily I was wearing my leather jacket, it being a chilly morning, and only my hands came to any harm, with an assortment of tooth punctures. The dogs, after a lot of wild snapping, all moved off, leaving me a bit shocked and feeling very stupid, and not sure what to do. So I walked to the next farm, not very far, and my neighbour drove me down to Kitale. The doctor there patched me up, cheerily advising me to come back in a week to see if I had rabies or not. I did not develop rabies, but I certainly learned not to walk round the farm without even a walking stick for my defence.

When Mr. Hanlon eventually returned he seemed pleased enough with the state of his farm, and never pursued the matter of his dead horse. I suppose from his point of view one horse down the drain, or down the well in this case, was not too bad a result if the rest of the farm was all right. He gave me a good reference, and other jobs followed, so that I began to acquire some real knowledge of the farming scene as I moved round this and other districts. At different times I worked on regular mixed farms, cattle farms, fruit farms, even a farm growing cut flowers.

I made friends with the young manager on another farm in the area, and we went climbing on Mount Elgon, a few miles to the north west. It was alleged to be the second highest peak in Kenya, at fourteen thousand and something feet, but from a distance it didn't look like a very serious climb. In fact from the distance of our farms its peak appeared quite flat and uninteresting, no more than a slightly elevated part of the rolling moorland that made our horizon in that direction; not much more than an afternoon stroll. Still, if it was an official mountain peak it was worth having a go at it, and as my friend knew some people who had a farm on the lower slopes he suggested we visited them. They said that they would come with us and show us the way, so off we went early one Sunday morning; but when we arrived at their farm we found that they could not come after all. One of their dogs had been bitten by a puff adder and they were worried about leaving it; in fact it did not look well at all, lying in its basket, swollen up, and scarcely breathing. So they stayed at home with the dog and we set off from their house by ourselves, using a farm track which we were assured would lead us in the right direction.

Like all East African mountains the lower slopes are swathed in thick forest, which was supposed to peter out by about the 12,000ft mark, and from there apparently it was mainly open grass land, and little more than a gentle walk to the summit. We slogged away all the morning through this forest, with very little idea of exactly where we were going, except vaguely upwards. The main thing about thick forest is that you can't see more than a few yards ahead, so we could only follow the track and hope for the best, which is what we did for a couple of hours or so. It was hard going, and the path became more and more uncertain, but eventually we reached the open country above it. The change was abrupt, one minute dark damp, green gloom, then the next we were in the open, and at last had a view of where we were going; rolling brown moors, with one ridge after another, and in the distance what appeared to be a low cliff and above that the flat summit. So far so good. But what we did not quite understand, never having tried it before, was the affect of altitude on this final walk up the last two thousand feet to the top. We must have been reasonably conditioned to altitude; after all, the white farming areas of Kenya were mostly at several thousand feet above sea level, but we found that we were not conditioned enough. By the time we had climbed up through that forest we had realized that it was going to be anything but a casual stroll to us. We had suddenly, and seriously, run out of breath. Added to which the moorland, seen close to, was not at all like the grassy lawn it appeared to be from a distance. It was dotted with strange plants, many taller than we were, and there was a sort of giant heather which covered most of the ground, and was shoulder high. There was no path now. You might have said there was no need of one, the summit was there ahead in clear view, and we only had to walk towards it. And indeed an elephant could have walked towards it without much trouble; but we could only make progress by finding a way round the thickest and tallest clumps of the high, tough heather, and it was very slow going.

Our friends down below with their sick dog may have known an easy route, but we could only just toil on up to one ridge, down the other side, then up the next one, then down again, on and on towards that flat looking summit in the distance. The top of each succeeding ridge gave a nice clear view of it, but we did not seem to get much closer, and by now we had to rest every few yards. It was also afternoon, and we were beginning to wonder how long it would take us to get back. If, on the way home, we were still in the forest when it got dark, it could be tricky.

In the end we decided to call it a day, get back to base while there was still plenty of daylight left, and leave the conquest of Mt. Elgon for another time. We stopped at the top of the next ridge, got our breath back, took one last look at that mysterious flat summit with the low cliffs round it, and retraced our steps. Of course, in the way of such things, it seemed easier going back; we found the path through the forest without any trouble, and arrived back at our friend's dog's sick-room by tea time. To everyone's relief the dog was better. It had the look of a dog that would leave puff adders alone in future, but no longer seemed to be at death's door. We left them with our best wishes for the animal's continued recovery, and their promises to definitely come with us the next time, and show us the best way, but somehow it never happened.

As I moved round from temporary job to temporary job there was sometimes gaps between these jobs, and I had the chance of going off and visiting other parts of Kenya that I had not seen. Once my mountaineering friend and I filled in the odd week with a trip down to the coast. The highlands of Kenya are several hundred miles inland, so living there you never see the sea in your normal daily life. In the old days early settlers living in the highlands would hardly have seen it at all, having once been delivered to Mombassa by your ship, and having taken the long trek inland. I missed the sea a lot, having been born near the coast, and having spent most of my young life within a short distance of it. So one day, between jobs, and my friend having a weeks holiday due, and willing to accompany me, I decided to go and have a look at it.

The road from Nairobi to Mombassa is about three hundred miles and follows the railway track, a more or less level drive over a rather dull, and bad road. Nairobi is about four thousand feet above sea level, so the descent to the coast is considerable, but driving along you don't notice it. The main impression is of the great, level East African plain, all very similar scrubby bush and thorn trees. You left Nairobi town an tarmac, which lulled the driver into a false sense of confidence over the coming trip, but that surface only continued as far as Athi River, a few miles on the route. After that it was the usual murram surface all the rest of the way, and the only slightly civilised stop on route was the township of Voi; there you could get petrol and a drink or something to eat, before bumping on again in your private cloud of dust all the rest of the way. Mombassa, when you got there was a pleasant town with an air of solidity and age about it, virtually unknown elsewhere in East Africa. The harbour, guarded by the old Portuguese fortress, very picturesque, with its shipping varying from modern warships to ancient Arab sailing dhows. But the drawback was the climate. At sea level one suddenly became aware that one was on the equator, and it was hot and steamy. Up in the highlands it was very seldom like that, and even hot days usually ended in cool evenings, but on the coast it was very warm, day and night. We spent a few days there, met a few other people on holiday, and swam in the sea, which was very nice. But I was quite glad to get away from it again, bumping back up the long dusty murram road to Voi and Nairobi.

At another time I took the chance of visiting the Northern Frontier District, barren and beautiful semi-desert country on the way to Ethiopia. You had to get a special pass to enter that area, and you took your food, or anything else you might need, with you. There were no hotels, townships, shops, or anything else but the African bush, and you were by yourself, apart from any tribesman you might happen to meet, and who probably would not understand any word you might say to him.

The permit to enter the NFD was allegedly difficult to obtain, but in the event this proved quite easy; perhaps because as the old Colonial government ran down people were less fussy about such things. Anyhow, someone in the appropriate office in Nairobi simply gave me a piece of paper and told me to introduce myself to the District Officer when I reached Marigat, which I did. This was more or less the last outpost of civilisation, if you could call it that, consisting as it did of an office and a few huts. In the office sat the D.O., a young man with that rather detached from the world look that such young officials often acquired. He asked me politely where I was going and why, and I said I intended to visit Lake Beringo and take some photographs. It seemed better to sound as if I had some definite purpose in mind, rather than admit that I just wanted to swan around a bit and see what his precious NFD was like. He said OK, but to let him know when I left his area. I don't think he was that interested in what I was doing, but he didn't want me to just wander off and disappear, so that he would have to waste time sending out a search party. I left his little office, and feeling like Stanley or Speke or someone of that ilk, set off north to Lake Beringo.

There was a sort of road in that direction, through very rough bush country. The road was very rough too, more a vague indication of direction than anything else, winding between rocks and dense scrub, and sometimes it was not too clear what was road and what was not. It crossed a wide and rocky river bed at one point, dry at the moment, but it was a bit un-nerving to realise that if it rained there would no longer be a road there to return along. I drove on, through thicker bush, wondering just how wise or foolish I was being, not able to see far in any direction now; and the track wound on, and then ascended and came at last to more open country. Still very rough, but with more scattered trees and bushes; then as the scene opened up around, I realised I was on the edge of one of those dramatic escarpments that are such a feature of the Kenya landscape.

Away to the right hand side of the track which my car had been jolting along, the land now fell away, and a far vista of blue-grey hills marked a distant horizon that was visible for the first time. I stopped the car and walked a few yards, and found I was standing on top of a cliff. Down below, between me and those distant hills was a part of the Rift Valley, and down in the bottom of it, a mile or two away lay Lake Beringo, dotted with islands. My road did not seem to be going in that direction at all, but was running parallel with the lake, high above it, and still heading north; if indeed it was heading anywhere, or was in fact a road. I stood on the edge of the cliff, looking at the view and wondering what to do next. I knew there was a road of some sort that went to the lake, but this was obviously not it, and, assuming this primitive track I had been driving along was an actual road and went somewhere, I had not the slightest idea where it would end up. Or, assuming it did arrive somewhere, if there would be petrol available there. I had a fair amount of fuel with me, but not an infinite supply; so I stood there admiring the view with one part of my brain, and thinking about petrol pumps with the other, and soon came to the conclusion that I would stay where I was. I had told the D.O. that I was heading for Lake Beringo, and there it was; and there was not likely to be a better view anywhere else, so this would do. It was late afternoon by now anyhow, so I pulled the car off the road in to a convenient sheltered and level spot and set up camp.

This was a simple operation, as my car at that time was the old Peugeot, with plenty of room for me to sleep in the back. I also had a piece of canvas that could be attached to one side to make a primitive tent, but as the weather was bone dry there was no need for that. Other camping equipment consisted mainly of a primus stove, several tins of assorted meat and fish, a bag of potatoes and onions, and a five gallon container of water. This last turned out to be a bit of a mistake, as it was an old cod liver oil can from one of the farms I had worked on, and though carefully cleaned out never quite lost a faint aroma of its original contents. Still, it was all I had, and perfectly clean, so it had to do. Thus to set up camp meant little more than to find a suitable place, which I had done. The view was superb, taking in the wide sweep of the great valley below me and the lake. I made myself a cup of slightly fishy tasting tea, sat on a convenient log near the edge of the cliff, and studied the panorama.

The valley floor, about a hundred feet below at this point, and then sloping away down to the lake, seemed to be the same sort of fairly open bush country as on the top of my cliff. The lake was a couple of miles away and looked very elongated; in fact from where I was it appeared to be two lakes, but I assumed that this was because of a very large island in the middle that apparently divided it in two. Looking with binoculars, I could now see canoes moving on the water, and I knew there was supposed to be a fishery there, but nothing else was visible from where I sat.. At the end of the invisible road that did go in that direction was a depot of some sort, I had been told, where lorries went to collect the fish; but that was presumably at the southern end, several miles from here. There was no road out there in the valley that I could see, or any sign of activity of any sort, except the distant canoes moving silently on the lake. It was very quiet here on the cliff top too, just a bird or two hopping about in the scattered bushes; then as I sat there a wild pig with a line of small spotted piglets trotted by, taking no notice of me, and passed on. It seemed to confirm that I had found a really remote and unfrequented spot.

Nothing else happened, and, having had a good look round with my binoculars there seemed little else to do for the moment. It was late afternoon now, and as darkness would arrive promptly at six o'clock, I got out my modest provisions, chose a tin of fish for supper, wondering if I would be able to get fresh tilapia from the lake tomorrow, and did a little cookery. Hearing the tinkle of goat bells and looking up from the saucepan I was stirring over my primus stove, I discovered that a visitor had arrived. The goats were wandering quietly by my camp site taking casual bites at the bushes as they went, and a few yards away the goat herd, a boy dressed in a dusty brown garment draped from one shoulder, and carrying a spear, stood looking at me.

I tried a casual, 'Jambo, habari gani?' But he just continued to look. The Swahili language didn't seem to have arrived here yet, or if it had, he wasn't letting on. I continued the modest preparations for my supper, hoping that he would say something, or get bored and move on, but he did neither. I was unusual enough to be worth watching, so he just made himself comfortable leaning against his spear, and continued watching. Supper being ready by now, I sat down to eat it, and offered my audience some, which he took and looked at thoughtfully; but then thought better of it put it carefully on the ground and continued watching. He muttered something which may well have meant, 'No thanks, I'll just watch you eating yours.' I tried a word or two more of Swahili on him, to no avail, and then, his goats having moved on and disappeared, he decided to move on too. A lone white man eating something awful out of a tin wasn't that interesting. A cheerful, 'Kwaheri, then', still brought forth no reply, and he passed on and soon disappeared with his flock amongst the scattered bushes. The occasional goat bell tinkled faintly in the distance for a time, then I had the world on the top of the cliff all to myself again.

I decided that in the morning I would explore the cliff and see if it was possible to get down to the lake, and at daybreak this is what I did. Though quite steep where I had camped, it proved easy to climb down a few hundred yards away, where there seemed to have been a landslide at some time in the past, and it was merely a steep slope. Studying it from below, which always feels much safer than looking down from the edge of a cliff, I could work out a way of climbing back up near my camp, and so returned for breakfast. After that I thought I would try getting to the shore of the lake, and so it was down the cliff again, but now there was a problem. From ground level down there the lake was completely invisible, so I tried simply walking away from my cliff in what appeared to be the right direction. This worked for a few hundred yards, but the bush and scrub turned out to be thicker than it had appeared from above, and I soon reached a point where I was in danger of losing sight of the cliff top.

Not wanting to get lost, I returned to camp again, and spent the rest of that day scouting around about the campsite, and working out a more sensible plan to get to the lake. This time I made a sketch map of the ground between cliff and lake, and the next morning set out again, taking careful bearings so that I could be reasonably sure of my directions. After the now familiar scramble down to the land below my cliff, I followed my compass in what I now knew must be the direct route to the lake, but again did not get there. I reached a lone tree that I had made a note of from above, but it seemed now to be much further away than it had appeared. There was still no sign of the lake; the cliff was also completely out of sight, and all that could be seen was the same rough scrub in all directions. With the sun vertically overhead by now it was also very hot and airless, and I gave up the search again and made my way back, feeling quite relieved when my old familiar cliff came into view again.

I tried yet again the next day, and this time actually reached water, but there was no sign of the open lake I had expected. The dry bush country seemed to just merge into reeds and marsh, which was just as dense, if wetter, and still gave no view in any direction. There seemed no point in trying to wade on out into an invisible freshwater sea, so I filled my water bottle with lake water, feeling that this at least proved that I had reached it, and made my way back to camp again. I stayed there for a day or two more, and made a few sketches of the superb views, but by then the simple life had become boring, so I made my way back to the D.C.s office at Maragat; reported myself still alive and unlost, and returned to civilisation.

Life went on like this, from one temporary job to another, until I eventually took a job with a farmer at Londiani, on the high land of western Kenya, overlooking Songhor and Muhoroni and the great plain stretching to Lake Victoria. This turned out to be more of a permanent job, as the owner wanted someone to look after his farm machinery, which I was quite good at. This one was a serious sort of farm, very much on the standard English model, with cattle and sheep, and growing wheat, barley and oats. The only African style crops we grew were maize and pyrethrum, and our machinery included advanced technology, for Kenya, such as a combine harvester and a rotary bailer. This bailer was probably a very early form of that machine, a mass of whirring wheels and belts, and was a complete nightmare to keep working. I spent many an hour in the pitiless sun during our harvest season, trying to make the thing form neat bales, instead of tying its belts into knots and choking itself with great formless bundles of straw.

The job went on for a year or two, which was a long time for me to be in one place, and at one stage I was planning to join two other young farmers, who were managing the next door farm, in a safari to the Belgian Congo. We had planned a long trip that would have taken in many of the places that only a year or two later were to become notorious horror spots, as the Congo erupted into chaos and violence. No one knew it at the time, but the journey we had planned through then peaceful country, in which we expected trouble only from bad roads and tricky weather, would never be possible again. But in any case the safari did not take place. My boss became ill, and had to go to a hospital in England, and I found myself stuck where I was, looking after his farm and his wife.

This was an awkward situation, not least because the poor woman seemed to expect me to stand in for him at any social situation that cropped up, and she was a highly social person and chairwoman of the local Womens' Institute and other ladies' get-togethers.. On more than one occasion I hid on some remote part of the farm pleading pressure of work, while she sent urgent messages requiring my immediate presence at some social function or other. However, all turned out well in the end with her husband's health problems, and he came back and resumed his official duties as genial host when the ladies gathered at the big house. I, with great relief resumed my position as humble assistant and mechanic, and then after a decent interval, moved on.

But then eventually I found myself looking after a ranch for an elderly Irishman who, not having been home to the old country for many years, had asked me to keep an eye on his cattle for him for a month or two while he went back to Ireland. This was at Fort Ternan, to the west of Londiani and lower down on the railway line as it made its way to Lake Victoria, on the edge of the area that I had come to know well when I had lived and worked at Muhoroni. This was at the point where the railway left the true highlands and made its steepest descent over ravines on those wild-west style trestle bridges, to the flat plain on the way to Uganda.

The farm was in a different landscape again, of broad, grass covered ridges divided by deep river gorges; true cattle country, with very little other agriculture. I loved it instantly, and when my employer, after a few months at home in Ireland, wrote asking me to continue managing it for him, I was delighted.

It soon became clear that he and his wife, having become once more part of the hunting and racing scene at home, - and he loved anything to do with horses or dogs,- had no great desire to return to Africa again. He knew perfectly well that the land, with the approach of the end of the old Colonial regime, would be difficult to sell, and he suggested that perhaps I would like to take it over? Well, I had little or no money, but it seemed to be possible to get a bank loan; and in the end we worked out a scheme whereby I would continue to look after his stock, buy some of it, and by degrees take over the whole ranch. It was a strange time to be acquiring land in Kenya, but it was what I wanted to do, and what had I to lose? It might not last long, but who could say? Fate had presented me with the wholly unexpected chance to fulfil my unlikely dream of becoming a Kenya farmer, and this was it.

11
Another Safari

Before I took up the job at Fort Ternan I'd had a month free between jobs, and having just received an unexpected windfall of a hundred pounds, quite a fair amount of money in those days, I decided to fill in the time with a journey down south to visit some of the places I had never seen. There was Tanganyika, Rhodesia, and the Union of South Africa itself; all sounded interesting but were too far away to ever visit as a matter of course. All my travelling within Kenya had been over distances of a few hundred miles at the most, but South Africa was well over a thousand miles away. Now at last, with a hundred pounds in my pocket, and a spare month in hand, the moment had arrived when it would be possible to venture further afield.

I had done a few short safaris, alone or with friends, and knew it could be done. I had a stout, if unexciting, Standard Vanguard estate car at this time, which had replaced the old Peugeot, and had already carried me over many bad roads to fairly far flung places. Bad surfaces and almost non-existent roads had not worried it so far, and it seemed reasonable to expect that it could probably get me to the Limpopo River and back, given a bit of luck and a following wind.

As for camping equipment, I still had the standard issue camp bed that the Kenya Police had provided me with in those far off days when we young hopefuls had first left Nairobi to travel up country. A tent was unnecessary, as I could sleep in the back of the Vanguard if it was wet; and most of the time I could just sleep in the open under my old heavy tartan rug, that also dated back to those early days. It had been purchased at an Indian shop in Nyeri called, rather charmingly, Ladies Suitable Tailoring.

Food was no problem, and very little expense, as I knew from experience that a few staples like potatoes and onions, plus the odd tinned fish or bully beef, would keep me going for a long time. I had some basic cooking equipment, of course. I also had a battered old ammunition box full of tools and spare bits and pieces for the car, which I guessed, correctly, might be useful en route. My tool kit lacked one item, a good tyre pump. The one that went with the car had fallen to pieces, and I had been managing quite well without one as such things were always to be found lying about on farms. A good pump would be a fairly large bit of expenditure, and it was going to be necessary to stretch my hundred pounds as far as possible, so could I get by without one? A sensible person would have said no, of course not; who ever heard of anyone setting off on an African safari without a tyre pump? Well, here was one now. I had convinced myself that the price of a pump would buy quite a lot of petrol, so I would manage to get by without one. You could always borrow a pump along the road somewhere, and so the money was ear- marked for fuel; but I was going to learn that the rest of Africa was different to Kenya, and the spaces between which you might reasonably expect to borrow a pump or anything else for that matter could be very long indeed. Still, having settled that little argument with myself there was nothing to keep me; so I said farewell to a friend or two and set off south.

The tarmac, as you leave Nairobi, in this direction as in most others, soon peters out, but I had made a good start and was soon heading towards Arusha in Tanganyika, driving through typical East African game country. Whether or not it was officially a game reserve in those days I am not sure, but it was lonely, open bush country; that typical African landscape that is almost like an English park, grassland dotted with trees, except the grass is dry and brown most of the time, and the flat topped thorn trees are all the wrong shape.

Soon the great mountain mass of Kilimanjaro was ahead of me. It was shrouded in clouds, as these African mountains nearly always are, and looking merely like a pile of distant, fluffy white clouds on the horizon. But as the afternoon became evening the sky suddenly cleared and the mountain stood out startlingly sharp ahead; purple lower slopes and flat, white, snow cap, hard and unnaturally distinct against the blue background of the sky, and seemingly quite close in the clear air. By then it was getting towards the time when I would have to think about camping somewhere for the night, so I pulled off the road. It was easy to find a nice level place to park the Vanguard, so I just stopped there, did a bit of a fry-up on my primus stove, and arranged my faithful camp bed beside the car. That was all the setting up of a camp that was necessary.

I had decided to make a pictorial record of the journey with water-colours, and this was obviously a good spot for the first one, so I got out my block of cartridge paper, and did a sketch of the scene before me. It was not easy to capture on paper, and the mountain came out looking rather too much like a purple christmas pudding; but it was quite satisfying to feel that something more artistic than the usual photographic snap had been achieved. This accomplished, it was nearly dark, and there was little else to do but potter round my campsite a bit, and go to bed.

The first night passed peacefully enough, with a few distant animal noises, but nothing near or loud enough to be seriously worrying, and in the morning with the mountain concealed behind its covering of clouds again I fried up some breakfast and motored on to Arusha. The capital of Tanganyika proved to be the usual mix of corrugated iron shacks and smart modern buildings that was typical of East Africa, and in size something between Nairobi and Nakuru. I had never intended to stop there, and there was no reason to do so, apart from filling up with petrol, so on I went again southwards towards the next large town on the map which was Dodoma, about four hundred miles from base through more open country of plains dotted with thorn trees.

An hour or two later I was driving along enjoying the view, and thinking the road was not too bad, and surprisingly quiet and traffic free considering that it was virtually the only road from north to south. The country now was pleasantly green, and I was thinking that there must have been a good deal of rain about here, when the road came to a tree edged gully, did a sharp turn and then disappeared down into a donga along which a lot of brown, swirling, and rather uninviting water was flowing. Twenty yards ahead the road emerged from the water again and went on its way, but this ford looked a bit tricky, flooded no doubt by some of the rain that had been greening the countryside hereabouts.

Still, this was the trunk road south, and so must be used by many vehicles, and my old Vanguard was well used to negotiating fords. I pulled up and waited to see some other vehicle pass through it, to get some idea of its depth, but nothing came. The road had indeed been very quiet, I hadn't seen a vehicle of any sort for a time, and nothing turned up, so after a while I did a bit of investigating the watery obstacle myself. It was brown and opaque like African flood water is, and was gushing across the road with some force, but as far as I could see was not deep. Back in the car I started up, and drove forward gingerly down into the stream. The murky water was soon swirling up round the wheels, but I kept going steadily and seemed to be getting through it very well, when we hit some invisible obstruction, jolted to a standstill, and the engine stalled. I got out into the knee deep water eddying round the car, felt around with my foot, and soon discovered a largish rock wedged under one of the front wheels. That was easily moved, and I went to restart the car, then suddenly remembered being told that if you try to start a car when the exhaust pipe is under water, it can suck up water into the engine. I tried pushing it, but Vanguards were heavy, and I couldn't get a grip with my feet; the current wasn't helping either. I thought long and hard about whether I could risk starting the engine where it was, came to the conclusion that caution was the only possible course, and decided to loosen the manifold; that way, nothing could be sucked up the exhaust pipe.

It didn't take long; it was at least easy to get at anything on those old, very conventional engines. Then a single touch on the starter and it roared into life, in spite of the water surging and splashing all round, and in a matter of seconds we were out the far side. The exhaust manifold was soon tightened up again, and we were as good as new. Except that I now found that while under water, I had acquired a puncture. I got out the spare, and changed the wheel. Then I repaired the puncture, caused by a thorn forced through tyre and tube, but of course had no way of pumping it up. Thinking sober thoughts about the lack of any other traffic on the road, and Dodoma still over a hundred miles ahead, I pressed on. Within a mile another tyre went flat, exactly the same trouble again; there must have been the branch of a thorn tree down there in the murky water somewhere. The puncture was soon repaired, but of course, no pump to blow the tyre up again. I sat there beside the great trans-African highway for some time, reflecting on the stupidity of having no pump, and wondering what had happened to all the trans-African traffic. Was the road cut completely somewhere ahead ? Floods would often cut roads, and even railways. How long would I have to stay there ? Should I start walking the twenty or thirty miles back to Arusha ? Perhaps the great safari would end with a trip back to Nairobi by bus.

Then, in the distance behind me, was the faint sound of some heavy vehicle coming my way. You could clearly hear it grinding its way through the ford, then it hove in sight going hell for leather along our road to Dodoma and points south. It somehow didn't look as if its driver was going to stop out of curiosity or to pass the time of day, so I jumped up and stood in the middle of the road, waving. I thought that being dressed in khaki shirt and shorts, I might just pass for an official of some sort. The lorry skidded to a halt and the driver, a large, dark brown person in torn and greasy overalls, gave me a less than friendly look. He gazed at me, and then at my not very official looking car, and was clearly trying to work out whether he should treat me with deference, or merely drive on as quickly as possible. A manner of quiet confidence, I quickly decided, was called for.

'Jambo', I remarked in a casual sort of way, 'Habari gani?' He seemed disinclined to discuss the news of the day with me, and looked ready to drive on. I quickly added, 'Iko shauri kidogo hapa' - there is a little problem here, I am on an important journey, and I have foolishly left my pump at home, would you lend me yours for one moment only? He spoke for the first time, 'Hapana wesa simama hapa', he couldn't stop here, he said. So I pointed out that he had stopped, and that I only wanted his pump for a moment. He looked uncertain and clearly didn't know quite what to do, so I stepped closer and asked again, and he fished under his seat and brought out a pump.

I grabbed it and quickly pumped up one of my tyres, then as he seemed to accept the situation, inflated the other flat one too. I returned the pump, gave him a shilling for his trouble, and waved him on. Still looking uncertain, and clearly puzzled by the whole event, he jerked into gear and drove away. All the time this had been going on no other vehicle had appeared, either coming north or going south, and I began to wonder if there were any other travellers on the road, anywhere. It was all very different to Kenya I thought, as mobile again, I drove on in his wake, south towards Dodoma.

The great Tanganyika plain went on and on, occasionally broken here and there with rocky ridges, where the road wound up one side of a line of hills and down the other, and then went on again. Sometimes the view ahead of gently undulating countryside, and the road stretching into the far distance over it, seemed as if it must go on and on for ever; and the very sameness of the view in every direction gave me a new feeling of the vastness of Africa. I occasionally saw wild life of one sort or another in the distance, but hardly any sign of men or their dwellings. I went through one or two small, scruffy, townships, but then miles of empty, totally unoccupied looking bush country again.

Dodoma, sprawling, dusty, and looking probably much the same as it had when it was the centre of the ancient Arab slave trade, came and went. It was one of the very few African towns I had seen that seemed to have any feeling of history about it. Nearly all the townships I had been used to in Kenya looked as if they had been put together yesterday or the day before. But Dodoma in some strange, indefinable way, looked old. The imagination immediately conjured up nineteenth century illustrations of the expeditions of the old explorers, or of the Arab slave caravans, with their lines of manacled prisoners, making their slow way from Dodoma down to Dar es Salaam on the coast.

I drove on, through six hundred miles of the East African plain, via Iringa and Mbeya, which were two much more ordinary little towns, and came to Tunduma at the Rhodesian border. This was marked, not by a fence of any sort, but merely by a small hut on the side of the road inhabited by a single policeman. Even this was much more formal than the border between Kenya and Tanganyika, which was not marked at all, but it proved not to be a great obstacle to my further progress. The policeman emerged from his hut, and asked me where I was going. 'South, on holiday', I said. 'For how long?' 'Well, I've got to be back in Kenya in a month because of my work'. 'Have you got enough money with you for the trip?' I said, yes, I had plenty of money. That seemed to be the end of border formalities, and he waved me on. So, for the first time I was outside East Africa, and now in Central Africa.

Funnily enough, the country changed. The great plains had ended, and I found myself driving through a much more wooded landscape. Now, instead of being able to see many miles in every direction, the view became constricted to little more than the sides of the road. At first it seemed very pleasant, like English woodland, but it went on and on just as interminably as the plains; and the complete lack of view in any direction became claustrophobic. The dense bush right down to the edge of the road made finding a suitable camp site more difficult too, and that night I stopped at an official government rest house. There were two or three other young men stopping there for the night, minor government officials it seemed, who had business thereabouts, but no serious travellers. The great trunk road was still oddly empty and free of the heavy traffic in both directions than I had imagined it would carry.

In the morning the other travellers went off in their different directions, about their own business, and I pursued my course south, now heading for Lusaka, the capital of Northern Rhodesia. The road was good, still murram gravel surface, but well maintained, and I thought my great safari was now going to be almost too easy, but I was wrong. We were still about a hundred miles from Lusaka, and going up a steep hill, luckily very slowly, when the Vanguard lurched suddenly to the left, and subsided on to the sandy bank that formed the side of the road just there. The soft sand had been lucky, for no damage was done, but when I had dug the front wheel out I found that the suspension had come apart.

On the Vanguard each front wheel pivoted on a single large bolt in a sort of wishbone arrangement, and this particular bolt had obviously given up after a long and hard life. I jacked the front of the car up, looked at it thoughtfully, got out my big box of tools, and removed the broken bolt. It was probably a very special one in the eyes of its manufacturers, but it looked ordinary enough, and I had plenty of assorted bolts and nuts in my box, so I got one out that was near enough the right size and fitted it. It looked as good as new and there was no other damage, so I drove on, slightly surprised that an apparent catastrophe had been remedied so easily. But fate hadn't finished with me. Several miles further on we were bowling along merrily again when I became aware that although the engine was roaring away lustily, we were actually slowing down. It was apparent that something dire had happened to the transmission, and the engine was spinning away without any power actually getting to the rear wheels; these cars were built long before front wheel drive became usual, of course. We cruised to a stop at the side of the road, and I sat there thinking that this could be the really bad news. Something that should be connecting with something else, in the gear box, or clutch, or differential, clearly was not doing its stuff. Lusaka was still the best part of a hundred miles away, and I now knew from experience that there were not likely to be any friendly roadside garages hereabouts, they just didn't seem to exist. Once more it looked as if we might have come to the end of the safari.

I got out and had a good look underneath, but there was nothing obviously amiss. A little experimentation seemed to show that gear box and clutch were working, so that left the differential on the drive to the rear wheels. Well, working on farms and tractors had made me fairly used to what goes on inside gearboxes, and clutches, but the differential of a Standard Vanguard was definitely unknown territory. I looked under the rear of the car, without any real expectation of being able to do anything useful, but then saw that the differential box had a sort of inspection plate on it, held by a number of small nuts, so I could at least look inside and see if I could find out what was wrong.

The car was soon jacked up, a tin put underneath to catch the oil that was going to gush out, and the inspection cover removed. I peered inside, wondering if I could work out what was wrong, much less fix anything; but then immediately saw that a small rod between two cog wheels had broken. So, that was straightforward enough, but how could I possibly get a replacement? It was no good waiting for the A.A. man to arrive, or thinking of phoning the nearest agent, wherever that might happen to be, so I went back to my old tool box to see if there was anything in there that could be used. There was. I found an odd bit of mild steel rod, part of a home made tyre lever, that looked to be about the right diameter. There were basic necessities like a hacksaw and some files in the box, so it was just a matter of time to cut the rod to the right length, and with a good deal of filing, fit the ends of it into the two cogs.

With everything put back together again, it all, unbelievably, seemed to work perfectly well. I tried the car on the road, very gingerly, and it moved forward and back. All, perhaps was not lost; but I had been working on it for several hours by now and it was getting dark, so the side of the road became my campsite for the night. I cooked up some food, and then turned in, with at least the hope of being able to push on towards Lusaka in the morning; if only I could get that far, it might be possible to get a proper repair carried out. In the morning when the car was started up my make-do-and-mend job was still working, so I packed up all the camping gear and the tools and set off once more. At first I drove very slowly, quite expecting my repair to come apart, and the differential to seize up solid with nasty grinding noises, but it did not. After a time my confidence grew, and in the end we bowled along with no trouble at all, and soon reached Lusaka. This was a clearly a much bigger sort of town with plenty of garages and workshops, and I soon found the local Standard agent. He was a bit surprised by my story, but looked through his stock of spare parts and found a replacement for the bit that had broken, and which looked exactly like the replacement I had made beside the road. Common sense suggested that we should stop there and get the whole thing fixed up by a expert, but that, it seemed would mean making an appointment with the workshop and staying in the town at least a couple of days. That would have meant a hotel, and the whole thing could have become very expensive, and anyhow I wanted to get on with my safari, so I bought the spare part and told myself that I would do the job myself when I got the chance.

Next stop would be Salisbury in Southern Rhodesia, three hundred miles further on, and then beyond and south of that town, I wanted to go and see the mysterious ruins at Zimbabwe. After that friends had given me an introduction to some people farming near Bulawayo, and also to an engineer at Kariba, where the new dam was being built; so I had quite a lot to do and had begun to work out a programme and a route.

After Zimbabwe I would carry on south to Beit Bridge over the Limpopo River, the boundary with South Africa, then turn north again, and north west towards Bulawayo and then further north to Victoria Falls. From there I would go north east to Kariba, thus completing a sort of rough circuit of the whole country. I hoped that the introduction to farming people might give me the chance of a temporary job, and so earn a few pounds to replenish the coffers. That could be useful; I was probably travelling about as cheaply as it could be done, but still money was being used up, and I would have a long way to drive home at the end of it all. On the way to Salisbury I had a couple of passengers. I met an old and grizzled miner from the copper belt who accepted a lift though he did not seem to be going anywhere in particular. He was full of gloomy stories about how there was no work in the mines now, because all the jobs were being given to black Africans, whether they could do them or not. He reckoned it was all political, and the mines would soon become too dangerous to work in anyhow, with black supervisors not knowing what they were doing. He was wearing an old wide brimmed felt hat, battered and stained with sweat, which he offered to change with my straw hat with the puffadder skin round it, on the grounds that changing hats was lucky. But lucky or not I didn't much fancy it and made an excuse.

He went on his way to nowhere in particular, and I gave a lift to a young South African minister of a local church who was making his way to Salisbury. He had just finished his training in the Dutch Reformed Church, and I was interested to hear his point of view as a member of that, allegedly, most racist of all sects. He chatted away amiably enough as we drove along, and seemed very well informed and open minded, but was quite convinced that black Africans were incapable of taking part in the government of South Africa. He was sure that the white race were much better equipped mentally to run the government of the country, and should continue to do so, while suitably educated tribesmen could run their own affairs locally. The fact that the rest of the world apparently did not see things this way did not seem to worry him very much, and you could see why. I was used to living in a small country, where the whole political policy had for a long time been leading towards a democratic government, with presumably a black majority. He lived in a large, powerful state, ruled by a white government that intended to remain in power for ever, and saw no reason why it should not. His point of view as a minister of religion was that it was his duty to take a benign and fatherly attitude to his black flock, teaching Christian virtues and helping them where he could. This was not, to him, at all a political attitude, but just the obvious and correct way to behave; and in the context of his world I could see that this was a perfectly reasonable way to see things.

We talked as the miles passed, and eventually I dropped him off at the place he was aiming for on the outskirts of Salisbury. By this time the scenery had change several times, from the great plains of East Africa through the rugged bush country of Northern Rhodesia and then a much more varied landscape as I had travelled south. It had become a more open sort of bush, with great boulders, as big as houses, dotted about in it, distant views of rocky hills, and some quite European like countryside. Now, in the outskirts of Salisbury, we could have been driving into any big European city. Smart houses, offices, factories, wide well paved roads, heavy traffic; we could have been anywhere; anywhere that is, except the sort of Africa I was used to. However, smart and interesting as Salisbury looked, this was not what I had come to see, so after a day which I sent in doing some running repairs to my long-suffering car, I was on my way again first towards the Angola border and then to Zimbabwe.

The diversion towards Angola was simply out of curiosity, to see what the Portuguese colony looked like, but I had no visa in my passport to enter that country, and so having reached the border simply retraced my tracks. Then it was south to Zimbabwe and after that Beit Bridge at the South African border. Beit Bridge turned out to be merely a big modern iron girder bridge over the Limpopo River, and the great Limpopo itself on that particular day seemed to be mostly sand banks. But Zimbabwe was every bit as fascinating as it was supposed to be. The name apparently means the 'the place of stones' and you immediately see why as it lies in a broad valley littered with grey, broken rock. There was a small government rest camp, just a couple of huts, and the African in charge said I could stay there. He spoke a word or two of English only, and I had already discovered that no one this far south wanted to use Swahili, and I was not able to find out much about the place from him; so I just set up camp, and then set out myself to explore.

In the centre of the barren looking valley stands the curious, famous, building with its double walls, built from the stone that lies everywhere. It was bigger and with taller walls than I had expected, and was certainly completely unlike anything I had seen in Africa, as everybody who sees it seems to agree. Just as it is unlike any native sort of building, it is also unlike old Portuguese buildings on the coast such as Fort Jesus at Mombassa. It gave no clue how long it had stood there, but also gave absolutely no indication of any recent use or habitation. Trees and bushes grew amongst the walls, parts of which had collapsed or had been torn down at some time in the past. It suggested some sort of prehistoric fortification, perhaps something like the small round forts called brochs in the Highlands of Scotland, but built on a much larger scale.

Up on a rocky outcrop, separate and some way away were more rock walls, which also looked like a smaller part of the same fortifications. The rock is all a granite-like material, with a glittering surface and obviously very hard. The buildings seem to be built of quite small brick-like pieces of this rock, not large irregular lumps as you might expect. I could see no mortar, and these small, quite regular pieces of rock were merely piled one on top of the other. It looked as if the rock must naturally split into layers, that could then be broken up into rough 'bricks'; there were no tool marks to suggest any conventional stone-working activity. It was a very strange place, unnaturally quiet with no life, human, animal or bird stirring, and it would have been easy to believe that the valley had been like this, unknown and unvisited, for hundreds or thousands of years.

I stayed at the little rest house for a couple of days camping, and saw no-one else but an occasional glimpse of the custodian I had met on arrival. I felt that I could spend a week or two there, just studying it all, but no doubt other people, better equipped than me have done that. So I moved on again, this time towards Bulawayo, to where I had the introduction to a farmer. It was another long, hot and dusty drive, and when I got there the farm turned out to be just a portion of the same hot and dusty plain. The people were kind and friendly, and suggested at once that I might like to have a cooling swim in their water tank. This was a large structure of metal, about six or seven feet high, built beside their house. There was a ladder up the side, which as a teenage son of the household demonstrated, you apparently climbed up and simply jumped in. It was quite wide, the size of a small swimming pool, and it crossed my mind to wonder how you got out of it again, or if I was about to drown. However, pride decreed that I should jump, so I did, and swam across to the other side, then I could see that there was also a ladder on the inside of the tank too. So getting out again presented no problem, and it was certainly cooling.

I stayed at the farm for a couple of days, and was offered a job later in the year when there would be work, but there was nothing much going on just then, and no chance of some ready cash. The farmer had a friend on the way to Victoria Falls, who he thought might be more useful in the way of casual work, so I pushed on in that direction. It turned out that there was no work there either, but I was going in the right direction, so motored on again another two hundred miles or so to Victoria Falls. The coal mining centre of Wankie was on the way, and appeared to be a biggish town, but I skirted it and kept on, camping once beside the road.

This road itself was quite interesting, and famous locally as being probably the worst one in the world. The reason for this was that some road-building genius had constructed it of tarmac strips side by side and each about a foot wide, placed so that the left hand wheels of your car went along one strip, and the right hand wheels on the other. In theory this gave you the superior surface of tarmac, while being much cheaper than covering the whole width of the road in the same material. The only slight problem was that to pass another vehicle you were supposed to move over so that each vehicle could use one strip only. It may have worked all right when the strips were first laid down, but of course with this happening all the time, the earth between the tarmac strips was soon worn away, and to move over to avoid hitting someone else usually meant plunging into deep holes and gullies. It made for interesting motoring, but luckily there was very little traffic. Most people probably travelled by air to Wankie and Victoria Falls; or else by the famous Blue Train that came up all the way from the Cape in South Africa.

I had no choice in the matter, and rattled on along this infamous strip road over the flat, hot and dusty plain that seemed to be the norm in this part of Southern Rhodesia. But doing it like this meant that I approached the falls by much the same route as the first explorers, if a bit faster, and was rewarded by seeing the falls from the distance in the same way. A low cloud, apparently of white smoke, appeared ahead, and rose higher in the air as one approached. There was no other sign, just the same flat shimmering plain still ahead of me, as in every other direction. Then at last the dull scenery was broken by a few trees on either side of the road. Next a house or two, and then a large, low, rambling, very old fashioned colonial looking hotel appeared on the left, and then the road came to a bridge that spanned a deep gorge. I pulled on to the side of the road and stopped the engine, and then, instead of the usual sudden quiet, the air was filled and seemed to vibrate with the rumble and thunder of the great falls.

I walked up to the hotel and had a cool drink, which they seemed slightly disinclined to serve me; I was hot and travel weary, and probably pretty dirty looking, and I could see at a glance, not the sort of guest they were used to there. Still, I got my drink and also the information that there was a government rest camp a little further on, above the falls. This proved to be true, and turned out to be also probably the best camp site in the world. It consisted of the usual few huts with minimal facilities of any sort, but it was beside the Zambezi not far upstream of the point where it pours over and into the gorge. Here the river is very wide, though exactly how wide, it is impossible to judge because it is dotted with many islands, so that you cannot quite see where the far side is. The bank you are standing on is grassy, with a few trees, very like any English river bank. The water ripples blue and sparkling as it hurries by, and the islands are vivid green, grassy, and also dotted with trees. For the hot and dusty traveller it is a vision of cool delight, and must have always been so, and you can easily see why early travellers described it so rapturously.

I soon acquired one of the huts, there were only one or two other people stopping there, and stayed for several days; painting pictures of the river, with varying success, exploring the gorge, and even trying my luck at fishing in the Zambesi. My first day was spent at the falls themselves, where I found that you could get down a path to a position facing the great cascade, and there I spent an hour or two with my sketch pad and paints trying to get some idea of it all down on paper, while dodging the spray. The scene could only be described as unearthly, fantastic. At the end on the steep, muddy path, one found oneself standing in a little glade in the dense green forest that grew in the spray of the great river as it threw itself down into the rocky chasm. In front was the wall of broken water, thundering down into the bottom of the gorge, a mixture of white foam, mist, and streaks of blue; behind was the forest, and all around the great, enveloping roar of the falls. The space I found myself in was surprisingly small, for this great river, so wide and sunny and calm above the falls, is falling into a narrow dark gorge, where it becomes an angry rushing torrent, as it foams and crashes into the sides of the gorge and great detached rocks, as though trying to escape. The ability to capture this with paint brush and paper was way beyond me, but I managed a sort of colour sketch, mainly white paper, with touches of blue and green, and then gave up and spent the rest of the day scrambling about along the river gorge itself.

There were other narrow, precipitous tracks here and there, which made it quite easy to explore, and I climbed down to the river and up again in several places. The gorge zigzags away from the falls and doubles back on itself again and again, where the enormous force of the water has carved away the rock, so that you need a strong sense of direction to know quite where you are. At one point I scrambled up to what I had assumed to be level ground, only to find myself on a sort of knife edge of rock, looking down into the next zig or zag of the river. It was a dizzying prospect, and I turned in my tracks vary gingerly, and went back the way I had come.

Another day I hired a boat from the hotel and tried my luck fishing on the great lake-like expanse of water above the falls, but I am no fisherman and nothing came of it, though I did come upon some elephants on the shore. Well, I heard them moving away into some forest as I paddled along, and found impressive heaps of dung. Still, elephant dung is no good if you are looking for a fish supper, and as I was obviously not going to catch any myself I went along to Livingstone, the little town a few miles upstream, to see if I could buy any there. Amazingly all that seemed to be on sale in any of the shops there was some shark steaks out of a freezer, and that must have come all the way from the Indian Ocean.

The river above the falls was so inviting that I took a brief swim in it; very brief because there were alleged to be crocodiles about, but if so none fancied me and I emerged unscathed. There was plenty of other wild life about, including the elephants, but there was so much cover along the river banks that little showed itself. It was another of those places where one could have remained a long time, but I was running short of both money and time, and moved on again to Kariba.

There the big dam had just been built, and the new lake was filling, but engineers were still working on the power station that had been built deep in the rock beside the dam. The man I had an introduction to was able to take me into the tunnels that had been built there, and so I had the luck to see some of the great engineering works. Most impressive was the experience of standing on a metal plate that was part of an enormous turbine down below, even deeper in the rock. You could feel the gentle rumble of heavy machinery turning as water from the dam rushed through, and was then allowed to gush out through sluices into the valley below. It was a most impressive place, an isolated spot in the middle of the African bush, where the mighty Zambezi, running through another natural gorge was confined and made to turn the energy of its waters into electricity; and the most amazing thing about it was that apart from the white arc of the dam itself, everything was concealed in great tunnels inside the cliffs of the gorge. It was the most awe inspiring man-made thing that I had seen in any part of Africa, and it made a climax and in effect marked the end of my safari round Rhodesia.

After this the state of my finances decreed that I found a temporary job pretty quickly, or cut and run for home. I had one more go at finding a suitable job, without any success, and then set out back up north again. I was also getting worried about the state of my old Vanguard, which though it had survived well so far, was getting sadder by the day. Its main problem now was constant overheating, which did not seem to be due to any particular problem, but possibly just overwork and old age. It was using up so much water that I could not carry enough to keep it going, and had to stop and top up my water cans whenever I came to a stream. My last stop in Northern Rhodesia was beside a pool where I had stopped for this reason, and then camped for the night; and I was delighted when a couple of natives happened to wander up and spoke to me in Swahili. It seemed to be ages since I had heard anyone speak the language of East Africa, and it was like already being back home.

12
Fort Ternan

The Irishman's farm lay along one side of a wide valley, running up from the little township of Fort Ternan towards the hills to the north. There was little cultivation here, and most of the land bore only a mixture of coarse grass and scrubby bushes, with thorn trees dotted about here and there. There were two streams running down the valley, on either side of a low central ridge, and eventually joining at its southern end just above the township. Imagine a valley about two miles wide stretching from north to south; rocky and steep-sided to the west, divided by this low ridge along the middle, and with a higher but less precipitous side to the east. On that side there was also some forest, occupied by a tribe of baboons who shrieked at you and showed their large yellow teeth as you rode by. The farm's boundaries were marked by the rocky side of the valley to the west, and the second stream to the east.

Further up the valley was another farm, and down the valley was the railway and the Fort Ternan railway station; and on that side of the farm the winding railway and its great viaduct bridges formed my southern boundary. On the east side of the valley, beyond the stream, but before the baboon forest, was more ranched grassland which belonged to a doctor in Nairobi. It turned out that he too wanted someone to look after his land for him, and so I soon found myself managing several square miles of Africa, and up to a thousand head of cattle. But my part of the valley was by no means only occupied by me and the cattle; there were also a lot of people of the local Kipsigis tribe living there

This was just outside the official Kipsigis tribal land, but was still regarded by them as their country, and many Kipsigis families lived in the valley. Some of them worked, in a casual sort of way, for whoever happened to be the official owner of the land; they liked this, as it was quite a handy source of cash for them, but it was always on a strictly part time basis. Most of these Kipsigis did a bit of work on the farm, herding or milking, or looking after stock in one way or another; one or two even did a bit of domestic work. But this was all done basically because they happened to live there, and did not mind making themselves useful now and then for suitable emolument. These families lived mainly in an area of level land along one of the streams, where they used to till the land with teams of oxen, and grow crops of maize. It was a mode of life which suited them, and had suited the Irishman and, I suppose, had suited other official but temporary owners of the valley; and would probably suit me.

About a dozen of these Kipsigis worked quite regularly, most of them helping to bring in the breeding herd of cows to be milked first thing in the morning, and then doing the milking and separating the cream, which was to be dispatched to the Kenya Co-operative Creamery at Nakuru. The skim milk was regarded as a perk, and was distributed to members of their families who would turn up at about this time of the morning. Most of my farm 'staff' disappeared after that to get on with their own lives, while two or three took the cows out to their appointed grazing area, and then checked over the other herds. There were only two men who seemed to regard themselves as regular employees in any serious sense. One was Arap Langat, who was respected by all as the headman, although I never really knew whether he had been officially appointed to that position by anyone. The other was Kip Rotich, who ruled the dairy, supervised the cream separating, and saw to the dispatch of the cream on the railway every day. He also doled out the skim milk by his own particular system, with which I did not interfere.

They all seemed to regard looking after cattle, any cattle, as their normal way of life, and they hardly looked on it as work. Like the Masai and Nandi tribes, cattle had traditionally been the most important thing in their lives; breeding cattle, dealing in cattle and rustling cattle, fighting other tribes for cattle. As I got to know a little about them I found that they had a whole language of special words to describe cattle; type, colour, markings, and so on. Their life on what was technically my ranch seemed to be much the same as they had always lived, apart from keeping half an eye on farm livestock. At first I often wondered how seriously they did this, as rustling of cattle was always a real problem in Kenya, and as I rode round myself to look at the herds of cows, heifers and steers, there often seemed to be no one about visibly guarding any of them. But we very seldom lost anything, and that was the main point; to me it did not seem to be very important how this came about. The cattle were safe and secure, and that has to be the most important thing about any successful cattle ranching. If the local Kipsigis had not wanted it to be successful it would have been hopeless; for how ever much time I spent in the saddle and riding round, I could never have been aware of what was going on at any particular moment over large areas of my valley.

It was a lot of land, and it took all day to ride round it. I had acquired two horses with the farm, and they were my only transport over most of it. They were crossbred Somali ponies, stout and sure footed, as they needed to be on the rocky and broken surface that made up most of the landscape. One was a grey called Muffet, and easy to ride; the other, called Rufus, was a bit high strung, and given the chance was inclined to shy at nothing in particular and could scrape you off against a tree as he pranced about. Needless to say, I usually rode Moffet. Some of the land, especially the rugged ridge to the west, was not suitable for a horse, at any rate with an inexpert rider like me, so I always went up there on foot. It was good exercise, and felt a lot safer than being on top of a pony that was slipping and sliding amongst loose rocks on a steep hillside.

The grazing, on such rough, stony land, was not particularly good, but it was adequate for tough half-bred cattle, and there was this great feature of the valley, its water supply. The two streams were both permanent, and never dried up however dry the season, so that even in the most parched of times the farm livestock always had plenty of fresh clean water. Each stream ran down from the forest land at the head of the valley, sometimes through narrow strips of lush greenery, and sometimes in rocky gorges. In one of these gorges, half way along my valley, there was a hot spring gushing out of the rock. This was a strange place, only a few yards wide between sheer rock walls, and someone, perhaps the first settler there, had made good use of the hot water by excavating a bath in the rocky wall of the gorge. This bath still existed, though far from the farm house, and it was fortunate that the site was secluded, as I soon discovered that it often contained a naked Kipsigis.

This first white settler here had apparently been a German, sometime about the end of the nineteenth century, who had brought his house with him. It had been prefabricated from wooden panels, and no doubt dragged up from the railway on the usual ox cart, to where it was erected on the west side of the valley, at the base of the rocks. It was well designed and built to last, and was still in good order. It must have been the home for several different people over the years, and now it was mine, and the rather comical thing about it, in the middle of Africa, was that it looked exactly like a Swiss chalet.

At some time in the past a bathroom had been added to it, probably when one of its owners had grown tired of walking over to the stream to use the hot spring. This bit of mod. con. consisted of a tin bath in the middle of a large room which was probably originally a bedroom; a pipe ran from it to a forty gallon drum outside which was raised on two brick piers so that a fire could be lit underneath, and which then provided plenty of hot water. It was a typical piece of settler-technology, simple but quite effective, provided that someone remembered to light the fire under the drum when required.

Part of the good design of the house was that it had been built six feet off the ground on a stone base, so its wooden walls and floors were well away from white ants or anything else that might have eaten it. The gap between this insect- proof base, and the floor proper, formed a sort of ground level cellar, and made a very useful storage area; although as I discovered, occupied by several snakes. I never found out much about the house's previous owners, though I often wondered about them. At least one of them was still there, under a gravestone up on the hillside behind the house; and there was another stone cross some way away, which seemed to commemorate a child. In the early days in Kenya there must have been many settlers who, when they died, were simply buried where they had lived. The tomb behind my house had probably been someone's favourite spot, for it had a wonderful view, south west across Fort Ternan, and then many miles over Kipsigis tribal lands, towards the distant hills around Kericho. Above it the hillside steepened and became rougher as it climbed higher, culminating in an outcrop of angular grey basalt rocks, like octagonal columns, which must have been the result of ancient volcanic activity. It soon became one of my favourite places too, and I often spent time up there when I got the chance, just relaxing and taking in the peace of the place; and you could watch the hyraxes too, funny animals like large fat grey guinea pigs, that lived up there, hopping about among the rocks.

The Irishman, as well as leaving me his horses, also left me his dogs. Being the sort of Irishman he was, these were hounds; a foxhound and two beagles. My new neighbours told me that he used to run a hunt of sorts, and regularly rode round the rugged countryside with a motley pack of assorted hounds. However, the hunt, when I took it over, was reduced to these three, as he had given up some of his wilder sporting ways. I somehow never got round to asking him what had become of all the other hounds, but in the nature of things they'd probably had short lives, especially the bassets. Small dogs, unless carefully protected, tended not to last long in Kenya. There were plenty of natural hazards for them, especially snakes, and this area was snake country, with plenty of puff adders, mambas and cobras about, all bad news for a dog; and especially pythons, that were well known to be partial to a dog for dinner. Snakes were a fact of life at Fort Ternan, as I soon found out. I hadn't been there very long when one day I was sitting at the dining table doing some paperwork, when I became aware of a sort of strange sound near my feet. It sounded like leaves scraping and rustling together, and I assumed that something of that sort had blown in the door, which was open and only a yard or two away. I kicked vaguely in the direction of the noise, without bothering to look under the table, and continued with what I was doing. The noise continued, more violently, and I glanced down to see what was happening. To my horror there was a brown mamba, a good five feet long, thrashing about on the wooden floor; it must have come in through the open door, lost its grip on the shiny wood, and was slipping and sliding about like a beginner at the ice rink. I leaped to my feet and sprinted to the far side of the room to keep out of its way, and then wondered what to do next. All I could remember about mambas was that you had about ten minutes to get to a doctor when bitten, and that brown ones were the most poisonous. I slipped into the bedroom and got my rifle, then began to wonder how you hit a rapidly moving snake without also making lots of holes in the walls and floor. I was still trying to draw a bead on it when, luckily, it slithered its way to the door again, and left. I resumed my seat at the table, but thereafter always looked under it before sitting down. Later I discovered that there was also a big black snake that lived under the house, and used to come out and sun itself on the stone steps to my front door. I never succeeded in identifying it and so had no idea if it was harmless or dangerous, but it always slithered away down a hole in the stonework when I appeared; so we lived together peacefully, but in a state of mutual suspicion of each other.

The two remaining basset hounds disappeared soon after I took over. They were completely wild, and spent their time hunting round the hills above our valley; you could follow their course by their excited barking and yelping, but probably not see them all day long. One day their musical baying ceased, and that was that. The foxhound, on the other hand was a much calmer and quieter sort of animal, and stayed at home with me most of the time, and in fact was my more or less constant companion for the years I lived there. I called him Luke, and he used to sleep on a dilapidated old armchair that was part of the furniture and fittings when I took over the old house; and which gradually collapsed into a sort of dog-nest over the years. When not in his dog-nest he often trotted along behind as I rode round the farm, usually keeping so close that he worried the pony when his nose touched her leg; he probably understood more about the dangers of pythons than the bassets had.

The other neighbours of mine, the white farmers from whom I acquired such knowledge as I could about my valley, its inhabitants, and its history, were few. Up the valley lived an elderly man, not in the best of health, who was taken off to hospital soon after I arrived. Apart from one or two conversations we had, discussing various alarming medical symptoms, we can hardly be said to have had much chance of getting to know each other. Over to the east, beyond the two streams and the far ridge, lived the brother of the man I had met at Muhoroni, who had built his own gasworks. This brother, Tony, possibly being a touch more conventional, merely ran a large cattle ranch, much the same sort of set-up as mine. He and his wife had three small children, who seemed to have a busy but pleasant life running around the farm, and being educated by means of some sort of postal course. I had a feeling that their mother worked pretty hard at that, as well as being a farmer's wife, but I never actually caught the children doing anything so dull as lessons on the occasions when I rode over their way.

Nearer, but beyond the township and railway, on the land that began to slope up towards Kericho, lived my other next door neighbours, Colin and Molly Manners. Our houses were in clear view of each other, though two or three miles apart, and when I got to know Colin we used to sometimes signal to each other in morse code with our torches of an evening. He was one of the many second world war ex-service men in Kenya, and as he told me, having acquired his bit of land from the government just after the war, had gone off to look for a suitable wife. He spent some time over this quest, back home in England of course, as there were very few spare marriageable white women in our part of Africa. Molly had apparently been sailing a boat somewhere on the Cornish coast when he met her, and asked her if she would like to go to Kenya; she must have been a girl of quick decisions, said yes, and here she was.

They had more of a mixed farm than mine, including a lot of chickens. Why on earth they had taken up chicken farming I never quite understood, having learned myself, at Fort Hall, that Africa is full of creatures with sharp teeth looking for a chicken supper. So keeping them on any scale beyond a few pecking round the kitchen door, and roosting in a handy tree, was likely to be a doomed enterprise. Although they never said as much I always felt that this was their experience too, and I also deduced that there was not much money in eggs, by the way that when you were invited to a meal there, you always seemed to get omelettes.

Next to them, on the other side of the township lived an American called Fred Wicker. He lived by himself, and kept himself pretty much to himself, but I got to know him after a fashion. For one thing he grew oranges, and with a few other people including my friends the Robinsons, at Muhoroni, he had formed a co-operative to sell them. These Kenya oranges were odd, in that even when ripe they were not orange coloured but green; something to do with the altitude or the soil or the climate, I never understood quite why. But because of this they had never been considered a worth- while export, as most people in those parts of the world to which an export business might be profitable, seemed to expect their oranges to be orange. Nobody wanted to buy an orange, however delicious, that was a very unripe looking bright green. But Fred Wicker, who had been around a bit and was very knowledgeable about all sorts of odd things, managed to persuade a few people with some orange trees, that if they combined their operations and built a small factory they could break into the overseas market and make some real money. The secret, which he had discovered on his travels in South America I believe, was that green oranges become a much more saleable colour if they are passed through a gas chamber. The green for some reason then becomes yellow. They were still not orange, but they looked quite attractive, and his idea was, after the gas treatment, to market them under the name of Kenya Gold. It was quite a good idea in a place where citrus fruit grew very easily, but were worth very little, and the factory was built. Not much more than a medium sized shed really, but several people became involved in the project and duly took along their best green oranges, which were really very good apart from the colour, helped in the processing, and packed them in smart cardboard boxes marked Kenya Gold.

It was all fairly successful too, and the gold-yellow-oranges sold quite well, though nobody seemed to get very rich out of it. Fred's ideas were a bit like that, always very good, but tending not to be dramatically commercial. He was well known for such projects; some quite useful, others verging on the bizarre. His worst idea, on which he was very keen when I first met him, was to grow crops in a soil free, factory environment. This seemed to me to be completely mad, in a country where there was plenty of space and workers to grow crops in the normal, conventional, ordinary way. But this was a time when the news from home was always full of trade union unrest, and Fred reckoned that sooner or later this trouble would spread everywhere, and then this would be the only way to grow food. He had worked out his system quite scientifically, and it all sounded perfectly practical, if pointless; but he never put it to the test.

Fred also seemed to know all sorts of interesting people that he had met at one time or another, and it was through him that I had the chance of meeting the famous anthropologist Dr. Leakey, who was working in our part of East Africa just then. The Doctor's pursuit of the traces of early man in Africa had taken him to various parts of Kenya, and just then he and his team were encamped on Fred Wicker's land. Nobody seemed to know what they were doing there, but in this area there were fossils to be found simply lying about on the surface, so it was assumed that this was the attraction. Probably no one in the area, possibly excepting Fred, had any knowledge of such things, and as I'd had the odd conversation with him about some of the fossils on my land, he asked me to meet this team of experts one day. In fact I found myself invited to dinner at their camp, and so late one afternoon I rode over to see them.

It was a very civilized and well organized camp site with several tents of an almost military aspect, and a large table was set with a white tablecloth in front of the largest tent. Later on, as the sun set and the brief equatorial twilight deepened into darkness, lamps were lit and a well cooked meal appeared. I had hoped to hear all about the work they were doing, and what was being found, but no-one was saying much about it. That was disappointing, but I supposed that like all serious scientists, they were being careful that their work did not find its way to a newspaper in garbled form before they were ready for publication. I had brought one or two fossils from my bit of the valley for them to look at, which they politely did, but this was obviously just run of the mill stuff. Most was simply fossilised wood, which was clearly not their thing at all, but I had found one very odd item that I felt must be of interest. It was a small, spherical object, definitely stone, but very delicate and fine, like a tiny balloon, white and paper thin. It was passed round and inspected, but on-one had anything to say about it; I suppose it was outside their narrow field of study. 'An egg, of some sort?' I ventured to this rather unresponsive circle of serious faces. Fred laughed. 'No, of course not,' he said, 'Anyone can see that it's a fossilised fart !'

The serious faces round the camp fire managed a smile or two, and the subject was changed. Nobody was going to hear anything very exciting from this lot of specialists, that was clear; so we just ate our supper and chatted small talk, while sausage flies and other insects crashed endlessly into the lamp that had been hung on a branch above us. Then I rode home through the late evening on my grey pony, down to Fort Ternan and then up the valley to my strange Swiss chalet of a house. It was dark by then, after we left the little pool of yellow light that marked their camp, but there was a moon, and the pony knew the way home anyway. Horses always do.

It soon became apparent, as I got to know my neighbours at Fort Ternan, that no one seemed to be particularly well off. They all seemed to just about manage to make a living, mainly out of cattle, but no one was throwing money about. A reasonable degree of comfort seemed to be what most had attained, and I deduced that I was not going to get rich quick either. I had worked out very carefully that I could survive the first year or two, with a bit of luck, and then even begin to make a profit; but this plan depended on nature being on my side, or at least neutral. But it is always rash to depend on that possibility, and the first year was not as easy as it might have been. My only source of income at this stage was milk from the semi-ranching system that I had taken over, and a problem soon developed. This semi-ranching worked on the fact that most of the time an average sort of cow actually produces more milk than her calf needs, and so all our good milkers, as well as rearing their calves, were also milked once a day. The cream that was separated from this milk in theory brought in a modest but steady income, which I had worked out would be just enough to run the farm on. The out-goings were equally modest, as our only piece of essential machinery was a hand turned cream separator, and all the stockmen, milkers and general labourers were drawn from this pool of casual workers who lived on the land anyhow, and neither expected nor received very much hard cash. But my calculations, based mainly on hope and optimism, had not taken into account the fact that we were going to have a very dry year; and after that the Army Worm. The lack of rainfall meant, of course, less and less grass, and so less milk and less income. Then, when we had rain at last, and new green shoots appeared in the brown landscape, the army worm appeared too. This 'worm' was one of the well-known hazards of Kenya farming; just a small, dull looking caterpillar, that appeared every few years, and was very fond of new grass shoots.

The trouble was, that when it appeared, it increased so rapidly that it would have made a good plague of Egypt, and within a day or two it seemed to cover the land, marching across the landscape and eating every scrap of grass before it. After several months of drought, and when the first new growth of grass was beginning to appear, this was the last thing you wanted to see; but there was nothing that could be done about it, except wait for the plague to move on so that the grass could begin to grow again. So I waited; and then after a bit it did go away, or more exactly, it just disappeared. People who had experienced it many times before had a theory that it carried the seed of its own destruction, in the form of a virus that always developed with it and struck the worm down after a certain period of time. Or perhaps, having eaten all the new grass, it just died. Either way, it came and it went; grass grew again, and things carried on, if not as briskly as had been hoped.

Still, the farm survived, and I discovered that cattle, if they have a plentiful supply of good water, are surprisingly resistant to these troubles. So at the end of the first year at Fort Ternan, though cash money was in short supply, we were just about holding our own. My cows had produced only a modest amount of cream for sale, but had produced a fine crop of calves, and were in good condition. In the weeks when there was very little grazing available they had spent most of their time standing in one or other of the two streams, and seemed to come to little harm.

After that first year we did not have a serious drought again, and the cattle did well, but no one tells you this in advance. So like every other stock farmer I soon learned to worry about rain, and especially the lack of it, more than anything else. My predecessor, who seemed to have preferred to do his worrying sitting down, had installed a rain gauge on his mantelpiece. There was a funnel on the roof, and from there a long pipe ran down to a calibrated cylinder above the fireplace; thus, even while sitting there with his back to the window, he knew instantly when there was any rain, and how much had fallen.

Even without a drought, there was always a dry season of course. Throughout East Africa rain was always very seasonal, and you knew perfectly well that you were always going to have several dry months every year. It was also obvious that when it rained, most of it flowed swiftly away down the rivers; so water conservation had to be a very good idea. I had noticed two places where, after rain, the water gushed in a torrent down the hillside on my side of the valley, and then disappeared. It probably eventually found its way to the stream at the bottom, where of course the cattle benefited from it, but it would be much better to keep it on the west side of the valley, where they would then have one or two extra drinking places. I'd had a go at dam building, at Fort Hall, and it had worked pretty well there, so I thought I would try it again.

My casual crew of herdsmen hadn't done that sort of work before, but for a modest extra wage they had already tackled a little light clearing work for me, and soon understood the point of the un-Kipsigis-like digging work required. In one place we simply dug out a water-hole, that obligingly soon filled with water, and was instantly useful. At another site, in a gully which seemed suitable, we built an actual earth dam. I tackled this a bit more seriously, and engaged some charcoal-burners who were working in the area to do the hard labouring. It was a big job, and took a couple of months, but was a great success in the end. These charcoal burners were a band of men who wondered around farming areas, clearing bush and making charcoal, and getting some sort of living out of it. They, because of their profession, were well able to wield shovel and spade and were good workmen, not averse to earning a little extra money.

Half way through its construction, when the dam was only five or six feet high, we unexpectedly had a heavy fall of rain. It poured out of the sky like buckets being emptied on your head, and I rushed over to the construction site to see how much damage had been done, but our work must have been good. Water was cascading down the hill side, the half built dam was full and running over, but the wall was holding perfectly. With this new source of water we were able to graze one of the herds round it, drinking from it and puddling the bottom of the dam with their hooves. It took another month to finish it off, and then we had to wait for the rain to fill it again, but when it had it was a very useful drinking point for cattle half a mile from the river. Cheered by this success, I next decided to put a hydraulic ram in the nearest stream, to pump yet more drinking water on to the dry western side of my valley.

There was already in existence an old and rickety pump, driven by a water wheel, that brought water up to the house, and to a tank near the cattle dip; but it was going to have to be replaced by something more reliable. It was a good bit of rough and ready engineering of the type that you often came across in Kenya, owing more to ingenuity with local materials than anything else, and it had probably done good work for many years, but it was near the end of its days. In my time of travelling round and visiting many farms, I had come across hydraulic rams here and there, and had been very impressed with their solid reliability. Of course I had no money to buy a new one, but the local press advertisements were a fruitful source for old and unwanted agricultural equipment, so I had a go at advertising for a second hand ram. Sure enough there were one or two available, apparently waiting for a new owner, and after a modest amount of negotiating on the telephone [there was one down at the station], I found myself the owner of a second-hand Hydram and the piping that went with it. It was fifty miles away, but its owner said he would put it on the railway for me, so I sent him a cheque, and a couple of weeks later a ton or so of cast iron duly arrived. Fortunately a little work with spanners soon reduced it to a number of small pieces, and in a day or two the entire labour force on the farm had carried it, in pieces, up to the site we had selected. A hydraulic ram pumps water by utilising the force of water itself, falling down a wide pipe, which by a system of valves, in turn forces part of the water along a much narrower pipe to wherever you want it to go. You need a good steady source of water from a stream to work it, but once installed in a suitable situation it is almost magical in its efficiency. I had found a good place, where the stream fell about twenty feet pretty rapidly; and we soon had it working and pumping large amounts of water across the valley, day and night. With that, and the new dam, and some new fencing, the utilisation of our grazing became quite a lot more efficient.

Life went on here at Fort Ternan, pretty smoothly on the whole, for four years. We had no more droughts, grass grew in the appropriate season, cows and bulls did their stuff, calves were born and eventually grew big enough to become beef. Most of my time was taken up with routine farm business which would have been similar anywhere else in the world, and my routine was the usual early rise each morning, seeing to the milking down at the dairy, riding round and checking fences, and once a week the dipping of all the stock. This cattle dipping was the most important routine of all; grassland in Africa is full of ticks, which carry an assortment of diseases, so they have to be killed off regularly by dipping or spraying all stock with insecticide.

I had inherited with the farm one of the usual cattle dips, which consisted of a long concrete bath, through which every beast on the farm had to swim every week. It was a simple procedure, but very important, and had to be carefully done to keep the ticks in check. So on the appointed day all the cattle would be brought in, counted to make sure none was missing, and swum through the bath. It was a pure wild west scene, with clouds of dust swirling about, cattle milling round and bellowing, the shouts of the herdsmen driving them forward, and the steady thump and enormous splash as each beast in turn dived in and swam through the pungent smelling dip.

The controlling of cattle disease was absolutely vital for any sort of cattle farming, but there was a very good local veterinary service, and someone would come and check things over at any sign of trouble. Some cattle plagues like East Coast fever could be killers, but I lost very few. Deaths were more often due to predators, like leopard or hyenas, or a simple accident like a broken leg in the rough, rocky terrain. Sometimes a steer was reported as having had an unfortunate accident just before a local feast day was due, and I just put that down to natural wastage. No one could have run a successful ranch without the co-operation of the local tribesmen, so why make a fuss? We once had an outbreak of foot and mouth disease in the district, but in Kenya this was dealt with by the enlightened method of inoculating all cattle in the immediate neighbourhood, and apart from loosing some milk, it had very little effect. The veterinary department also bred bulls of suitable hardy types to improve local stock, and I managed to buy three that happened to be surplus to the government breeding scheme. They were Sahiwal, an Indian humped breed, beautiful big, docile creatures that produced big beefy calves. These three bulls were regarded with great pride by 'my' Kipsigis, who gave them Kipsigis names, took great care of them, and made quite sure that they were not spirited away by rustlers.

There was inevitably a certain amount of rustling going on, with the tribal land so close, and rustling of cattle being a sort of local sport; probably not unlike the borderland between Scotland and England in the good old days. So every now and then a gang of cattle thieves, and some cattle, would be found by the police where they should not have been, and wild pursuits would take place, with a good deal of indiscriminate firing of guns in all directions. Once I was called out by one of my Kipsigis herdsmen in the middle of the afternoon, when most people would usually have been having a bit of a siesta or at least taking things easy. He told me that there was a fight going on and I had better come quickly, which was very unusual as I normally only heard of such an incident long after it had taken place, if at all; so I hurried off to see what was happening. It soon became apparent why I was wanted, when a young man who I had never seen before was produced, dripping with blood; he was 'mgonjwa sana', very ill.

He certainly was, as he had fairly obviously been shot, and must have already lost a lot of blood. A group of police askaries could be seen in the distance waving their rifles and running about, and it was fairly obvious what was going on. It seemed that I was required to think of what to do next in this rather tricky situation, but the priority was clear enough; whichever side of the law this man happened to be on, he had to be taken to a doctor, and quickly. So I bundled him into the back of my car and drove off to Kericho, that being the nearest place with a hospital, where the only doctor on duty took a quick look at my patient and said, 'He'll need some blood. Will you help?' Thinking he meant hold a bottle for him or something, I said I would. 'Right', he said, 'Lie down on that bed, and I'll check your blood group.' I hadn't realized that it was my blood that he intended to use, but didn't like to back out at that stage, so did as I was told. After a quick test of some sort he decided that it was suitable for the job, took a pint or two, and transferred it to our dying cattle rustler; but without any affect. That was the end of the story. I never knew who the young Kipsigis was or where he had come from, or how he had got himself killed in a gun fight, and no-one was saying anything.

There was a court case about the stolen cattle some time later, and I had to go up to the court at Kericho and tell my story in the witness box. I was a bit worried that I might find myself on the wrong side of the law for having impeded the arrest of our young rustler and interfered in the police chase, but that aspect of the case was skated over by the judge, who congratulated me on my apparently high-minded action. When it all appeared in the national newspaper, the East African Standard, I found myself represented as a local hero, at least for one day.

But an event like this, which might appear in the national press, was way out of the normal run of things, and my life as a rancher was normally very peaceful. Daily life, ninety nine percent of the time, was uneventful to the point of dullness, because most days after say, ten o'clock in the morning, all there was to do was ride round checking fences. I sometimes used to say to myself, 'Look, here you are, living in one of the most beautiful places on earth with this wonderful climate, sunny and warm most of the time, and with nothing much to do but watch cattle get fat enough to go to market; and how do you feel about it? You're bored!' But I needn't have worried, things would change soon enough.

13
Uhuru

About four years had passed since I had settled down to live in my valley at Fort Ternan, and nearly ten since I had, more or less by chance, come to Africa. The life we had all lived in far away Britain now seemed quite unreal, life on another planet. I used to think about this sometimes, and wonder how it could be that the life I had known for my first twenty years or so should now seem almost foreign, while everything about East Africa seemed completely normal. The seasons for instance, with no winter or summer, and the way that our days and nights were divided into twelve hours dark and twelve hours light all the year round. You would think that these things would always seem strange to someone born in northern climes, but somehow they did not. Anyhow, my life was now an African life, and it was also a settled routine of farm work, book keeping, housekeeping, and now and then visiting neighbours or the friends I had made over the years. Occasionally, on one excuse or another I even went as far as Nakuru or Nairobi, and one of the few trips to the capital I made was when, after selling some cattle, I at last had enough cash available to treat myself to a new vehicle.

Up to then I had still been using the old Vanguard that had so gamely carried me around on my safari down to Zimbabwe and the Limpopo river; but it was really showing signs of its hard life by now, and I badly needed something more reliable and useful on my farm. So one day with my newly acquired wad of money, I walked down to the station and boarded the morning train down country to Nairobi and the car sale rooms. It was the first and only time I had ever been on one of these great steam trains, that puffed and rattled their way over the two hundred miles from Fort Ternan up to the highlands, then down to Nakuru, on up the Rift Valley, and at last to Nairobi. In the first mile or two it crossed the three great girder bridges on the edge of my farm, which I had looked up at so many times from down in the river gorges below, and had occasionally frightened myself by walking across. For someone on foot they provided a tempting short cut from one ridge to the next, but you had to step from sleeper to sleeper all the way, and there was nothing else below you but the criss-crossing metal work, and far below that the rocky river beds. The longest bridge, which had a span of about a quarter of a mile, I walked across only once; the trouble was, at about the half way point I began to wonder what I would do if a train suddenly appeared at the other end, and I never tried it again.

This railway journey across Kenya from the Lake Victoria plain to Nairobi, must be one of the most dramatic in the world, and I had often thought when I watched the great black steam engines with their many coaches and trucks, that I would like to do the trip on it one day. But then, by the time that the moment came, I knew all the country we passed through so well that it was a bit of an anticlimax; and in the way of steam travel it seemed desperately slow. But we arrived in Nairobi eventually, and I did a quick round of the car dealers. This time it was no good looking at MGs or anything remotely like a sports car; it had to be something very practical, with room in the back for milk cans, and so I chose a brand new, smart but sturdy, Ford van. The salesman seemed a bit taken aback by this customer who dashed in, chose a car, handed him money, and drove away, more or less in one movement. It probably hadn't happened to him very often, but I did not have any time to waste, and the next day I was back on the farm again.

This was the period when Kenya was working towards independence, and there must have been a certain amount of excitement going on in Nairobi and government circles, but it hardly reached us up country. The attitude of most white farmers, at that time, varied between 'wait and see and hope for the best', and a sort of depressed fatalism about the whole thing. Even the most optimistic had to admit that however calm Kenya might seem in the run up to independence, the sort of chaos that we had already seen elsewhere as colonial government withdrew could also happen here. There seemed to be no sign of it then, with the government being slowly and calmly handed over to local politicians of all races, but the more thoughtful realized that the future was going to depend on more than politics. Kenya's stability depended on commerce and trade and its basic prosperity continuing, so the big question was, would it in fact continue? Some saw no reason why it should not, but others had their doubts. As some people saw it, it was all very well for political matters to be handed over to local politicians, but the same was happening to all sorts of important non-political firms and organizations and businesses; and it sometimes looked as if, here and there, someone with a black face was being put into the top job just for the look of the thing, whether they were any good at it or not.

Kenya depended on farming, and farming depended to a very great deal on the Kenya Farmers' Union, Kenya Creameries, Kenya Meat Commission, and similar long established and pretty well run organizations, which handled the sale and export of the meat, cereals, coffee and so on that the country was producing in large quantities. So people of a pessimistic frame of mind could see these businesses, which were so important, getting in to the wrong, and incompetent, hands. But then again, if you were an optimist you could hopefully assume that these organizations would go on, much as they were, into the foreseeable future. Most local Africans in Western Kenya seemed to take little notice of any of this, or what was going on politically, apart from uneasily observing that their old enemies, the Kikuyu in the Central Province seemed to be becoming more powerful in the new world of politics. They, with others, had formed a political party called Kanu, which was always in the news, and was becoming the dominant political power as the old colonial government withdrew. Belatedly, tribes like the Masai and Kipsigis began to realise that they might find themselves in a subservient position to their old foes, and started their own party, which was called the Kenya African Democratic Union, Kadu. It had little to do with politics in the usual sense, but was all about trying to maintain power in their own areas, with vague gestures towards a multi-racial government that would include Europeans and Asians.

Some white farmers joined Kadu, as I did, and when elections were held, in the run up to independence, every one in our area duly voted Kadu, just as all Kikuyu voted Kanu, and a fairly evenly divided government was set up. Our local politician, Teita arap Towet, a Kipsigis of course, who had naturally received virtually all the local votes, was made Minister of Agriculture in the new government. That at least pleased everybody, whether or not they had any idea what a minister of agriculture was for, or what he was going to do. He was in fact a very shrewd man, and began immediately to work out schemes for local tribesmen to take over any European owned land that became available. The U.K. government had arranged that there would be money available for this, and some white landowners, especially in other areas of the country, were showing signs that they wouldn't mind leaving to avoid the general upheaval that they felt would be coming. Rumours soon began to circulate about what land might, or might not, be taken over in one of these schemes, and Teita arap Towet came to see me one day, to have a little talk about the whole matter.

He had a cup of tea with me; a neat, almost dapper little man, and we chatted about this and that in English, which he spoke well. The land I was managing on the far side of the valley between my farm and Tony's was of course owned by an absentee landlord, the doctor in Nairobi, who apparently would not be too worried about it being taken over. The truth was probably that he regretted his original investment, and would be glad to be rid of it. Mr. Towett seemed to know about this, and of other land that his Kipsigis co-operative might be taking over, and was full of plans for the future. There was nothing threatening to the white farmers in the area in his perfectly open and straightforward plans, but I began to wonder how many of them would stay in the end if these takeovers went ahead.

But while all this was going on my life continued as before, although I now began to be less certain about how long I myself might remain there. I was quite a lot younger than all the other Europeans farmers around, and with no family to worry about, and I had been thoroughly used to moving about and never staying long in one place. So I was not too worried about having to move on again if I had to, but it was less simple for others.

The same talk of the land of white settlers being taken over for African run co-operatives was also being heard to the west, where my friends the Robinsons lived. Their big estate on the plain at Muhoroni was apparently in the sights of local Luo politicians, and there was casual talk about the possibility of a takeover there. Then, all the talk began to turn into action quite suddenly. The money necessary for buying up large areas of land had materialized from the UK government, and the owners of some farms had to decide very quickly what to do. To everybody's surprise the land that the Robinsons had farmed for so long seemed to be at the top of the list, and then one day Struan's mother told me that their old home was being sold, and she was going to live in Nakuru. She said that the price they would receive for it seemed quite reasonable, but at the same time this meant the very abrupt end of a way of life, especially for Struan, who of course had been born there, and had probably assumed that he would live there for the rest of his life. Within a few weeks everything had changed for him, and the settled life of running a big farm was finished. All the different aspects of the business had to be wound up, contracts ended, cattle sold off, horses found new homes. I had always remained friends with the family since the time when I arrived in Muhoroni, as a rather undedicated young government official, years previously, and now I found myself helping with this final packing up of a whole family's life. Cattle and goods and chattels of all sorts to be disposed of, arrangements to be made for staff, including old men who had lived and worked there all their lives. Some of the cattle were moved to my land at Fort Ternan, we were only about twenty miles away, while their final disposal could be worked out. All this was happening, luckily, at a time when we had plenty of grass, having had good rains, so there was space and feed for them, and they remained with us for several months. I even had one of the Robinson's buildings parked on my land for a time; it was an unusually well made wooden structure that had been built as a nursery cum school room when the children had been small, and Margaret decided that she would take it with her to Nakuru. I had told her in a careless moment that I thought it had been made so well that it could easily be taken apart again, transported there, and re-erected. So, I then found myself landed, on account of my big mouth, with the job of doing it. Having said that all you would have to do was mark every piece with a number, make a plan, and then dismantle it, it somehow became my job to climb all over it with a piece of chalk in my hand, numbering everything. There were more pieces than you would have thought possible; then of course it had to be taken apart and packed carefully for its journey. It turned out at this point that the site it was supposed to be going to at Nakuru was not ready for it, so it got as far as Fort Ternan, like the cattle, and then stuck there for months before it could be moved on.

The breaking up of an old family home involved many such jobs, and the process went on for quite a time. Then, one day, it was suddenly all finished and everything had gone. Struan and his wife went 'home' to England; where his twin sister and her husband, the policeman, had already arrived. They had been caught up in the communist take over of Zanzibar, where he had been working at the police training school. The government of the Sultan had suddenly collapsed, there had been chaos and a complete breakdown of law and order, and they had been lucky to escape at the last moment on the Sultan's yacht. The younger sister was at college in England now, and thus well out of the way, and so the big family that I had come to know so well over the years had disappeared. Some of them I never saw again, though I used to go up to see Margaret in her new home at Nakuru when I had the chance. She had not wanted to leave Africa herself and had bought a little house on the slopes of Menengai, the ancient volcano that rises up above Nakuru. She knew a few people who lived in or near the town, and seemed to feel that it could be a sort of half way house between her old life, and what ever the future might hold. It was a little house above and away from the town itself, with wide views over the Rift Valley, and Lake Nakuru. This sheet of water was famous as the home of thousands of flamingoes, and sometimes when I visited her we used to go down to the lake to watch them. It was a strange place, not far from the town, an area of dry bush with distant hills to the south, and just this wide shallow expanse of water edged by dry mud and covered by the elegant pink and white birds. Apparently the water was very alkaline, and nothing seemed to live in it or near it but this great flock of flamingoes. What they lived on was not visible to human eyes, but they waded back and forth in the shallow water all day, with their heads down and crooked bills obviously sifting out something that was edible to them. Every now and then, perhaps because they were startled, or on some sort of whim, a whole flock of many hundreds would take to the air, suddenly flashing pink and white as their wings beat; then they would circle round, and settle again. It was an extraordinary sight which you could watch, fascinated, for a long time. The immediate landscape itself was dull and flat and colourless; pale water, the dry whitish coloured mud shore, and those dark hills in the distance, but then in the foreground this ever moving spectacle of the great flocks of spindly legged birds.

Menangai itself was an interesting and unusual sort of place to live, but Margaret said she liked it simply because it was quiet and unfrequented, though only a few miles from the town. It is a low, flat volcanic cone, from a distance more like a large, grass covered hill than anything else. The crater, only visible when you have climbed to the top, was wide and filled with rough scrub and jumbled rocks, and showed no sign of any recent volcanic activity. Perhaps it had blown its top off, some time in the remote past. It does not seem to have been active within living memory, though there were supposed to be steam jets in the middle of the crater somewhere, and Nakuru had known mild earth tremors. I had tried to walk across the crater once, with a friend, to see if we could find these steam jets, but we got less than half way to the centre. We spent a day climbing down into the crater, which was easy, and then making our way across it, which was difficult, but when darkness descended we were still struggling slowly and painfully through the tangled scrub and large, jagged lumps of rock; and we spent a bitterly cold night in a cave, keeping a fire going with odd bits of wood and twigs. In the morning we gave it up, and made our way back the way we had come, and home.

The cottage on the slopes of Menengai became Margaret's home for some time, and the building that had been so laboriously dismantled down at Muhoroni eventually was transported there too, and she seemed quite cheerful creating a new garden and homestead. But then, in the end she followed the rest of her family back to the British Isles that she had left so long ago, as a very young woman. It was this departure of whole families that for many years had been part of Kenya life, and the disappearance of familiar faces, that soon began to bring home to everybody the reality of the great change that was now irrevocably set to happen, and people began to take the future very seriously.

Soon the long discussed and awaited day of 'uhuru', or freedom from colonial rule, had come and gone, but without much really seeming to change. There seemed to be no particular sense of hostility towards Europeans, as some had expected, even in those parts of the Central Province where MauMau had been strong. Yes, the Union Jack had been lowered in Nairobi, and the rather smart new flag of Kenya raised; one or two of us had even been up to Nairobi and had seen it happen, and there was plenty of vague talk about probable future problems. All just talk down at the club. But this was reality, and a long established and well known white family had suddenly left the country. Now some others, especially those with young families to educate and worry about, began mentally to start packing. But I had no family or dependants in Africa, and certainly felt no threat, so I just carried on with my now well established life as a cattle man..

Months passed, and perhaps a little ironically things were beginning to go really well on the farm now. The years of work and slow improvement were beginning to show, fences were in good order, water supply was better than it had ever been. My first 'crop' of big beef steers had gone to the butcher for a good price, and plenty more were coming on. I had at last been able to buy that new car, and give my faithful old Standard Vanguard to a couple of teenagers who lived not far away. We had even gone in for luxuries like a farm school. Many large estates had their own school for the children, but there was none in our valley, so when some of the Kipsigis helping down at the dairy suggested it would be a good idea, we converted an empty building and started one. A nearby mission provided a teacher, the people living in our valley agreed to pay him some modest salary and provide him with a house, and we had our school.

Then Teita arap Towet came to see me again one day to say that his plans for a co-operative in the area were going well. It had been officially registered now and was to be called the Chiilchiila Co-operative; so now they hoped to buy the land and cattle of the Nairobi doctor. We got round to the subject of my land too, and I indicated that I would not be averse to selling, as long as it went to the Kipsigis who already lived in the valley. He readily agreed to that, and we began a long drawn out negotiation involving the Chiilchiila co-operative, me, him, and of course the bank that actually owned the land. It would be of prime importance what happened to the cattle, and it was agreed that I would dispose of the young beef stock, but my 'employees', if they could be called that, would want to keep the breeding stock. I decided that if they agreed to give me a fair price for the land I would throw in the cows and my three bulls, and arranged with the head men in my valley how this would all be done. Then one day I heard officially that the Chiilchiila Co-operative had arranged to buy my farm and others round about, and that they would like to take over in a couple of months' time. Next Teita arap Towet turned up with a lot of forms to be read carefully and signed, and after that everything happened quickly, leaving me with the immediate prospect of having more money than I had ever had before, but no farm or employment, or any idea at all of what I would do next.

My friends who had the ranch to the east, beyond the baboons' forest, were made an offer for their land too, so that the whole block could become all one large Kipsigis co-operative. Previously they would have had no intention at all of leaving their farm, where their family were growing up, and where they were happily settled. But then the whole situation had suddenly become so different, and the existence of their young family, in itself, made them think again about their future. That which had seemed a reasonably secure future was now full of uncertainties, and they had to give a lot of thought to what would be best for their children. Tony and his wife had to try to visualize a different future for them, instead of the farm life that had once seemed ordained by fate. No obvious future was visible, so after a lot of hard thought they decided that the only sensible action was to sell up, while they had the chance, take the family to the UK, and start again. Tony's brother, with his homemade gas works, said that he would definitely stay, and in fact did just that, and was still living in the area years later.

As far as I was concerned, I just kept the farm going until it was taken over officially, and I had to begin to negotiate the sale of my young stock, as arranged. That was dealt with, and then I was busy handing everything over as neatly as possible; which was fairly easy, since the same people would be running it all on a day to day basis when I had gone. Someone else would have to keep the books and deal with that side of things, but no doubt the new co-operative would be able to produce a clerk to do that. Suddenly all I had to do was pack up and go.

But a slight complication arose. Several times during the last few years, while I had been living at Fort Ternan, I had suggested to my family in England that one or other of them might like to come and visit me. Once or twice someone had shown signs of coming, but it had somehow never quite worked out, and they had never come to Africa. Then suddenly, more or less at the last moment, my sister Avril must have woken up to the thought that it was now or never, and wrote to say that she was coming to see me, and Fort Ternan and the farm. In a way it was quite a good moment, because I had plenty of free time, having nothing much to do but hang about while the last days of my life as Kenya settler passed. I had really very little to do, so there was nothing to stop me leaving the farm in the hands of those who would soon be its new owners, and spending some time in showing my sister round the country.

Accordingly, a week or two later found me driving up to Nairobi, to meet her plane at the new airport. Times had changed since my arrival at the old airport all those years ago. Gone were those scruffy huts, set in a wasteland of dry grass under the searing sun; the airport was now smart and very modern, a vast building thronged with people, and looking just like every other airport in the world. Her plane arrived, and after the usual delay Avril appeared, looking a bit uncomfortable in clothes that suggested at once that she had not known exactly what to wear. Well, it was midwinter in the UK, so I could remember my own arrival in Africa, and sympathize. We collected her luggage, went and found my car in the vast car park, and set off up country; me reflecting that soon I would be at that airport for the last time, probably leaving Kenya for ever. I had decided to take Avril to Nakuru first, and break our journey by introducing her to Margaret at her new home on Menengai. It seemed to me that it might be the kindest way to begin to show her this very different world; everything she saw was going to be pretty new and strange, but Margaret always remained rather old fashioned and very Scottish. This was a good idea too, because by the time we reached there my sister was already showing the strain of coping with too much, too different, too quickly. The whirligig of traffic in Nairobi had been a startling new experience to begin with, and I had already received a lecture about hooting at pedestrians. She was obviously still very much the elder sister, though we had seen little of each other for many years, and felt it necessary to point out my errors in road etiquette; I just explained that if I did not hoot, they would not move, and we would be involved in a succession of nasty collisions.

At Nakuru we stayed with Margaret in her new little house for the night, making a break in the long journey, and then went on to Fort Ternan. She met several of the Kipsigis on the farm, but of course had no idea what anyone was talking about. The fact that I was also talking in a foreign language most of the time seemed to worry her also, so after a very quick look around, I took her across the valley to meet the Stokes, and other white folk, who at least could talk to her in English. The high point of that visit was when Molly warned her that she might see a snake in their very basic outside lavatory. 'But don't worry, if it's a green one it's not poisonous'.

Still, she liked the Stokes, they were recognizable as small farmers, who apart from the snake, would have been much the same in Norfolk. A day or two were spent in similar visits, and riding round the valley on the ponies, which she enjoyed, as she had always liked that sort of thing. Then I had a batch of cattle to send off to the Kenya Meat Commission, so she was able to join in the job of herding them down to the railway and loading them. Having sent them off, we went off ourselves, back to Nairobi again, to check out the grading of the cattle. Some farmers did this as a matter of course whenever they dispatched cattle to the KMC, but I never had. It had always seemed to be a pointless waste of time and much traveling, and I never had much stomach for watching my cattle being slaughtered. Anyhow I thought we might as well do it this time, so off we went.

We arrived a bit late, perhaps fortunately, after the cattle had become beef hanging on hooks, so I just looked at the grading book, for the first and last time, and wondered what to do next. No point in rushing back to the farm again, so we went off on a tour round Kenya and Northern Tanganyika. Avril, naturally enough , wanted to see a game reserve, so we headed south to one of the well known ones and stopped for the night at a safari lodge. It was very comfortable, if a bit dull, though we did hear assorted animals snorting and roaring and so on all night. Next day we went on to Arusha and stopped there briefly, but I was not able to show her the spectacle of Kilimanjaro, which had decided to hide itself in the clouds as usual. We visited Voi, and the coast, and then back we went to Nairobi, and then home to Fort Ternan. We did another round of local acquaintances, who were probably mostly thinking mainly of their own departures in the near future, and then back to Nairobi airport again. Avril bought the usual set of touristy carvings from roadside dealers on the way, stuffing a mixture of assorted animals and miniature warrior figures into her luggage, and off she went back to the English winter. I think she had quite enjoyed it all, and picked up some idea of my world in Africa; but it had all been so hurried and hectic, dashing about here and there, and briefly meeting people who were the background of my whole life, that she must have had pretty vague and confused memories of it all. For me then, it was back to the farm, for probably the last time.

There followed a week or two of tying up the odd loose end, and that was the end of it. Teita arap Towett came to see me for the last time, to say that the financial side had all been tied up, money had been paid over, and now the new co-operative would take over at the beginning of March. I worked out with all our residents and workers, exactly who would have which cows, and produced a certificate for each animal. There was no way of knowing how long these new agreements would last, or what was going to happen in the long run, but everyone seemed happy with the arrangements for the moment. I was a bit worried about the only non-Kipsigis resident on the farm, an old Luo who seemed to have been living on his little plot there for many years, and who's arrival there long predated me. However the new owners seemed happy to let him remain there, so as far as I could arrange it, the takeover would be smooth. There was no problem with any other livestock, as my chickens would go with the farm, my old dog Luke was dead, and the two ponies were taken over by another farmer, one of the few who still had no intention of leaving the district. The contents of the house I just left for whoever came next, but there was a certain amount of personal luggage that would have to go somewhere, so I made a large wooden crate and packed my guns and a few other things inside, and arranged for a shipping agent to get it to my parents' address at home in England. Then I drove down to Nakuru in my fairly new Ford and did a deal with the agents there, to hand it over to them at the airport when I left the country, in exchange for a new GT. Cortina, to be picked up at the airport when I arrived at London. It was quite nice to be able to do that, as the Cortina was the fashionable car at that moment, it having just won the East African safari rally. It was the first time in my life that I had been able to spend money as freely as that, and to casually order a new car. It was a bright spot in what was otherwise a strange, sad, and rather confused time. I went round saying goodbye to old friends, and suddenly became so emotional about it that I had to pretend that I had been taken ill with a touch of flu.

All that had to be done then was to go down to Nairobi and get on a plane. I had another nasty twinge when the girl who sold me my airline ticket looked at my passport and said, 'Oh, you're lucky, you've got a Kenya Resident's permit, it's impossible to get these now. We'd all mad to get one'. At that moment I felt completely stupid, and so pretended to the girl, and myself, that I would probably be coming back, but I wasn't sure exactly when. I had an couple of hours or so before it was time to hand over my Ford van, get on the plane, and leave Africa; and on a sudden impulse I thought I would drive out to Ngong and round the Nairobi game reserve for the last time, a reprise of that very first drive outside the town with Derek and Ken in his Landrover, years ago. Half an hour later I was trundling along happily near the place where we had seen the lions and got stuck, when I suddenly remembered that, thinking that my car was about to be handed in, I hadn't put much petrol in the tank; in fact the gauge was showing empty. There was also now less than two hours to get on the plane, and I was miles away from the airport. Feeling foolish, and wondering if it would be possible to get a refund on the ticket if I missed my flight, I drove very carefully back the shortest way I could think of, waiting to hear the engine splutter and stop at any moment. It didn't, and I got to the airport in time, handed over the van, had my luggage weighed, and went aboard. I wasn't completely sure that I would have minded very much if I had indeed missed the plane, and had seen it flying away without me.

The flight home to England was in a VC 10, a smart new aircraft of East African Airways, and we had a good trip. Towards the North African coast the sun shone down on us out of a brilliant blue sky as I watched the seemingly endless empty miles of the desert slip away below, and then the blue Mediterranean. Then the snowy Alps, clear cut and looking only a short way under our wings. After that the land below seemed to become less clear, and then we were above the partial cloud cover over northern Europe. By the time our plane was flying over England there was still a brilliant blue sky above, but nothing below except white cloud tops. Then the steady note of our engines changed, we began to descend, and the brilliant white clouds mysteriously changed into drifts of grey, while the blue sky we had been traveling in all the way dimmed. Then at last, there below us was London, vast, sprawling and shades of grey. I was home, just past my thirty third birthday, and without the slightest idea what I was going to do next.

14
Scotland

When my plane landed at London airport I was probably in a state of shock. A ten year slice of my life had ended abruptly, and I really did not know what I was going to do next.

Well, I had one thing to do, which was to follow everybody else through the arrivals procedure and customs. This had never presented itself as a problem before and I casually dumped my luggage on the desk expecting the bored looking young man to scribble a chalk mark and wave me on. He didn't. He began to open my case and enquired if I had anything to declare. As I had a rather nice camera I thought perhaps I should tell him before he found it, so I did. 'Where did you acquire it?' I had 'acquired' it in Kenya, of course, and explained I had been living there for the last ten years. Did I have documents to prove where I had acquired it, and how much I had paid? No, of course not. When had I acquired it? About two years ago, I thought.

The bored young man in the custom officer's uniform was beginning to dislike me; I was not taking him seriously enough. 'If you have no proof that you have owned the camera for more than two years it will be subject to full duty.' He opened a large reference book and began running his finger down the columns. 'On this item the duty payable is forty two pounds seventeen and eleven pence. Have you anything else to declare?' I said, 'You must be joking, that's probably more than I paid for it,' and added foolishly, ' are you going to charge me for my watch too? I've had that less than two years !' It was definitely the wrong thing to say. He held out his hand and I found myself handing it over for his inspection, and heard him adding another twenty pounds to the bill.

I told him it was completely unreasonable and I would not pay it. He said that if I wished to dispute the charge I could fill in this form and the items in question would be held in the bonded warehouse until the matter was settled, or I decided to pay. Well, I had walked into that one. We exchanged looks of mutual loathing, he handed me a receipt for my camera and watch, and I moved on, and out into the open air. Home again ! It was also late afternoon by now, dull, and drizzling slightly.

Still, the next item on the agenda was more promising, the new car that I had ordered that day, long ago in Nakuru, was to be picked up, that at least was a more cheerful thought. I looked for and found the Cortina, waiting for me as had been arranged, and told the man delivering it all about my troubles with Her Majesty's customs; but I think he had heard it all before. He had certainly delivered cars to airports often before, and managed to complete the hand over in about five minutes flat and disappeared home for his tea. He had probably told me how everything worked, but when I had finished admiring the lovely new, pristine white, Cortina GT, and putting my luggage in the boot, I discovered that I could remember how to start it, but nothing much else. Having driven it a few yards we stopped again, got out the driver's manual and worked out how the windscreen wipers and the lights functioned; for it was raining seriously and getting dark now. That attended to I drove on, but it seemed a bit late to head for Norfolk, and I had a vague invitation to visit some members of the Robinson family, Margaret's daughter and son in law, who I hadn't seen since they'd had to flee from Zanzibar years ago, and who lived just south of London now.

I found the place easily enough, a modern little house in a rather smart suburban cul-de-sac, very unlike Kenya. They seemed fairly happy there and cheerfully provided me with a meal and a bed for the night just as though we had still been in Africa. We had a long talk, comparing notes, and they told me that they were most impressed with the different attitude to work here in England. For instance, the lad who brought round the milk every morning did it all by himself, and at the double; whereas we all knew that if such a thing as delivered milk had happened in Kenya, it would have been done very slowly and inefficiently and probably by several people all assisting each other.

In the morning, having duly observed the amazing speediness of the milk rounds-man, and said our farewells and assurances that we would soon all meet again, the new Cortina was started up once more and off I went on the final leg of the journey back to Norfolk. After the dull evening it had turned out to be a nice bright morning, cool but with a splash of sunshine and white clouds scudding by in a blue sky. Much more encouraging, and I drove along in my nice new car feeling more cheerful and ready for what life had to offer. But actually life had another trick up its sleeve.

Away from London the road was almost empty of other traffic, and I was beginning to really enjoy driving on tarmac instead of the surface of gravel and rock and mud that was the norm in Kenya. I zoomed along happily for a long time, and then began to notice a loud whining sound from somewhere in the transmission. End of happy zooming, as I began to wonder where the noise was coming from. What could be whining in a brand new car ? I was used to old gear boxes and differentials that whined like sad banshees, and you accepted that as normal. But a new car ? As I thought about it I became convinced that something had not been lubricated properly at the factory. Well, you heard all sorts of horror stories. Say the lad who was supposed to fill the differential with oil had been having a fag when my car went by ?

I came to a town with a garage which acclaimed itself as Ford Main Dealer and drove up on to the forecourt, found myself a mechanic, and explained that I had taken delivery of the car a matter of hours ago, and suspected that there was no oil in the differential. My mechanic assumed the sad aspect of a mechanic who has been asked to pick up a spanner beyond the call of duty, and shook his head. 'They can't have sent it out without any oil in it.' 'Well, it could happen, couldn't it ?' 'No guv.'

I thought, he doesn't believe me and I am making a fool of myself. But there was a car hoist standing there with nothing on it, and he allowed himself to be persuaded to have a look. The new car was hoisted up, the filler cap unscrewed, and the differential checked. Yes. I had made a fool of myself, the oil level was OK. 'Nothing wrong there, guv.' The car was returned to ground level, the sad mechanic thanked profusely, and I drove on. Of course, the whining sound wasn't so loud now. In fact you hardly noticed it. In fact I had been winding myself up. Oh, well, I said to myself, you've had a busy day or two; time to go home and have a rest.

Home was now Wells in Norfolk where my mother and father were living, so it seemed the obvious place to go, but I had no idea what I would do when I got there beyond saying hallo to people. And this was indeed what happened. It was all very comfortable, there was a room for me in my parents house, but they had their own lives which they had lived quite well without me for the last ten years, and there was nothing much for me to do.

Loafing around was not really my thing, nor did the rather chilly early spring weather encourage it, and I soon started looking round for something more positive. A search round for some sort of employment did not reveal anything very interesting, and no-one I talked to seemed to have any good ideas. I had to go and see the local bank manager one day about some routine matter concerning the modest amount of money I had brought home with me, and I was talking to him about the possibilities of perhaps starting a business of some sort. He said that there was an estate agency for sale near by, and suggested that as a good business project.

I thought, well, that's an idea at least. Then I thought again, wait a minute, do I know anything at all about running an estate agent's office? No. And I went 'home' wondering what, if anything, I did know enough about to make a living.

The answer was obvious. I was not an expert at anything at all, but I had enough general knowledge and aptitude to run a farm and breed cattle. After all, I had done that pretty successfully for several years under some fairly tricky circumstances in Africa; why not here?

This was a positive thought, and I could do with a positive thought or two, so I worked on it. What sort of farming and where? Not in Norfolk obviously, farms were big and land too expensive for me to even think about. Anyhow I didn't really want to be a Norfolk farmer, too dull. What about a croft in the Hebrides or something like that, or a hill farm on top of a mountain in Wales? I began to cheer up, this was more like it. What to do about it was more of a problem. Should I just set out in my shiny new car and drive round hopefully in the more remote areas of the British Isles and see what turned up? Yes, that appealed as an immediate objective; better than sitting about in Wells and feeling rather an unwanted extra in other people's lives.

My sister, who had been on holiday in Scotland recently, said she knew a lady living in Glasgow from whom they had rented a cottage in some remote glen, who probably knew about crofting and things like that. This seemed as good a start as any, so I wrote down her address carefully, filled the car with petrol, threw a few things in the back, including a cake supplied by my mother for the journey, and set off. This was before the days of motorways and driving up to Scotland was a slow business with main roads narrow and clogged with traffic, and usually passing through the middle of each town as they came to it. Even in my Cortina GT which I liked to think was pretty fast and nippy, it took all day and I arrived in Glasgow in the early evening. The address was easy to find, and turned out to be in the north west of the city, in an obviously rather good class sort of area.

The lady I was going to introduce myself to was called Joan Tebbutt and she lived on the top floor of a block of flats, so I just left my car outside, this being also before the era of double yellow lines; walked up the stairs and knocked on the door. I had no idea what to expect, except apparently a woman who owned and let country cottages to holiday makers, and so I was not quite sure what to say when an attractive, casually dressed young girl with dark brown hair and a hole in her stockings, who somehow did not look like a property owner, opened it. 'Joan Tebbutt?' I said rather doubtfully. The girl shook her head, 'No, I'm afraid she's not here.' 'But this is her flat ?' 'Oh, yes' she said, 'But I'm her lodger and live here too, we're both at the art school. I'm Anne.'

Art school, I thought, an art student, obviously. But what about Joan Tebbutt then, she couldn't be a student too. I had been imagining a middle aged woman, and anyhow art students don't own property. Rather at a loss to say anything intelligent I blurted out, 'Er, I had been given her name, I had better come back later .' The young lady smiled and said, 'Come in and wait if you like, Joan probably won't be very long. Come and look at what I am working on.' Slightly surprised by the friendly, casual, welcome I went in, thinking: well I suppose art students are like this. I only found out later that Anne had supposed that I, because of the African tan still on my face, was one of the group of explorers and mountain climbers and others of that ilk who were Joan's friends.

It was a large flat with several rooms; built for a family residence no doubt in the old days when these very solid blocks of flats went up all over Glasgow. Anne showed me her work, which apparently was a 'pulpit fall' designed for St. Giles Church in Edinburgh. I had never heard of such a thing before, and knew nothing about embroidery of any sort, so she explained it all to me; and said that she was having trouble with it because someone was complaining that the design was off- centre. Anne said indignantly that it might appear off centre, but that was simply because they didn't understand it, and it was optically quite correct. She obviously did not have a high opinion of people, be they ever so important members of St Giles, who did not appreciate her work.

This conversation soon exhausted my ability to say anything intelligent about church embroidery, and not having had much to eat that day, I had a good idea and asked this interesting young lady if she could tell me where one could get some food in the neighbourhood; and would she perhaps like to have something to eat with me while waiting for Joan Tebbutt to appear ? Rather to my surprise Anne said yes, she would come and show me a near by restaurant; and yes, she would quite like something to eat. Without further ado she strode off, with me following, and after collecting my car we went off into Glasgow. The car immediately ran out of petrol, I had forgotten that the tank must be low, so Anne first had to take me to the nearest garage, then we went to rather modest cafeteria sort of place; she told me later that she hadn't wanted to embarrass me by going to somewhere expensive. After that we went back to the flat again. Joan Tebbutt had appeared by this time, turned out to be the sort of age I had expected, an obviously highly intelligent woman of the world, but just as friendly as Anne, and offered me her spare room for the night.

In the course of much chatting that evening I discovered several things. One, Anne was not a student, she was a lecturer at the Art School like Joan, though she hardly looked old enough. Joan was not some sort of property tycoon, but just happened to own a tiny house on the Mull of Kintyre which she sometimes rented out to visitors to bring in a little cash. In fact she was a very prestigious but somewhat impecunious calligrapher. Normally she went there herself at weekends, and had in fact just returned thence in her little open tourer car. Often, it appeared, Anne and various friends and acquaintances went with her, but hadn't this time, so that was a bit of luck.

I was beginning to think that I rather liked this Anne, and when it came out in the general conversation that she was going up to her parents' home at Nairn in the north of Scotland an a couple of days, to see her father, who was not very well, I asked her if I could drive her up there? All part of my touring round the country and looking out for a farm or croft or something, of course.

Anne took to the idea at once, and said she could introduce me to one or two people in the area who were farmers and could perhaps help. She told me later that she was already thinking that it was a pity about the farming, because though she would not mind marrying a farmer, she did not like chickens very much.

Joan told me that she knew a chap in Edinburgh who was some sort of official who worked in, or possibly ran, an organization called the Land Bank. This was all to do with helping young people to get into farming in Scotland, and sounded an intriguing possibility. It was soon worked out for me that I would go and see the important man in Edinburgh, have a look round some of the nearer bits of Scotland, come back again on Wednesday evening., and drive Anne up to Nairn to visit her parents. So the next morning I drove Anne down to the Art School, arranged exactly where I would pick her up when I returned, and went off on stage two of my Scotland safari.

The thought of living on an island had always appealed to me, so I wanted to go and look at islands. The port of Oban from which boats went to Mull, and I supposed other islands, seemed a good place to start, so I headed north.

The map told me that a road ran up the side of Loch Lomand, and that from there I could head west to Inverary, and then round the coast to Oban. It was fine weather, though early in the year, and the road, which soon left the town behind, was charming. It was narrow and pretty tortuous in places, and you did tend to get stuck behind the odd slow vehicle here and there, but it was beautiful and I drove along cheerfully singing bits about the bonny, bonny banks as I went. After miles of this loch-side road, which wound along above the water most of the time in a partly wooded landscape, we climbed up to the grander open moorland, and then eventually down again to a rocky coastline and the sea.

Oban turned out to be a pleasant enough little town with a few shops and a quay filled with an assortment of small craft, fishing boats and little steamers of one sort or another. I had a walk round and enquired about ferries to the offshore islands, but soon discovered that the scale of things was larger than I had imagined, and there would be no nipping out to islands and back in a couple of hours. Since I had said I would be back in Glasgow in two days, and I was supposed to be going to Edinburgh too, that didn't leave much time for visiting islands near or far, so that adventure would have to be left for another day. For the moment I would just spend a bit more time in Oban, get some lunch, and go on up the coast and see what I found there.

What I found was a little town called Connan, which had a nice old traditional looking hotel within sight of the sea, which appealed to me, and as it was mid afternoon by then I thought I would stop and have a cup of tea and book myself in for the night. I did not want to go any further North because you could see from a map that it was going to be a long drive the next day, right across Scotland from west to east via Crianlarich and Stirling to Edinburgh.

I enquired about a room and was told there was indeed a single room available, so I took it, and was shown up. I had to laugh at myself then as, going to the window to admire the view I found that it overlooked the railway sidings behind the hotel, not the sea in front. Still, I thought what did it matter for one night, and if I wanted to see the sea I could always go and look at it. I went down and asked if I could have some tea, thinking a cup of tea and a biscuit or something like that; another mistake. I was shown to a table in the large, and otherwise empty, dining room, and left there. Sitting in this room all by myself I was thinking that it was a bit unnecessarily formal for a cup of tea when the waitress came back again struggling under an enormous tray covered with every imaginable thing you might possibly eat at teatime including bread and butter, several pots of assorted jams, two or three varieties of sandwiches, scones, and a selection of cakes. Then she went back and returned with a large shiny brown teapot, sugar, milk and cup and saucer. A cup of tea and a biscuit was obviously not what travellers received at a hotel in Scotland. I should have known that, I supposed. Well there was nothing for it but to make some sort of show of eating some of it, and then the equally generous dinner that followed a couple of hours later.

The next morning saw me up betimes, breakfasted on kippers, and off and away from my room overlooking the railway sidings. It was, as I had supposed a long drive right across Scotland to Edinburgh, but I enjoyed the wild moorland that I was travelling through most of the way and arrived there in plenty of time to find the office of the man Joan had said might help me to find a croft. He turned out to be a very nice sort of chap, and was encouraging about taking up farming in the Highlands, but did not have anything in particular on offer. I understood that if I found something myself I could expect to get financial help through his organization but I would have to find my croft first. I thanked him, made notes of names and telephone numbers, and moved on.

Edinburgh was a fine city and I spent some time looking round, and feeling I should buy something Scottish, went into a gentleman's outfitters knee deep in assorted tartans and bought myself a thick woollen dressing gown; it had been quite cold in the room with the view over the railway yards. It was by then mid afternoon, which gave me, I reckoned, plenty of time to get to the Art School in Glasgow by five o'clock. Alas, another mistake. It didn't look far on the map, about half an hours drive I thought; but I had reckoned without a lot of heavy traffic between the two cities, and the fact that it was approaching the rush hour for people leaving work just as I reached the outskirts of Glasgow. By the time I was supposed to be picking up Anne at the Art School I had been ploughing ever more slowly through ever thicker traffic to somewhere vaguely in the centre of the town, then had to admit I was completely lost. I drew up to the pavement where a group of young lads were standing, they looked street-wise enough to know where anything was in the vicinity, and I leaned over and held out half-a-crown, "Do you know where the Art School is?" I shouted. A cheeky looking ten year old grabbed the half-crown and jumped into the car, "I'll show you mister ", he said, and proceeded with great aplomb and a rich Glasgow accent to pilot me through the traffic. Oh my god, I was thinking, I am going to be arrested for kidnapping children, and was just deciding to stop the car and throw him out again when the unmistakable square outline of the Art School appeared in front, and there miraculously stood Anne still waiting for me. Her friends, she told me later, had been telling her she was completely mad to be waiting for this stranger she had just met, and who was, even if he was coming at all, over half an hour late. But she did wait, and thus our fate was decided; or perhaps she had already decided it for herself. Anyway, off we went together, out of Glasgow again, she directing me this time, and off on the long road north.

I only had the vaguest idea where we were going. Somewhere

near Inverness, it seemed, and all I knew about that town was that it was somewhere in the far north of the British Isles. But then I always liked driving long distances, and off into the darkness of the Highlands with this jolly young lady was really very romantic. We passed Stirling, where I had at least been before, and then on into the unknown through places I had hardly heard of. Perth, Pitlochry, Blair Athol, Kingussie (I couldn't have even pronounced that one), Aviemore; further and further on we went along that dark, lonely road. At the start of the journey I'd had the very English idea that there would be lots of jolly pubs along the way where we would stop and have something to eat and the odd glass or two, but of course there weren't. Jolly pubs were few and far between along Scottish roads in those days. Even at hotels, of which there were some, casual passers by seemed hardly welcome, and if you asked for a meal after about six p.m. they thought you were joking.

At long last we arrived at the little town of Nairn, drove through it and drew up at a very neat, very Scottish looking cottage. Anne's mother met us at the door, her father of course was not there, being at the local hospital for some sort of check up; but nothing, we were assured, to worry about. At last we had arrived, and could relax and have a very welcome meal in this bright little house, which was almost dazzling after the miles and miles of dark road sweeping on and on over the endless moors.

The next day we went into Inverness to the hospital to see Anne's father who turned out to be perfectly well. His doctor had been worried about a mysterious lump somewhere inside that turned out to be something quite normal that he'd had all his life, so everyone was much relieved. Anne still had the rest of the week off from her art school, and then there was the weekend; so she took me around the area and introduced me to a farming family she knew, and after that we went further north and looked at the coast beyond the Murray Firth and the Black Isle. It was all beautiful and wild country, often very bleak but with pockets of kindlier looking countryside in the valleys. It was not the sea lochs-and-islands sort of country that I was seeking, for that was all in the west, and we were on the east coast, but I was happy enough touring around with Anne and seeing it all. What was the hurry after all, there was plenty of time to find a farm, and driving about with a pretty Scots girl was fine for the time being. All too soon she would go back to Glasgow to do some work, and then I could resume my vague search for a farm.

I discovered that she was part of an amateur theatricals gang who were putting on The Merry Widow at the near by town of Forres that very weekend, and I found myself booked in to go to that, and the party afterwards. I wasn't sure if I was ready for Scottish local theatricals, and was quite relieved to find that Anne was not actually on the stage; she had been putting her art to good use by making all the exotic hats for them, that was all.

Saturday night found us at the theatre at Forres, where I was bowled over at the unexpectedly professional performance, and of course at the beauty of the hats. Afterwards I met the whole crew at their party; not at all the village "do" I had imagined, but a glittering affair which could well have been going on in the West End of London. The leader of the group, a tall handsome man, who talked and acted rather like Noel Coward with a fine Scottish accent, was clearly on the most cordial terms with Anne, which I found oddly irritating and I was slightly relieved to be introduced to his wife. They were both old friends, Anne said. Everybody else seemed to be old friends too, the whole thing was a bit overwhelming for me, and I was quite relieved and more than ready to go when Anne agreed to leave about midnight, and go home to Mum. I heard afterwards the this was noticed by everybody there, as it was the first time Anne had ever been known to go home so early. There were a lot of knowing looks exchanged.

Next day we were back in Glasgow again almost exactly a week after we had met. Only a week? We were well aware that in some mysterious way life had changed for both of us, but neither of us could really believe that things like this could happen so quickly. That evening we went for a meal in a Glasgow restaurant again, but this time a rather nice little Italian place that Anne knew. We had a very pleasant meal and a bottle of Chianti and afterwards went and sat in the car. The fact was that neither of us was thinking about the quality of the food or drink, and there seemed to be nothing else to say but would she marry me? Anne said she would. I think we were both bewitched by the moment. It all seemed so obvious that there was nothing else to do or say and we were very happy. But in the cold light of day later on I was horrified. Here was I with no prospects of any sort, without a job, without an income, without anywhere to live even, coolly expecting this young woman with an excellent, well paid career in front of her, to just pack it all in and leap up on my horse and gallop off into the sunset. Well, for horse read Cortina. We were clearly both mad. She went back to the Art School and I went back to Norfolk for the moment, and then to continue my interrupted search for a farm, but for two people now, not just one.

Fate had decreed, rather conveniently, that Anne was going down to London shortly for some reason connected with her work, and we agreed to meet again there. Then Easter would be upon us soon and she would have several weeks off, so we would be able to resume our driving round together while we both looked for this imaginary farm. That would be very pleasant, and fun.

In due course we met again, and Anne came to Norfolk and met my family, who were bemused by the whole business. My parents didn't know what to make of me anyhow after I came home from Africa, different from the boy who had gone there ten years ago, and with a beard and all. And now here I was suddenly appearing with a Scots girl I had just met and saying we were going to be married. Nobody knew quite what to say, and anyhow I soon disappeared again as Anne and I went off on various safaris to search for our farm.

We looked at assorted places in Scotland, and then in Devon just for a change. Well we had been told that there were lots of small, picturesque farms in the South West, and so there were; but the ones we found for sale seemed to be dull and mean looking and usually situated in a sea of mud. It was probably not the time of year to see them at their best, but some were so muddy that you had to change your clothes after looking round. On one occasion on returning to the car I took off my muddy trousers, put on clean ones, and threw the dirty ones in the boot. The lid slammed down, and then I realized the car keys were still in the pocket of the trousers inside the boot, and with that particular car the boot could only be opened with the car key. So there we were, standing beside the Cortina at the side of the road somewhere in Devon, with the car keys securely locked inside the boot. And we hadn't liked any of the farms anyhow. Such tools as I had were also in the boot of course, but we had to something or stand there until I died of exposure, so with the aid of a penknife I hot-wired our vehicle, and drove on to the first town we could find. There was a Ford agent there; thank goodness, there nearly always was a Ford Agent, so all we had to do was drive into the garage, find a mechanic, and explain the I had locked my trousers and keys in the boot. Could he please open the boot for us? He looked from Anne to me, and back again, obviously trying to work out exactly what had been going on; then without batting an eyelid said he would see what he could do. He went to the office and we could see him regaling his friends with the story, probably the best one they had heard for some time, and then returned with a bunch of assorted car keys. We soon found one that fitted, obviously Ford car security was not great in those days but who cared? My keys were retrieved and the mechanic thanked ; there was no point in trying to explain what had happened, he knew what he thought, and we drove on. That was our Devon experience, and our next hunting ground was Wales.

Anne had friends who lived in Anglesey and they invited us to visit them and look round there; I think Anne's friends all wanted to see this unknown young man she had suddenly taken a shine to. Anyhow we drove to and through Wales on a weekend of wonderful clear weather. There was not much traffic, and we zoomed up and down the hills and valleys, at one time racing another sports car, and had a wonderful time. The large rock we saw by the roadside with "English go Home" painted on it caused only merriment, but in fact we did not find our farm there either. Our friends showed us a nice looking one that was for sale and very reasonable, called Plas Bedaden, and I loved the name whatever it meant, but it was not for us. Anne said she did not like the idea of producing Welsh speaking children, so that was that.

The end of our search came at length in Scotland, where we were looking at the last of a long list of small farms offered by a local agent. We had been all round the country from a smallholding near Glasgow to a rather grand looking place with moor grazing rights on the Mull of Kintyre, but couldn't find what we wanted. This last one was back in the highlands near Loch Ness and sounded at least a romantic spot. But it turned out to be a bleak hillside, cold and dreary, and a piece of forest marked on the map as being part of the property had all been felled. To provide some fuel to warm them up, I gloomily assumed. The only signs of life, or at least recent life, were several dead sheep scattered about the old farmstead. The final straw was that on our way there we had found ourselves following along behind a car with the registration letters BUY; this must at last be a good omen that we had found our little nest. Some nest, we said, this idea of a farm or croft is a wash out, so what shall we do?

We had decided by then that we would get married in July when Anne's term at the Art School ended, so we had to have at least somewhere to live by then. We had a quick think about it. Anne had this arts background, my family had always been in business of one sort or another. There must be something we could work out between us. Anne said, what about a business of some sort? She had always fancied running an antique shop. What about that?

15
Antiques

We really had no idea what we were plunging into. We read a lot of books about the antique trade of course; in fact we bought so many that we said perhaps we should start a book shop instead. We read up on furniture, we read up on china, on silver, on pewter, on treen (which we discovered meant small objects made of wood), we never stopped reading up. Stuffed with our new-found knowledge we began going to auctions to see what we could pick up. After all it was no good having all this knowledge, and books, if we had nothing to sell. But going to auctions meant that we had to know what to buy when we got there.

Anne was ready to buy on her hunch of what was a good idea, and to tell the truth we had nothing else to go on, except a certain caution about how we spent our limited resources. We discussed this aspect at some length, and agreed that we would, to start with, not spend more than five pounds on any one item. This resolve did not last very long, for even in those days five pounds did not go very far, unless you limited yourself to bidding for lots that, basically, no one else wanted very much. In fact in those early days Anne's flair and my caution generally ended with us loading up at the end of the sale with all manner of odds and ends that might be described as quite interesting, but of no commercial value what so ever. Our speciality was mixed boxes of odds and ends that contained perhaps a piece or two of porcelain that our new found knowledge told us were highly 'collectable'. The fact that such pieces were usually chipped, and therefore unwanted by collectors, took time to get through to us in our youthful enthusiasm.

Getting our shop ready was more straight forward. We had found a little place in Burnham Market, near Wells where my parents were living, and I started working on it straight away.

It was an interesting antique in itself. We bought it simply because it was cheap and, we hoped, would be suitable for an antique shop. In the village there were already two other antique businesses, one run by two very ladylike ladies and another run by a rather sinister looking father and son. It seemed a good idea to start up in a place where there was already some antique trading going on; and we reasoned, quite accurately as it happened, that we might get some spin off from the other two shops. We knew hardly anything about the antique business world, but we had noticed that antique dealers seemed to circulate amongst others in the same trade, and reckoned that some of these dealers might drift in our direction after visiting the other two.

All we knew about our physical situation, when we arrived there, was that we were going to live in a rather scruffy looking old building in the middle of an unknown Norfolk village. But we felt that this house would suit us very well. It had a double shop front, a yard and stables at the back, and a nice sized garden, even if it was filled with old sheds and pigsties. There were about a dozen rooms, so lots of space, and we just sort of liked it. After all, we had to live somewhere.

It needed a lot of care and attention, being more than somewhat neglected, but we felt we could deal with that, and make it look and feel a lot better. It was going to be a challenge, but then so was everything else in this new life, and I knew that at least I could turn my hand to the many odd jobs that we were going to tackle. Luckily Dad, now at long last retired and living not far away, decided that he would help and lend a hand with this and that. He even did some carpentry for us, to my mother's amazement; she said the last time he had done anything useful about the home was lost in the mists of time.

Our new home was in fact an old pub. It was called the Black Horse, and had been recently de-licensed and sold off by the brewers who had owned it. The rooms that we intended to convert from pub to shop were in quite good condition, and needed little more than a good clean up and some work with a paint brush. It still took time, and quite a lot of work, especially removing many years accumulation of tobacco staining from walls and ceiling, but this required only simple slogging, which we were both well able to deal with.

There was, it is true, a problem with what had been the tap-room. This was at the front of the house and would be part of the shop but had a completely rotten floor, due no doubt to the very damp beer cellar underneath. Luckily at the time we did not know quite how damp this could be; we only found out much later that it was not only very damp but, from time to time, flooded up to six feet deep in water. Still, that came later, and for the moment we got a local builder to put in a new floor to replace the old wood, so that no-one would actually fall through, and after that we more or less ignored what was underneath.

All this was done in the late summer and autumn, and at the same time we hopefully accumulated our stock in trade. We had decided that our stock would be interestingly mixed, and at the same time that we were making our rather strange purchases at local auctions, we were also visiting trade warehouses to find amusing and useful items that could be mixed in with our fascinating antiques. Trade warehouses were as much a foreign country to us as the auctions, more so in fact, and we had never even known they existed until a helpful 'gift shop' owner introduced us to our first one. These places, with their endless shelves of items that were described vaguely as gifts, meaning for the most part things that you might be given on your birthday but would never find a use for, left us bemused. Should you stock up with these things? They were usually cheap enough to be well within our five pound limit. But would anybody want to buy them from us? It seemed unlikely. Still, someone must buy this stuff, or else what was the warehouse for? So we bought a few assorted items here and there, from warehouse people who always seemed amazed that we didn't want to open an account and have van loads of the stuff delivered.

When our shop opened, in November (why November? We just happened to be ready to open, so we opened) it consisted of two rooms filled with probably the strangest mixture of goods that had ever seen the light of day together. Our stock ranged from good modern kitchen ware, through horrendous modern 'gifts' , to an assortment of antiques that seemed to be bargains at the many auctions we had visited.

We had happened to open in what was probably the worst week we could have chosen; it snowed. Unusual to have a snowy week in November, in Norfolk, but we had managed to pick it.

In those days Burnham Market was a quiet little place at any time, but especially so if it happened to be snowing, and hardly anyone came in that first day. Luckily for us one of the ladies who ran the high class porcelain business at the other end of the market place, came in to see us, out of kindness no doubt, and perhaps curiosity. Being a friendly person, she chatted and bought a trifle from us and asked, did we 'do trade'? Having no idea what she meant, I played safe and said I didn't think so.

Oh, dear. Of course she was merely asking for the usual trade price which all antique dealers gave each other. We became good friends and remained so for many years, but that little exchange of her 'Do you do trade?', and my 'I don't think so' always remained a bit of a joke against me at least in my own mind.

Still, our shop was open, and we were in business. Our stock was not great, but we did have some interesting bits. Between working on our house and our frequent forays to sales and warehouses, we had spent a lot of time studying our new subject, and had begun to acquire some useful knowledge. We had also started to appreciate something about the world of antiques, and to understand why some things were valued more than others. We still bought things at auction that had less commercial value than we had hoped, but at least we could begin to tell the difference between good quality, damaged, but still desirable, and things that were frankly rubbish.

Most of the things we put on display had some interest about them. The very first good antique we had was merely an early nineteenth century coarse pottery mug, but it was unusual and had a certain quality about it, and it sold quickly enough and made a profit. Amazing event! We had bought and sold something at a profit. We were dealers! We also bought and sold a pretty Regency period chair, sabre legs and caned seat. That had cost a good deal more than the prescribed limit of five pounds. We splashed out ten pounds, and sold it for fifteen. At the end of our first week we had taken thirty pounds and in our third week we took one hundred, which I took to our bank and handed over with a flourish. We were away!

While this was going on we were always still working on our house; in fact this was a job that never really finished, as we found that over the years there was always something that needed doing, and we never reached that state where we could stand back and feel that everything that could be done was done.

Our plan for working on our new home was always simple and practical. We started with the kitchen and one bedroom, which covered the basic essentials, and worked slowly outwards. With these rooms at least liveable in, we felt that our life style was reasonable, if not luxurious. Next came a little room behind the shop, which also needed a new floor, and after that our sitting room, which in the traditional style would be above the shop. This was actually quite a big room with a fine Georgian sash window looking over the market place; but it had been divided, making two rather nasty mean little bedrooms, with the dividing wall even cutting through the window. Removing the dividing wall was simple, but this left a problem, because one of the two little bedrooms had its original beams, while the other had a modern white plaster ceiling. We would have liked to have restored this so that the whole room was beamed again, but that looked like being a big job and it was quicker with some plaster board to extend the modern ceiling over the whole room. At least for the time being, we said, and the original look could be restored later.

I the end we began to realize that the restoration of the Black Horse was going to be a much bigger job than we had thought at first. We also began to understand that the building was much older than it appeared and was not just another Victorian pub. This became apparent when we worked our way up to the top floor where there was an attic that ran the whole length of the house. This had seemed to be just a sort of loft space full of old plaster, dirt, and rubbish; but on closer inspection when we got round to it was a fascinating old room with superb oak beams, a window with very ancient ironwork, and a strange little extra room at the end of it. This was scarcely bigger than a cupboard but had a little arched door with a bolt on the inside. A bolt on the inside of a cupboard door? Someone must have slept in there in times past.

With this attic cleaned out and refurbished we found that we had, according to experts, a genuine original 17th.century room; and the lockable cupboard at the end was where the daughter of the house would have been kept safe and sound.

So we now realized that we were not living in a nondescript old pub, but an historic building that needed to be carefully preserved. Still we kept to our original plan of doing a bit at a time, to make it a comfortable home but with no sweeping modernisation; and thus almost by accident most of the old structure was preserved, where many old houses were gutted and virtually destroyed inside. Years later we were told by an expert that we had one of the best preserved old houses in the village; and that was mainly because from the beginning we were spending very little on it, not having much spare cash to spend, but just giving it plenty of care and attention.

Furniture was needed too of course, but that was quite easy to arrange. Local auctions in which other peoples' cast offs were sold for a pound or two, or less, happened all the time. Every week there was a sale on one of the greens at Burnham Market in which old bicycles, bits of ancient farm equipment, and sticks of rejected furniture were the staples, and there we very quickly acquired several useful pieces including a kitchen dresser. On the green this had merely looked old and sad and tatty, but it was basically sound, and we bought it for ten shillings. Taken home and cleaned up a bit and then painted white it looked quite smart. Dad, in his new role as carpenter and handyman, made us a plate rack to go on the back and we painted that also. We then had a rather nice, and definitely useful piece of furniture which still stands in our kitchen. Other pieces came in the same way, and our rooms were soon quite comfortable if not smart.

We needed something a bit better to go in our big sitting room upstairs, with its nice Georgian window and wide windowsill; and our village porcelain specialists, Lady Margaret and Miss Sumpter chanced to have just what we wanted. They did buy and sell furniture, usually Georgian, but it happened that a set of early Victorian settee and two chairs appeared in their shop one day. They were upholstered in a stripy material and would set off the room nicely; the price was affordable, special trade terms of course, so we bought them and carried them through the village home.

We had a bit of a struggle getting them upstairs, with one of the ladies getting stuck behind the settee half way up, but we made it in the end and it looked very nice. Incidentally it was our first experience of that bane of the antique dealer's life, getting up and down stairs with awkward bits of furniture. We were a bit surprised to see the two ladies taking this in their stride, but soon learned that this was a normal part of the life of any dealer.

At all events our antique shop was up and running by the end of that year and we had proved to ourselves that we could buy and sell antiques. What we did not realize then but which must have helped us, was that we were dealing on a rising market. We were often told by people we met about the amazing bargains they had bought a year or two ago, which we assumed was due to their cleverness or good luck, or something; but the truth was that the market was buoyant and prices rising. The fact was that antiques were fashionable and were going to become more so as time went on. I don't know if anyone realized that at the time, we certainly did not, and it is only over a period of years that such trends in business become obvious. We were just learning a trade, and by hook or by crook making enough profit to keep going while we learned.

And one of the first things we learned was that there was no point in having the same goods to sell as other people. Our modern stuff, which we had bought hoping it was interesting enough to bring people into the shop, was not a success. The fact was that our customers, who from the beginning were people who lived out there in the big wide world and drove into the village in their motor cars, were not particularly interested in things they could buy in the shops elsewhere. In Burnham Market they wanted to see things that were not around in the big modern stores. It didn't take long to cotton on to this, and after that first Christmas we decided, like the other shops, to have a sale of our modern gear, and from then on no more was purchased. We had tried the amusing mixture idea but no-one wanted to know.

Our last attempt on the modern trade was to go in for painted furniture, which was fashionable at the time. We reckoned that we could do a bit of good with that; I could paint things and use a spray gun, and Anne, for goodness sakes, was actually an artist. But it didn't work. Painted furniture was in all the fashionable magazines, and we did some quite nice bits, even a table decorated with a union jack, but nobody wanted it. I suppose if they did want that sort of thing they could get it in the King's Road in London, but they certainly did not come to our village for that sort of thing. Fair enough, we said, it's antiques only from now on.

Of course, for all our hard work at learning the trade we knew we were not going to immediately make a killing in the real, serious, antiques world. We were not going up to London to compete in the big auction houses with the serious people. We were well aware that we were not in that league, but we had already bought things in local auctions and sold them successfully, so we would just carry on doing that. Our hunch that being in a village with other antique shops would help us had turned out to be correct, and most days a dealer or two from perhaps many miles away would turn up, chat, look around our modest stock, and maybe buy something.

A lot of book knowledge and a lack of practical experience can be a strange and even dangerous mixture. All our spare time had been spent in reading up on the antique collectors' world, and so we often knew about antique items in a theoretical sort of way, without having handled them or ever seen them in the flesh. In those early days we could easily be looking at something in an auction with casual interest, and suddenly realize that it was a real example of something only previously read about in a book. I well remember one day poking about the serried ranks of assorted jugs at a typical country house sale, noticing a rather quaint one with a scratchy picture of cows on its dull, buff surface, and suddenly realizing with a shock that I was looking at the work of the famous Hannah Barlow. A book on the Doulton factory stood on the shelf at home and I had been reading all about the story of this pottery and how it used to produce everything from drain pipes to fine household ware. I had also read about how in the late nineteenth century this the firm began to employ young ladies from a nearby art school to decorate their finer pots and jugs, and that these items were now sought after by collectors. Their work had been described in great detail and illustrated; Miss Barlow was one of the best known, and she was very collectable indeed. I knew without doubt that though I had never seen it before I was looking at an example of her work. Had anyone else spotted it, I thought. No one seemed to be looking at it, so I casually picked the jug up and glanced at its base. There it was, the word Doulton. Amazing. I was like an explorer in the jungle who has just discovered a splendid and hitherto unknown orchid. I pretended complete indifference, looked idly at one or two other items on the table, and sidled over to where Anne was looking at a piece of furniture. I said, 'Don't look round, but there is a Hannah Barlow jug over there. No one seems to have noticed it.'

Such innocence. We waited patiently for its lot number to come up, then casually put in a bid for it. The bidding started at two pounds, and crept up slowly, I bid twice and it reached seven pounds, I bid seven pounds ten shillings, and the bidding seemed to stop. I thought, I've got it. The auctioneer glanced round the room, 'Eight, I'm bid.' I looked round to see who was bidding against me, but then someone else increased the bid, and the price went up quickly. So much for having spotted something that nobody else knew about. It was bought by someone at the back of the room. There were a little group standing there who didn't seem to do much but mutter amongst themselves and occasionally bid for something. I had vaguely recognized them. This was the Ring, a mysterious group of dealers who seemed to hang about at the back of auctions where ever you went. We didn't know anything about them, except that they obviously knew what they were doing, and knew what was worth buying. So there was little chance that nobody but me had noticed our Hannah Barlow jug.

We had one or two mild brushes with the ring in our early days. At whatever little remote local auction we went to, and we went to most of them, they were always there. Not always all of them, but always at least one or two standing at the back of the room, barn, village hall or whatever it was, and keeping an eye on things. I suppose they were also keeping half an eye on us, in case we seemed to want to muscle in on their trade. Once, in the very early days, we had spotted another nice little thing, a Stephengraph woven silk picture of Wellington and Blucher at the battle of Waterloo, in a box of prints and pictures. Again a very collectable item, our books told us, so we bid away hoping as usual that no one else had seen it. This time it seemed to work and we bought it. A few minutes later one of those watchers at the back of the room sidled up to Anne. 'I let you have that,' he said, 'How much ?'

Anne looked at him in mild surprise, 'You can't have it. I want it for our shop.' The watcher from the back of the room gave her a rather baffled look and sidled away again. We half expected to be mugged on the way home, but nothing happened, and the little silk picture duly appeared in our shop and was sold. Another time a more friendly approach was made, and I was, I think, more or less invited to join in with them. This was tricky because we certainly did not want to make enemies, but nor did we want to be hangers-on of this shifty looking gang at the back of the room.

Rings at auction sales were strictly against the law, though nobody seemed to take any action against them. So we just made a point of minding our own business, usually not bidding for the obvious desirable pieces, and so we avoided getting involved.

The way they operated of course, was to size up the sale before it began, work out the prices of items that they wanted, and then agree amongst themselves that only one member of the gang would bid so that they never bid against each other. Assuming that they knew, between them, more than the other people in the room about the value of what was on offer, - and this was probably often the case, - they could then buy very cheap. After that, at the end of the day they would have a little knock-out auction amongst themselves. The result of this was that the original seller did not get the proper price, the leaders of the ring got all the good stuff, and the minor hangers on got a fiver or a tenner for their trouble. Fair enough, we reckoned, if that was what you wanted to do; but we did not go to these sales to get paid off for co-operating with the ring, we wanted stock for our shop.

In fact as time went on we bought less and less at auctions and found it more profitable to spend our time elsewhere. It was true that great bargains could sometimes be picked up at the sale of the old country mansions that frequently came on the market then. Quite often in these sort of auctions there would be large boxes of assorted items that the auctioneers had not bothered to sort out, and there could be real treasure trove. One day at a crumbling old rectory, apparently previously inhabited by one of the old time vicars who used to pass their plentiful free time as amateur scientists, we bought a trunk full of bits of brass. They looked to me like parts of old scientific instruments and I bought it for a few pounds on impulse. Back at home with mounting excitement we extracted, sorted out, and fitted together the parts of a fine old microscope, two or three lesser ones, and lots of other Victorian laboratory equipment. The bits of brass had simply been jumbled up, perhaps by someone who had no idea what they were, and the trunk contained all sorts of exciting and even valuable items.

Well, that could happen, but the trouble was that usually at these sales, often quite a social event where the locals met to gossip over the grand folk who used to live there, a lot of time could be wasted and then at the end of the day you might go home with little to show for it. We came to realize that you could be much better employed spending the same amount of time visiting the many antique shops that used to be in nearly every village in those days, and picking up a piece here and a piece there. You could always get a good trade price, and since we soon had our own 'style' in our shop we could usually take our finds home and put a good profit on them; the point being that some unconsidered trifle in someone else's shop could with a little of Anne's careful arranging be much more saleable in ours.

Another good source of stock was the large warehouse type of place that house-clearance merchants often ran. They made their money by clearing whole houses, often after a death, and usually for a pittance, and then passing on the good bits to others in the antique trade. As we were mainly looking for odd, quirky items, rather than the obviously valuable antiques we could often buy well. Soon too, people were dropping into our shop and asking if we wanted to buy this or that from them, perhaps a piece of old fashioned furniture or an unfashionable tea service; and of course what was unfashionable to one person could be highly desirable to someone else, so that was a useful source of stock too. We always tried to give people who brought us things a good fair deal. Apart from any other consideration, we really wanted to build up a good connection with our general public, so we always gave as much as seemed reasonable.

This could be really difficult, we had to have some idea of the value of anything from a sideboard to a tea cup; and even a tea cup, we had soon learned, could be worth anything from several hundred pounds to a penny, or less. This was in the days before thick, glossy books gave at least some idea of the value of anything you cared to think of. We had to make up our own prices as we went along, and the strangest things were brought in to us. Often we might be landed with something we knew absolutely nothing about, like a folio of old prints; were they rare and valuable or just so much waste paper, and worth nothing ? We had to decide quickly. In extreme doubt our attitude was simply, if it looks attractive someone will want it; and usually offered our favourite price of a fiver, which as often as not was accepted. In the early days little old ladies from the village were always coming in with odd ornaments from their mantelpiece or perhaps something very strange and dusty, but indubitable old, from their outhouse. Small, broken bits of furniture were popular items to sell to the two young people in the new antique shop; and these could often be repaired, polished up, and passed on at an excellent profit. I was quite good at little repair jobs, and Anne had very useful knowledge of style and historical period from her art school training; and we stumbled along through the mists of our ignorance learning, learning, all the time.

Sometimes we bought something because we felt it must be "good" but then had no idea what to do with it next. As time went on we became sophisticated enough to take things to the museums or the big auction houses in London and get their opinions, but that came later. On one occasion in these very early days I bought an attractive and unusual china cow for my usual fiver, and it went into the shop at seven pounds ten. That evening I was going through some of our many antique books trying to find out where it might have come from, and came upon a reference to a Leeds Cow. These cows, I learned, dated back to the very early days of figure pottery in England, they were very rare, and of course collectable. In a word, valuable. Unfortunately the book had no illustration of this wonderful beast, but the description sounded very like the item standing in our shop window at its very modest price. Thank goodness no one had spotted it and bought it, I thought, as I rushed in and removed it. It spent the next day or two in our sitting room being studied thoughtfully while we went over all the books we had which might have information on Leeds cows and their value.

Well, we had plenty of books on antique pottery and china, but there seemed to be very little on Leeds cows, and certainly no picture anywhere. We studied our cow day and night. Sometimes we thought it must be very rare and valuable, sometimes we thought it was just a china cow, and worth about seven pounds ten. But we could not find out any more about it. No Internet in those days of course. In the end we put it back in the shop, but with no price ticket. This was pretty cunning, we thought, because if one of the dealers who were always dropping in saw it and seemed excited about it we could make up a price on the spot and see what happened.

The next day it stood in its accustomed place in the window when a man we knew to be a knowledgeable china expert came in. I watched closely to see what his reaction to the cow was, but he didn't seem to notice it. I adjusted its position in the window while he was looking round, but again no reaction. He left without mentioning it. I felt he must have seen it, so why no reaction? Was he being clever, and didn't want to appear interested in a fabulously rare item? He had probably noticed there was no price ticket and was going to be cagy about making an offer. We took our cow out of the window and it went back into our sitting room. I half expected our china expert to ring up later and ask about it, but nothing happened.

The Leeds cow spent the next few days in our sitting room while we decided what to do next. But, since we were supposed to be dealing in antiques this seemed a bit pointless, and at last we thought we would put it back on sale, but at a higher price. So back into the shop window it went, but no one showed any interest in it; dealers and members of the public came and went, but no one seemed to want our lovely Leeds cow. Time passed, one or two people looked at our cow casually, but no one was interested enough to pay our price. Then, one day we happened to be in London, went into the V&A museum and saw there, in its glass case, an actual Leeds cow. Sadly, it was not like ours at all. Ours was coloured and that one was white and quite, quite different. So back ours went into the shop at our original price, and some one bought it; not a crafty dealer, just someone who thought it was quite pretty. So it went to a good home in the end.

We also tried advertising in the press, to the effect that we were in the market for buying old and interesting items, and this brought us odds and ends; and one strange adventure. We received one day a letter from a lady called Mrs. Wellbeloved, who lived in Brighton, which we knew perfectly well was more or less the centre of the antique dealing world. There must have been literally hundreds of dealers there in those days, but none the less this lady wanted to deal with us. She said she had been in our shop and was impressed with our honesty and so on, and decided to come to us instead of one of the local men, who, she hinted were not altogether as straight and upright as they should be. Flattered, but a bit puzzled about why she should have picked on us in our little shop a couple of hundred miles away, we decided that none the less this particular avenue, like all the others that might be open to us to obtain suitable stock, must be thoroughly explored. We duly telephoned her and were told that an elderly relative had recently died and left her a lot of antique china, glass, and so on, and she would like to sell us some of it, if we were interested. We certainly were, and we were already getting into the habit of travelling round all over the place looking for suitable stock, so why not go to Brighton and visit Mrs. Wellbeloved? We went, and then it all became even odder.

We had accepted that she did not want to sell to local dealers; a trifle odd, perhaps, but then she might have perfectly good reasons for not liking any of them, and it was no reason for us looking this particular gift horse in the mouth. We were told, in the course of another phone call, to be careful not to park outside her house but on the other side of the street and wait. She would then contact us. What was going on? Had she been watching too many gangster movies? Or was she a gangster herself? This was Brighton, after all. Anyhow we were committed to turn up, so looked for the street, found it; a very ordinary little street of Victorian terraces in one of the less interesting parts of the town, found her house number, and parked as required on the other side of the road. It was a very quiet little street, no sign of life at all, not even the traditional dog sniffing round a lamp post. With our car engine switched off silence descended and we sat there waiting for something to happen and gazing nervously at the house on the other side of the street. What would happen next?

Would anything happen, or were we just going to sit there feeling sillier and sillier. Did Mrs. Wellbeloved actually exist, or if she did exist, was she mad? But then as we watched a curtain suddenly twitched in the little bow window opposite, an elderly lady waved a hand at us, then beckoned urgently and a moment or two later the front door opened. We got out of our car and scuttled across feeling very furtive, and went in.

Mrs. Wellbeloved greeted us effusively; she was so pleased to see us again, she said, and then without further ado began showing us various china and glass items standing on her mantle piece and sideboard and dotted around the room in general; good quality decanters, pretty little porcelain groups of shepherds and shepherdesses, all nice stuff. No boxes of assorted bric-a-brac as we had vaguely expected, but everything clean and tidy and displayed as if in a shop; and this was the really odd bit, - ticketed and priced. We looked at each other doubtfully, but didn't like to say anything about it; after all, if the lady liked to put price tickets on her things, why not? But then again, it did make it all look like the stock out of someone's shop. Was it all stolen? Or did Mrs. Wellbeloved run a shop in her front room? Was the recently dead relative a sort of polite fiction? We could both sense these ideas running through each other's minds like some stage thought- reading act, and we easily came to the same conclusion and decided to buy. After all, there was nothing to tell us that anything underhand was going on, just that we seemed to be dealing with a pleasant but highly eccentric old lady; and we had learned enough about the antique trade already to find eccentricity par for the course.

Her prices, neatly marked on everything on display, were reasonable, and these were just the sort of things we wanted for our shop and were hard to buy in auction or elsewhere. Pretty pieces of china and glass were very saleable and in demand in the trade, so if she wanted to sell exclusively to us that was fine. We did a deal, soon packed it all in our car, trying not to look round to see if we were being watched, and we were on our way. We went into the town to get a meal and have a look round while we were there, decided we rather liked Brighton and would be back, and then we were on our way home again.

We never found out anything more about this strange little old lady. Looking back it still seems odd, for nobody else ever mentioned her, and in time we got to know quite a lot of dealers from that area. She seemed to know the Brighton dealers, at least to the extent that she had decided that she didn't like any of them, but they didn't seem to know her. Was she in the trade and using us to get rid of some dodgy items on the quiet, or was she just a harmless old lady who liked to amuse herself with the cloak and dagger stuff? We went back to see her two or three times, but we never found out any more about her.

Having got the idea of going to Brighton we often went back in those early days. It was an attractive, jolly sort of place and we soon found that though these dealers in the Lanes were no doubt very knowledgeable and not prone to give their stock away, yet we could always find unusual and relatively undervalued bits and pieces that we could take home and sell well. Staffordshire pottery, especially dogs, were good; and all sorts of small, very countrified pieces of pottery, wood, or almost anything of that sort. At home on the Norfolk coast people were beginning to buy up property to convert to weekend cottages, and they all wanted this sort of stuff, still underrated in the smart Brighton market. Staffordshire dogs there stood dusty and forlorn on a shelf at the back of the shop, but at home in North Norfolk the weekend cottage set loved them.

Our stock in trade, and our business as a whole had definitely developed its own character by now, just as the other two shops in the village were both specialists in their own lines. Lady Margaret and her business partner Elizabeth Sumpter were very much the high-class end of the market, as indeed seemed only appropriate for these two ladies. Their speciality was fine porcelain, and we knew there was no point in our trying to compete with them even if we had wanted to. The other shop was run by a character of the old school called Billy, who dealt mainly in what the trade called brown furniture; that is, your conventional and potentially valuable good English eighteenth century mahogany. He and his son looked as if they took no prisoners, but they turned out to be quite friendly when they found we were not trying to compete with them either.

Our particular line had soon developed into country furniture and quaint, unusual, but not too expensive, interesting bits and pieces to go with it. Pieces of Staffordshire and other nineteenth century pottery, good but not fabulously valuable china such as Spode and Wedgwood, nice but inexpensive country things like milking stools and modest furniture, glass cases of stuffed birds and fish were all grist to our mill.

At one time our shop was full to bursting with cases of stuffed birds and frankly rather grisly animals, moth eaten and with the stuffing coming out. We could hardly get enough of them, and as quickly as they came in to our shop, out they went again. The well-to-do weekend cottage brigade were at one time mad for a tatty old bird or stuffed ferret in its case hung on the wall. We got so carried away by this brisk trade that on one of our trips down to Brighton we fell for and bought an enormous glass dome about a yard high full of exotic birds. I knew it was a mistake, but Anne was enchanted by it so quite a lot of money changed hands and into the back of our car it went. In those early days we did not have a van, but like many others a Cortina estate with a big roof rack on the top. Well, you could not put this fragile, and of course irreplaceable, glass dome on the roof, so into the back of the car it went. There is no need to explain what happened on the way home. The back of the Cortina was also full of other treasures that we had sifted out of various shops, very full indeed, and a Victorian glass dome does not need much pressure to make it die with a sudden heart stopping creaking sort of slow cracking noise which is impossible to describe, or once heard, forget.

16
The Trade

One thing that we could never have guessed before we became antique dealers ourselves was the amazing variety of people that we would meet in The Trade, as everyone called it. There were some long established dealers of course; they had all been in the trade for a long time, often for more than one generation. Some ran shops on the high street, as everyone knew, but then there was a whole level of dealers who did not operate from a conventional shop at all. Often their place of business was a grand country house which the general public hardly knew about, and they dealt almost exclusively with other members of the trade or private collectors. We soon found that such people could be good 'calls' for us. Once through the grand façade they often proved to be friendly and helpful to talk to, - we could learn a lot from such people, - and they had items to sell to us that were not quite up to their top quality, and therefore quite reasonable to buy. Then there were the many small dealers who were doing it as a sort of part time job or hobby, often one half of a married couple, while the other half, usually hubby, went off to do a proper job of work. Village stores sometimes had a sort of antiques section, school teachers were part time dealers from their homes; as were retired army majors, in fact in the seventies almost everybody either was, or wanted to be, an antique dealer. All these people were good sources of stock for us, often because they would have just the sort of countrified, modestly priced amusing bits of Victoriana that we could sell well in our shop at Burnham Market. Sometimes these antique shops came and went like mushrooms on an autumn morning; they would start up with a nice little collection of things probably inherited from Grandma, sell out, and then have no idea how to continue.

One strange example of this 'now you see it now you don't' situation was a smart little shop that appeared one day in Dereham. We were driving through that busy market town, as we often did, and spotted this new shop, slipped into the nearest parking slot and went to have a closer look. They had some good quality nineteenth century china in their window, and we went in and bought a good fish service and some plates. There was more nice china inside, in fact a really good stock, and we left saying that we would certainly be back. True to our word, a week later we returned to see what else they might have for sale; and they had gone, vanished, disappeared. The shop was still there, so it wasn't just a dream, but there was nothing in the window , nothing inside, just an empty building.

We never heard what had happened to them; perhaps a passing dealer had spotted them like we had, simply bought everything up, and moved on. There were tales of such things happening in those heady days; usually concerning some wealthy American dealer who had chanced to come by, bought the entire contents of a shop and loaded it into a pantechnicon for shipping back to The States before moving on to the next village. We were never visited by any of these fabulous foreigners, if indeed they existed; but anyhow we didn't really want them to come and empty our little shop, not after having worked so hard to fill it in the first place.

With the rapid increase in numbers of antique businesses of one sort or another some towns became famous as centres of the trade. Long Melford in Suffolk was our favourite example of this; where a very long street seemed to be entirely lined with antique shops on both sides. Lavenham, not far away, was almost as bad; and there the added effect of the many mediaeval half-timbered buildings gave the impression of the stage-set for an opera called The Antique Dealers of Suffolk , or maybe even a T.V. series.

Norfolk never had such extreme examples of the growth of the trade, but Swaffham, in the south of the county sprouted a good number of shops and galleries. One of the more interesting businesses was run by a pair of young men, great experts in the more rarefied world of miniature paintings, decorated snuff boxes and the like, who we always visited when we were in the area. We seldom bought anything from them, their goods were far to smart for our shop, but it was interesting to look at, and we were friends for many years. We had first met at a smart charity auction in aid of Norwich cathedral. We didn't expect to buy much there, as the prices would be probably sky high, but we went along as we went to virtually everything in those days. All sorts of good stuff had been donated to the sale and one of the things which had immediately caught Anne's eye was a beautiful little oak cradle from one of the great houses of the county. We were expecting our first baby at the time and Anne's appearance made this pretty obvious. We agreed that we would see if we could buy it and duly put in our bid when they came to it in the catalogue.

Of course, in the circumstances, we behaved like rank amateurs with Anne whispering audibly, 'Go on, bid a bid more !' as the price rose steadily. In the end we dropped out, we had to be sensible, and it was knocked down to these two obviously dealer-looking men. 'Oh, well' I said, 'we tried.' That was that, except that afterwards the two men came over and said, 'It looks as if your need is greater than ours, you have it', and refused to take a profit. Thus began a friendship that lasted for years, and both our children started their lives in a very high class Jacobean oak cradle.

We always said that this ancient crib was much better than the modern sort. It was very steady on the floor, it stood beside our bed as it had no doubt stood beside many others through the last three or four hundred years, and could conveniently be rocked by sticking out one foot. It also went very well with our quaint old house, even if it had spent most of its time in grander surroundings.

Dealers operated on all sorts of different levels, but to do much good they all had to be pretty straight amongst themselves. There has always been a popular idea that all dealers are a bit dodgy and always ready to cheat some trusting soul. What the general public never seemed quite to understand was that a dealer who went round cheating everyone would soon cease to be a dealer, because no one else would do any business with him. The first and basic requirement for dealing is that your word is your bond; if the people you are hoping to do business with don't see you in that light you can forget the whole idea.

One stratum of dealers who acquired a really bad name were the 'knockers'. These were the ones who used to operate by visiting houses at random, knocking on the door and asking if there was anything for sale; and they were often regarded as rogues who would cheat their own grandmother out of her best tea spoons. Well, there may have been some like that, but we used to do business with one or two who were perfect gentlemen.

Our favourite of this genre was a strange, shaggy sort of man who drove round in an ancient car with no seats in the back, the better to carry anything from a single chair to a wardrobe. He often called on us with something to sell, and was clever enough to quickly understand what sort of things we were looking for, especially Anne's taste for the odder sorts of Victoriana. Many a day he turned up at our shop with some strange object such as a religious grotto made entirely of shells in a glass case, almost exquisitely horrible, but obviously once beloved by a long past Victorian; and now saleable again to the right customer.

He would unload such treasures from that old car of his, and then come and sit in our kitchen to drink a glass or two of our home-made beer, and gossip about the trade, and where he had found things in the past and where he was thinking of trying next. He also had excellent taste and could spot the value of things other people failed to notice.

Once he brought us, stuffed into the back of his car, a piece of furniture that was a collector's delight. It was dirty and dusty and knocked about a bit, but under the grime you could see, and he had recognised, a very early example of that popular Victorian item the Davenport writing desk. But this one was definitely pre-Victorian in its design, very plain and severe, and clearly Georgian. We recognised it at once as being rare and desirable, cleaned it up a bit, put it in our shop and sold it immediately to another dealer. A month or two later we saw a picture of it in one of the smart antiques magazines, much polished but still recognisable, and were amazed at the value it had acquired since we saw it last. Then for years afterwards we used to see it every now and then in someone's glossy advertisement, each time a bit more polished and 'improved' and at steadily mounting prices. Where our old friend found that unique piece of furniture we never knew; in some dim and dusty attic no doubt. He just had this real genius for sniffing around the countryside and finding such things.

Another favourite dealer of ours, who was far from being a knocker, was a retired, or resting, ex-actor called Charles. He had a shop in a near-by village and we often did a bit of business with him, usually buying minor pieces of good quality porcelain. He did a rather more exotic sort of trade than we aimed at and was something of an expert on fine china and porcelain, but was not averse to selling us odd bits and pieces at really good prices. He was also a very kind man, who once, when he came into our shop and found us looking a bit glum about something said, 'Just wait a minute, my dears', went out again and came back with a bottle of champagne and another of dark stout and mixed up three doses of Black Velvet. 'This will cheer us all up in no time,' he said, and he was right.

On another occasion when he decided that we needed to be cheered up (I think it was just an excuse, really) he took us to the wrestling at the Corn Hall in Kings Lynn. His idea of an evening 'at the wrestling' consisted mainly of drinking champagne and eating smoked salmon sandwiches, but it was all very enjoyable.

There were so many people in the antique business in those days, and so many facets of the antique world that we had to learn about. Some of the important people we did business with were collectors who would hardly have considered themselves in the trade at all, such as a very formidable American lady we often met at one time. She was a great admirer of Lord Nelson and had a magnificent collection of items connected with the great admiral. Such items were rare even then but she often called in at our shop, no doubt hoping that something interesting might have turned up so near his home. Odds and ends did come our way from time to time; we once even had a black mourning brooch with what was supposed to be a lock of his hair in it. At another time we were able to pass on to her a fine miniature portrait bust of the admiral . She was a great character who we used to enjoy meeting and talking with; very intelligent and knowledgeable on her favourite subject. In the end she vanished from our little world, and we discovered that she had gone back to the U.S. and donated her collection of Nelson memorabilia to the museum at Portsmouth. Then there was Gordon, a great collector of glassware, who never actually had a shop, but used to 'do' antique fairs and ran a stall at an antique centre. He had a wider knowledge of antique glass than many a specialist with a big, smart shop in a fashionable street, and we did many a deal with him.

Perhaps the last part of the world of antiques which we ventured into was the realm of the big, very grand, London auction houses. We were often told that they could be a good source of the more ordinary goods because their main clients didn't want such things, and perfectly good pieces of mahogany furniture and the like could often be bought cheaply. Well, it may have been true or it may have been wishful thinking; anyhow we never got round to testing that theory, but we did eventually find our way past their august doors, mainly because we were sometimes offered items that we suspected were valuable, but would never reach their price in our shop in a Norfolk village.

The first time that we were precipitated into this world of international dealing was when a lady who had sold us several nice bits and pieces asked one day if we would like to make an offer for her collection of dolls? We had no idea what to offer. There were early French dolls, costume dolls, probably of the thirties, we thought, Mickey Mouse dolls and others. We were lost in a sea of dolls, and only had a feeling that some of them were really valuable to guide us. After wracking our brains and being forced to admit to ourselves that we were probably going to make a terrible mistake about prices one way or the other whatever we decided on, we said we would sell them on commission for her through one of the London houses.

Thus we were suddenly precipitated into a new world and had to learn how it all worked, and we learned straight away that these experts were not always as clever as we had imagined. The first two people we dealt with differed wildly in their idea of the collection's valuation, which was a bit worrying. However, we eventually got to a top doll person, and found that we had at any rate been wise not to value them ourselves. These dolls were, in a word, serious money. We also found out what a long drawn out business it was dealing with the big, serious antique and art world. It took months for them to take on these dolls, value them, insure them, decide what international sale to put them in, produce a catalogue, and eventually inform us about when they would be sold. It also, we found, took just as long for anyone to be paid. But the prospect of entering this new world was all quite exciting, when we went up to London with the nice shiny catalogue featuring some of our dolls on the front, to see them sold.

This was quite a different experience to the sort of auctions we had been to before, and instead of the usual country style big, bustling sale room, we found ourselves in a quiet, small room, with very serious looking people sitting decorously on a few rows of chairs. No cross section of village life here, with people meeting and having a chat and expecting to be entertained; these people we assumed, were the top level of world doll experts. The auctioneer sat at his desk flanked by several assistants with telephones, and we sat quietly on our two chairs, no doubt also looking serious; and hoping that everyone was in a buying mood.

Well, they were, it seemed, though not a flicker of excitement crossed any of their faces. They quietly and steadily bid sometimes against each other and sometimes against the unseen bidders on the telephone, nearly always to the exact estimated price, but occasionally to our great excitement well above it, and our first venture into that world was a success. We earned a nice little commission, and the dolls' ex owner was delighted with the cheque that eventually came her way. Having discovered that the proceedings of the top level art and antiques world were not particularly daunting, just very slow, we used them from time to time thereafter, especially if we came across something we could not put a value on ourselves.

Probably the oddest example of this was The Mughal Button, which sounds like a story featuring Sherlock Holmes, and was almost as interesting. It started with one of the assorted boxes of odds and ends that were always coming our way. The box contained the usual mixture of good but broken bits of china and glass, one or two saleable items, and a collection of buttons in a tin; the sort of thing you would have found in any house where a housewife had kept useful bits and pieces. The buttons, though of no apparent value were mostly quite old and at least interesting enough to have a look at, and one was big and very unusual. It was round, as buttons usually are, about two inches across and pale greenish white. On closer inspection it had some fine carving on it, which might have been Chinese, and it could, we decided, be jade; and possibly quite old. And with that we more or less forgot about it, after all we were always coming across things out of some old house or other, that might, or might not be interesting. So the button was left lying about, until we happened to be going up to London one day, and I slipped it in my pocket thinking we might be able find out if it had any value. There were plenty of experts up there in town on any subject you liked to think of. The big auction houses always had a front office where you could drop in and get a casual opinion about values, so we dropped in on one of them in the West End to see what they had to say about our button.

There behind the desk sat the usual sort of young man, beautifully suited and plummy voiced, and straight from University. He looked very doubtfully at the button I produced; he wasn't used to looking at things that came out of trouser pockets, and his expression made this quite plain. I said, apologetically, 'We thought it might be jade, and quite old.' His disdainful look slipped slightly. He didn't know much, but he recognised the word jade. Something warned him that he ought to tell his boss, he had probably been told that it was a funny old world, and one day an idiot would wander in with a Picasso wrapped up in a piece of newspaper. 'Would you mind waiting while I refer this to our jade expert?' said he. We said fine, carry on. Time passed, our button was clearly puzzling others as well as the boy in the front office, and at length we were invited into the inner sanctum. More waiting, as the first jade expert called the even more elevated second jade expert, and then everybody became much more friendly.

Would we like them to handle the sale of this item? Taking our cue to be a bit disdainful in return, we said well, yes, possibly; would they care to value it for us? Difficult to say, said the very important second jade expert, unusual to see one of these, they would have to refer it to an even more elevated expert. But it was certainly interesting, and probably from Northern India, of the Mughal period. They would be able to tell us more when it had been thoroughly assessed, and there would be a special sale of artefacts of the period in two months. Stunned by this information, but trying not to look too surprised, we agreed that they could handle it for us, were handed a long printed document in exchange, and departed.

Time passed. Well, we knew by then how slowly things happened in that particular world. Letters passed back and forth, and our button was entered for one sale, then mysteriously withdrawn, perhaps they still hadn't quite made up their minds what it was. But at last it reached the saleroom, and was sold. According to the catalogue it was indeed Mughal, of the same period as the Taj Mahal, and was sold for several hundred pounds. But the substantial cheque which we eventually received was almost an anticlimax. How on earth had such an item, once worn by some leader of the Mughal empire, perhaps even Shah Jahan himself, ended up in a tin button box in a country house in Norfolk? The sheer romance of having found, and handled, such an object far outweighed the monetary value; nice as it was to occasionally make a good profit.

Still, anyone in business has to make a financial success of it, and earning our day to day bread and butter was mainly to do with buying and selling fairly ordinary antiques at a modest price, and as time went on we tended more and more towards furniture. There was a long period through the eighties and into the nineties when, though we were buying and selling almost anything over a hundred years old, our main business was just good, nice quality chests of drawers, tables and chairs, and generally useful objects of that sort. It was the heyday of antique furniture and the many people who were setting up second homes in North Norfolk all wanted it.

There was one period when Victorian pine was the thing, and so much of it was passing through our hands that we ran a second shop just for pine and the sort of country things that went with it. Our roof-racked Cortina, - we had worked our way through several different models by then, - was permanently filled and draped with pine of all sorts. Anne had a particular knack of going out, driving round several contacts she had in Norfolk, and coming home with the roof rack piled up like a hay stack. I used to fear that the whole lot would fall off in the middle of a busy main road somewhere, but she always had everything securely tied on and it never happened. It was I who once did manage to shed a large table when I was driving, which flew gracefully over the carriage way, missing all the other traffic, and landing in the hedge no more than slightly 'distressed'. In the end we had to face the fact that we needed something bigger than our faithful Cortinas, and we bought a van.

We had two children as well as two shops by then, and we had to take turns going out and buying. Life was so hectic that when our second child was born Anne had only left the shop for a day or two, and laughed about how a friendly customer asked her one day, 'Isn't your baby due soon?' Well, not really, she had said, he's already here!

Luckily we had two very capable girls, who lived close by, to help with the two babies at different times; but even so running two shops in the end proved a bit too hectic, and we reverted to just the one shop again.

We were still just as busy, but at least it was more sensible working from one shop than trying to work from two. By this time we also had to do a lot of journeys delivering furniture, which was easier with the van, but of course we had to employ someone to help with the shop. More and more our weekender customers wanted pieces of furniture delivered to their home base, which was usually London., so this had to be dealt with as well. Of course there were always commercial carriers to do this sort of work, but they were never cheap and usually slow; and we would often sell several pieces of furniture to various London customers in the course of a week, and then load up the van and take them down ourselves.

Finding where they actually lived was always a bit of a problem, if you were dealing with London traffic, one way streets, parking restrictions, and trying to read a street map all at the same time, and we found it an enormous boon when mobile phones came into general use. We had one of the very early ones, which was so heavy you wouldn't have wanted to carry it far, but it was very useful in the van to be able to contact your customer by phone; home in on them, and know that there would be someone there when you pulled up at the pavement by their front door, probably on a double yellow line.

This hectic period in the antique world did eventually begin to calm down, and we could at last slow down and catch our breath a bit. A good deal of the calming down process was probably due to the long term effect of VAT entering the once carefree trade. People who had never kept an accounts book in their lives suddenly found that they were expected to keep all sorts of precise details of their day to day trading, and found themselves in a much more serious and difficult world. Quite a lot of dealers had no idea how to keep books at all; some could hardly even read and write. We had always kept reasonable accounts, but could hardly believe what details we now had to record every time we bought and sold anything. The vatman was now likely to call and inspect all your records and wanted to know exactly when an item had been bought, from whom, with full name and address, price given, to whom sold, full name and address again, and a signed sales document countersigned by the purchaser. No one quite believed this at first, and some customers were not at all happy about signing pieces of paper. One well known actress who happened to be in our shop, - the village was becoming very popular by now and there were always a few well known people about, - thought I was trying to get her autograph.

Possibly the most irritating aspect of all this was that the Continental dealers who came to this country and had also discovered Burnham by now, used to simply ignore our typically British attempts to keep to all the rules and regulations. As we understood it, our cumbersome VAT regulations all came from Europe anyhow, but their attitude was that in their own countries nobody took it seriously. Dutch dealers in particular often came round looking for old oak, for which they seemed to have plenty of customers, and they were quite good buyers if the price was right. But sign documents? Give names and addresses? We were surely joking. If pressed they would sign a name of some sort, but it was as likely to be Donald Duck as anything else. This we had to accept; after all Duck could well be a Dutch name, for all we knew to the contrary.

Our own most ridiculous experience of a vatman was an occasion when one of them called to check that we were not having too much fun, and spent a whole day going through our accounts, only to announce in the end that there was some sort of irregularity in the way we had accounted for the tax on picture frames. Pictures were never much more than a sideline to us in those days, but of course we had some in our shop, and our vatman said he would have to take all our books away to check the anomalies he had found. Now I would never have claimed that our book keeping was beyond reproach, and it was not a pleasant feeling that the full fury of the VAT department was focussed on our accounts for several days. It was anybody's guess what they might find if they looked hard and long enough, and the return of the vatman was awaited with trepidation. On the Monday of the following week he duly returned and announced sombrely that, yes, they had found that our figures were incorrect. There was an error he said, of £4.50, which we had overpaid. But the computer at headquarters did not recognise repayments of less than £5, so our £4.50 could not be returned to us. With that he returned all our books, snapped his briefcase shut, refused the offer of a cup of coffee, and left.

This business of having to keep meticulous books that were likely to be checked by a vatman at any time made an enormous difference to the trade, and many who were operating on the fringes of it simply faded away. The more serious dealers who were depending on it for their living, as indeed we were, simply had to accept that life was now more difficult, and get on with it. Only big businesses and auction houses that could afford full time clerks and accountants could really deal with all the extra work; the rest of us had to bite on the bullet and do out best.

We felt we were pretty fully employed anyhow, but we just had to make time to keep the necessary records; you were told that you might go to jail if you did not. But keeping these sort of details for small, amusing, saleable, but cheap, items was just not worth while, so our business became mainly classic, fairly expensive pieces of furniture.

A new sort of dealer came into our lives now, because we had to find sources of such furniture, and there had never been too much available in really good condition. From now on we were often buying from good restorers, the sort of men who were experts in finding pieces of first quality furniture in poor condition, repairing and tidying it up, and even making new legs, knobs, and other bits and pieces that had come to the end of their natural lives. There was still a brisk demand for good looking items for furnishing, and we spent some of our time now going round collecting things such as side tables and desks and chests of drawers from these restorers, setting them up in our shop, selling them; and then putting them back in our van and delivering them to the new owner. I sometimes felt that we were now not much more than furniture porters, but it was still good business; though we had somehow passed from a world where everyone was interested in antiques for their own sake to one in which our customers merely wanted a nice looking piece of furniture.

Then in the nineties this interest in smart, highly polished furniture of previous centuries began to fade at last. There was a change of fashion towards modern, minimalist styles, and there was definitely less interest in suites of furniture that were brown and shiny and old. Since there was less interest on the part of the public, we had to shift our interests too; there was no point in sitting there with a shop full if things that few people now wanted.

At about this time the world political picture was changing and trading with China began again in earnest; and the sort of fine porcelain that the Chinese had always been famous for trickled into this country again. At first some of this was actually antique, then soon bowls and pots that might have been old, or might be very good copies appeared, and then a deluge of frankly modern copies of good antique porcelain.

For a long time pottery that looked like this had not been available except as rare and expensive items, and there was a tremendous public appetite for it all. Some pieces looked Chinese and some were skilful copies of old European porcelain, but it was very well done, often almost indistinguishable from the rare and valuable, and it was cheap. We got to know some of the dealers and importers in this trade, and bought and sold a lot of Chinese porcelain for a year or two, until this good quality stuff mysteriously dried up again. The Chinese were also producing amazingly good copies of all sorts of other antiques too. We never handled any of these as they were precisely the sort of clever 'repros' that we had always avoided, but we saw them all in the hands of importers we knew, and often had a quiet smile at some dusty and even cobwebbed 'antique' we saw offered for sale in shops and at auctions. The Chinese craftsmen were very clever, and these things were often got up to look very like the genuinely ancient items that used to come out of dusty attics in the good old days; but we knew that their true age could often be measured in months, or by the time it took for them to travel from China to the U.K. So as time went on the genuine antique trade became steadily less rewarding, and the trade in our shop slowly moved into other areas.

The people who shopped in Burnham Market had changed over the years too. No longer did we have only people in our shop who were seriously interested in antiques; there were many more customers than there used to be, and often these days they were simply visitors who were looking round the village. Our shop was just one of twenty or thirty round the greens that families trooped in and out of as part of their holiday. We were very much on the tourist route now, with the rest of the Norfolk coast, and our new public were more likely to buy some small amusing article for a few pounds than a piece of furniture for several hundred.

One very lucrative line was started almost by chance when another antique dealer asked if we would like to sell the cards he was producing. He had collected Victorian greetings cards over many years, and had hit on the idea of reprinting them. We said we would try a few, which went so briskly that we immediately ordered more. This lead to stocking other individual, unusual and interesting greetings cards, and there proved to be a great demand for cards that were different to the usual modern ones.

Then, on a hunch that turned out to be a very good idea, we started a new department of local country crafts; brand new, but good quality and always interesting simply because they were not mass-produced.. It was almost funny that after all these years we were back to our original notion of selling antique and modern together. The great difference was that now our 'modern' was work being produced by local craftsmen and women; every piece was in its own way unique, and warranted a shop in which it could be displayed and sold. We reckoned that many people would be glad to be able to buy something knowing that it was the work of human hands, and not pressed out in plastic like so much in the shops. This latest of our ideas worked well too. Enough of the general public clearly understood our purpose, and we were as busy as ever. Of course there were always some who couldn't understand why something made down the road might cost a bit more than something that looked similar but came from the far east. But you can't please everybody.

Yet another of our departments was now fine art. Our son Tom had developed into an artist, with a gene inherited from his mother no doubt, and we began to sell his work. This became our fine art gallery, and we soon had occasional exhibitions of other local artists as well. Thus our shop went through many changes but still continued over the years. It is true that every now and then we would hear a remark like, 'This used to be a nice little antique shop. Have you been here long?' But still, most people seemed to be happy to accept us in our latest reincarnation as a mini-department store, and the business remained very healthy. A bonus for us was that after the rather dull and serious later antique period, it was fun to be dealing with the very varied and interesting people who inhabit the arts and crafts world.

Burnham Market had changed completely in the forty or so years we had lived in it, from the quiet little village with half a dozen shops and no parking problems to a busy tourist destination with cars jammed in every possible slot where it is possible to stop. But still, every now and then, someone turns up from our early days in the village. Only the other day an elderly lady wondered in and announced rather imperiously that she must be one of our most regular customers. She had bought something from us when we had first opened, she said, though she couldn't remember exactly what. And then she had made a purchase from us again twenty years ago, and now here she was once more, buying something ! Don't leave it so long next time Dear Customer, I thought, or the shop might not be here,

Still, the Old Black Horse has been here in the form of one sort of a shop or another for a long time. Probably since medieval times when the village consisted of simple stalls and shops round the open space that people now call The Greens. I have little doubt that in fact it will still be here in twenty years time; though what will be on sale here then, who knows ?